INSANITY *and* SANCTITY *in* BYZANTIUM

INSANITY *and* SANCTITY *in* BYZANTIUM

The Ambiguity of Religious Experience

YOUVAL ROTMAN

Harvard University Press

Cambridge, Massachusetts, & London, England

2016

Second Printing

Library of Congress Cataloging-in-Publication Data

Names: Rotman, Youval, author.
Title: Insanity and sanctity in Byzantium : the ambiguity of religious experience / Youval Rotman.
Description: Cambridge, Massachusetts : Harvard University Press, 2016.
Identifiers: LCCN 2015051254 | ISBN 9780674057616
Subjects: LCSH: Psychology and religion—Byzantine Empire. | Mental illness—Religious aspects—Byzantine Empire. | Mental illness—Social aspects—Byzantine Empire. | Religion and sociology—Byzantine Empire. | Christian saints—Byzantine Empire. | Holy fools—Byzantine Empire. Classification: LCC BF51 .R64 2016 | DDC 204/.209495—dc23
LC record available at http://lccn.loc.gov/2015051254

to Drora Rotman

to Vered Amitai

Contents

INSANITY *and* SANCTITY *in* BYZANTIUM

PROLOGUE

Insanity and Religion

In every period in history the definition of insanity is pertinent, and its meaning is different. We owe this perception to a large movement in the scholarship of the 1960s and 1970s that changed our concept of what constitutes sanity and insanity. This scholarship examined the ways in which such concepts were formed as part of the medical, mental, social, cultural, but above all political settings. A number of important studies on psychology and psychiatry, whether in the fields of social sciences, the humanities, or medicine (by Michel Foucault, Roy Porter, William Bynum, Gladys Swain, Marcel Gauchet, Franco Basaglia, among others), has radically changed the way we look at insanity. These studies brought insanity out of the individual dimension, and made it a social, cultural, and political phenomenon.[1]

In a way, the wave of study of psychiatry in the 1960s and 1970s was a response to the development of psychoanalysis in the first half of the twentieth century, which concentrated on the psychological dimension in the individual. These new directions of thought shifted the understanding of what constitutes insanity from the individual to the social and political dimensions. Nevertheless, they still placed the individual in the center, affected by the social settings, mental constructs, and politics. This perspective was conditioned by the link between psychology and medicine, according to which the insane person was perceived as sick.

The present study chooses a different line of investigation. In a way, it goes in the opposite direction by focusing on societies that sanctified what today we consider insanity. These societies looked for spiritual values in abnormal, or insane, behavior, and legitimized it by attributing a unique spiritual character to figures who portrayed it. In this they were changing the social and cultural norms related to abnormality and normality. A parallel process can also be detected in contemporary societies. Only few decades ago, people in Western societies who turned to healers, clairvoyants, and mediums were themselves considered to be not in their right mind. Today, not only is such behavior legitimized, it is even becoming a norm. These so-called New Age phenomena express the invasion of the religious sphere into modern secular societies. We do not call them "religious," but "spiritual" in order to reject the religious establishment and its historical framework. However, such expressions of spirituality have long been the realm of the religious sphere. The question is why secular societies today have become more and more inclined to adopt and legitimize these expressions of spirituality, and justify their functionality.

As for the borderline between sanity and insanity, in today's world this has become a large field of mental disorders that cannot be arranged on a sliding scale. Moreover, these disorders are intricately woven into the social and cultural fabric of Western modern life. This raises two questions: Where do we draw the line between normal and abnormal behavior? And what is the place of individual abnormal behavior in the social fabric especially in situations when the individual's behavior disturbs the social?

The present book does not deal with modern societies, but proposes analyzing the same question in a different period of great changes: the Christianization of the Roman world, a process of transformation which marked the beginning of a new age, the monotheistic age. As this book will show, the development of new religious settings necessitated the use and abuse of what constitutes abnormality in order to produce a shift. This shift was religious, cultural, political, social, and mental. The borderline between normality and abnormality, one of the most important borderlines of the social setting, proved in the period under examination to be extremely elastic. In the center of our examination lies the question of the relationship between the elasticity of these definitions and the historical changes that were produced in the Roman world between the second and the seventh centuries, changes that transformed it into a new civilization and created the world of

Byzantium. In other words, the main question that this study addresses, concerns the way in which historical processes develop and can be realized as a product of changes of a psychological nature. An analysis of the development of early Christian societies will clearly demonstrate this. The book thus focuses on different types of social abnormality that were sanctified in the new Christian framework and reveals their social functionality, while comparing them to their contemporary Jewish equivalents.

The Abnormal as a Social Engine

The phenomenon of sanctification, attributing holiness and sanctity to human beings, became prevalent in the period under examination, the period of Byzantine antiquity. Many of such figures portrayed an abnormal behavior to their societies. Attributing holiness and sanctity to figures of abnormal behavior should be seen also as means to normalize abnormal forms of behavior. We can observe this in figures of martyrs, ascetics, and liminal figures whose abnormality reflects the breaking of accepted norms in order to define new ones. This of course creates a shift in the borderline between what is considered to be an accepted and unaccepted, normal and abnormal, sane and insane behavior.

But the sanctification of abnormal behavior also presents a problem of uncertainty. The historian who analyzes such phenomena can never be sure whether holy persons whose behavior was abnormal, consciously and intentionally defined new norms to their society, or whether they were chosen as symbols of transformations regardless of their *real* mental state. This problem of uncertainty reveals the ambiguity that such figures portray. Moreover, the ambiguity about the interpretation of their state applied also to their own society. In order to challenge the norms of their society, they needed to portray ambiguity to their surroundings. Their behavior was seen as both insane, but at the same time as intentional and courageous. This ambiguity, as this book will show, proves to be central to religious experience and serves, moreover, as a vehicle for change.

The present book examines the role that abnormal social behavior plays in the definition of holiness, and reveals the circumstances and reasons for sanctifying such patterns of behavior. We will see that their ambiguous character makes such figures particularly useful to society by challenging both the perception and definition of the borderline between sanity and insanity. First of all, the ambiguous holiness of such ecstatic figures does not permit any definitive demarcation of this border. In this way it renders this borderline unclear, and in fact transforms it to a less rigid borderline between normality and abnormality. Second, this shift in the definition of what is considered normal and abnormal behavior is employed by society in order to implement a change of mentality and a change of its settings. In fact, these changes result in changing the perception of reality and reality itself. The sanctification of abnormality proves here to be socially functional in shifting the borderline between what is normal and abnormal behavior. This regards not any type of abnormality, but abnormality that can be used in order to challenge the perception of reality. This is the reason why the present book is concerned with what we define today as insanity, that is, mental abnormalities. As we shall see, forms of sanctity that are specifically designed in order to challenge the perception of reality and the borderline between sanity and insanity appear to be essential to the development of a religious society and are used to generate social movements.

In what follows we will use intentionally the terms "insanity" and "abnormality" without qualifiers in order to be able to follow the elasticity of the definitions of these terms in view of the social, cultural, and mental conditions and needs. As Foucault has shown, the notion of the borderline between sanity and insanity as a rigid concept may not apply to every society. In fact, the present examination of the borderline between normal and abnormal social behavior will reveal its elasticity, which rigid definitions of insanity and sanity preclude. In other words, the religious realm employs the borderline between normal and abnormal behaviors because it can render it ambiguous much more easily than the borderline between sanity and insanity.

In using the terms "insanity" and "sanity" we follow the modern definitions of what constitutes abnormal mental condition. But defining insanity as a mental condition of the individual, constructs it at the same time as a social phenomenon in view of the boundary it sets between what is considered accepted (i.e., "normal"/"sane") behavior and unaccepted (i.e., "abnormal"/"insane") behavior. In contrast to unaccepted intentional behavior, insanity and mental abnormality refer to unintentional behavior and are understood as disease, sickness, or disorder. The use of the term "mental disorder" itself reveals the ways in which such an individual behavior is understood today. Like the term "insanity," it conceptualizes certain behaviors as disruptions of the sane mental condition which is perceived as "order," and in the same time as disruptions of the "normal" or "sane" social order. We will therefore leave aside the binary definitions of sanity-insanity and look at insanity as deviancy in situations when the individual's behavior disturbs the social.[2] This makes the borderline between sanity and insanity an undefined space, and creates an ambiguity about the definition of insanity. To society, such behaviors are abnormal "human noise." Nevertheless, referring to the deviant characteristic of insanity will enable us to shift our attention from the mental and medical states of the abnormal individual, and to examine the way in which society perceives and addresses it.

Although to society such behaviors are deviant, that is, abnormal "human noise," they can also become functional and serve as means to redefine social and cultural norms. As we shall see, in the religious societies under examination such "noises" or deviances that reflect an abnormal mental behavior, played an important role as means of change. This book thus analyzes the significance of insanity to the social fabric by focusing on the realm that has long used it: religion. By sanctifying forms of abnormality religion does not allow a static definition of insanity and sanity. In this, the importance of such an analysis exceeds the realm of the historical research of one particular culture in time. It provides a unique case study for examining the ways in which the phenomenon of insanity and sanity affects and determines social settings.

Between History and Psychology: Problems of Methodology

In order to investigate such questions the present study develops a unique methodology. Rather than choose between religious studies, history, and psychology, the methodology taken in this book combines all three fields. This approach aims to draw a parallel line between the dynamics of the psychological process from the one hand, and the evolution of a religious society on the other hand. It examines the conditions for abnormality to become socially functional, and reveals the social meaning of insanity that lies at the basis of religion. It aspires to find a new way to look at insanity, and in the process proposes a new method to use and analyze historical evidence. As we shall see, this method of analysis moves between the fields of history, religious studies, and psychology. We ask questions that relate to all three fields, but instead of combining material and methodologies from the three disciplines, the method taken in the present study aims to work in between them in order to analyze the historical evidence from both a historical and a psychological perspective. This methodology aspires to turn the relation between history and psychology (we use here "psychology" in grouping psychoanalysis, analytical psychology, and group psychology, though this study concerns mainly the first) into a two-way-street relationship, and to look into the historical evidence in order to challenge the way we conceptualize insanity today.

The disadvantages of this method are obvious: to the historian the religious studies and psychoanalytical discussions might seem superfluous. On the other hand, a scholar of religious studies might say that this book ignores much of the classic discussions of the field including the phenomenology of religion, and will find the historical analyses too specific to be interesting or fructuous. To the psychoanalyst, in contrast, both history and religious studies may seem irrelevant to the psychological questions that the book aims to address. Since the methodology taken here is unique in aiming to construct a shared analysis to the three disciplines involved, instead of importing accepted theories from one to the benefit of the other, this study may seem a priori as falling between the stools. Nevertheless, as we shall see, this risk will prove itself advantageous in presenting a way to analyze historical sources, which is set on the common ground of discussion between the three fields.

The book is divided into two parts that propose complementary approaches to address the question of insanity in religious experience. Part I, "Santified Insanity: Between History and Psychology," analyzes the phenomenon of sanctified insanity through a particular phenomenon: the Byzantine holy fool. It proposes a new historical-psychoanalytical perspective and employs it in a two-way-street analysis. Chapter 1, "The Paradox That Inhabits Ambiguity," includes a general introduction to the paradox that sanctified insanity presents to the modern mind. The chapter takes as a case study the phenomenon of the Byzantine holy fool and reveals the limits of scholarship in analyzing the borderline between sanity and insanity that such a phenomenon defines. Chapter 2, "Meanings of Insanity," investigates the social role of ambiguity in religious experience. This chapter focuses on the way the figure of the holy fool functions within the religious community as both a literary and social figure in order to produce a change in the perception of reality. The chapter concludes with the role of ambiguity of the mental state as a fundamental means for challenging the social, cultural, and psychological structure.

Part II, "Abnormality and Social Change: Early Christianity versus Rabbinic Judaism," presents a comparative analysis of early Christianity and rabbinic Judaism, and reveals the opposite ways in which these religious societies addressed the sanctification of abnormality. Chapter 3, "Abnormality and Social Change: Insanity and Martyrdom," confronts the historical analysis of insanity with the construction of the martyr as a figure of abnormal behavior in order to implement broader changes of mentality, society, and politics. The way in which normal and the abnormal social behaviors are defined appears here to be a formative factor of social changes, and not only their product. Chapter 4, "Socializing Nature: The Ascetic Totem," compares the phenomenon of asceticism in early Christian and rabbinic Jewish communities. A priori, asceticism portrays a withdrawal from society into nature, while the voluntary torments inflicted on one's body can be considered pathological. However, an anthropological reading of such a type of abnormal behavior reveals that in the religious setting exemplifying the "pathology" of asceticism serves a social function. It links the relationship of humans and nature with the relationship of humans and culture.

Finally, the Epilogue, "Psychology, Religion and Social Change," leaves the lines of investigation taken in the book in order to answer the main question raised throughout the book: What is mental abnormality? Taking as its base the concept of ambiguity between insanity and sanity in religious language, it aims to reconnect the study of religious societies to our understanding of psychological processes as social phenomena.

We therefore begin with the ways in which scholarship addresses the phenomenon of the sanctification of insanity, and their limits. The ambiguity embedded in this phenomenon appears to pose not only a paradox to the modern mind but also a serious problem for the scholar.

PART I

SANCTIFIED INSANITY

Between History and Psychology

1

The Paradox That Inhabits Ambiguity

> I am aware that the man who is said to be deluded may be in his delusion telling me the truth, and this in no equivocal or metaphorical sense, but quite literally, and that the cracked mind of the schizophrenic may *let in* light which does not enter the intact minds of many sane people whose minds are closed.
>
> —RONALD D. LAING, 1960

This chapter presents a unique historical phenomenon from Byzantine society: the figure of the holy fool (Greek: *salos*). The historical analysis of such a phenomenon brings into question our ability as scholars to fully comprehend its use and function. Our modern mind sees the existence of such a figure as a paradox that challenges the field of historical research. In this chapter we shall present this paradox, and argue that analyzing it forces us to acknowledge the gap between contemporary mental and social definitions and the mental and social definitions of the society which forms our object of research.

What Is a "Holy Fool"?

The etymological source of the word *salos,* which appears in Greek sources from the fifth century A.D. on, is far from certain.[1] It was used in Byzantium to designate a madman, and was applied to religious persons who feigned madness in order to achieve a high level of spirituality by fulfilling Paul's verses:

> If any man among you seems to be wise [Greek: *sophos*] in this world, let him become a fool [*mōros*] that he may be wise, for the wisdom [*sophia*] of this world is folly [*mōria*] in God's sight. (1 Cor. 3:18–19)[2]

In the same epistle Paul continues:

> We are fools [Greek: *mōroi*] for Christ's sake, while you are such sensible [*phronimoi*] Christians. (1 Cor. 4:10)[3]

The meaning of these verses is clear: wisdom and folly as we perceive them are cultural constructions of this world, not the *true* wisdom and folly in God's eyes, in fact quite the opposite. Moreover, the fervent revolutionary believers are those who challenge the social conception of being sensible (Greek: *phronimos*), that is, normal social behavior. By becoming fools for Christ's sake they follow in the footsteps of Jesus.[4] "Folly" seems to point to what is considered abnormal, unwise, and not sensible in the eyes of society, which here means following a new and revolutionary religion to the extreme.[5] Paul's meaning is clear: do not be content with being Christian, but fight to change the order of the world. Once Christianity was adopted as a state religion in the fourth century, Paul's revolutionary transformation of ideas would seem to have succeeded. Nevertheless, this did not mean that the battle between what is normal and abnormal, wise and fool, and we can also add sane and insane, was over. Paul's words had a follow-up by those who chose to read him literally, raising the immediate question: How can one become a fool? Is folly a state that someone can consciously choose to adopt and abandon at will? In the late antique *Sayings of the Desert Fathers* (*Apophtegmata Patrum*) this question is formulated in the following manner:

> A brother asked his elderly spiritual father [*abba*]: "How does one become a fool [Greek: *mōros*] for the Lord's sake?" The elder said to him: "There was a child in a *coenobion* who was given to a good elder so he might bring him up and teach him the fear of God. The elder would say to him: 'When somebody reviles you, bless him; and if you are sitting at table, eat what is decaying and leave what is good and, if you are to choose a garment, leave the good one and take the one that is worn out.' 'Am I a fool that you tell me to behave like that?" the child said to him. 'I am telling you to do those things for this reason that you may become "a fool for the Lord's sake," so that the Lord may make you wise,' said the

elder. The elder showed what one does to become 'a fool for the Lord's sake,' you see. . . ."

. . . An elder said: either escape people, or mock the world by making yourself a fool in many ways.[6]

This passage appears as an actual guide for young novice monks, and is presented as a way to escape the world and withdraw to an inner state, thus mocking the world of people, that is, society. This is precisely what another monk does when making himself a fool. By laughing instead of talking, he manages to stay by himself and is left alone by those who come to ask for his guidance.[7]

In this way abnormal behavior acquires a hidden spiritual meaning known only to the person who chooses to live it.[8] The individual abnormal way, here clearly an abnormal social and mental state, serves as a means both to be left alone and connect to the divine.[9] These two objectives are closely connected: holy fools act abnormally in order to disconnect themselves from society, but since this is done for a spiritual reason, their behavior bears a spiritual message to society. This is precisely the double message in Paul's phrase: flee from people or become a fool in order to mock the world, and through this you will become a spiritual magnet for society.

This theological setting was matched by Byzantine texts, moral tales, and stories of the saints' lives, which took up the theme of insanity itself and elaborated it into a peculiar type of sanctity: the holy madman, the holy *salos*. Though traditionally translated in today's English as "fool," the *salos's* sanctity did not consist only of acts of foolery, but also of acts of madness. The folly, *mōria*, which Paul talked about, was expressed by the act of presenting oneself to one's society as insane, a *salos*.

The earliest story that has come down to us about this sort of case is an account from the fifth century of a nun, a *salē*, a madwoman (the Greek feminine of *salos*) in a remote Egyptian monastery in Tabennisi. Palladius narrates this tale in his collection of stories from the fifth century about holy men and women in the Egyptian desert:

In this monastery there was another maiden who feigned folly [Greek: *mōria*] and demon-possession [Greek: *daimona*]. The others felt such contempt for her that they never ate with her, which pleased her entirely. Taking herself to the kitchen she used to perform every menial service and she was, as the saying goes, "the sponge of the monastery," really fulfilling the Scriptures: *If any man among you seems to be wise in this world, let him become a fool that he may be wise.* She wore a rag around her head—all the others had their hair closely cropped and wore cowls. In this way she used to serve. Not one of the four hundred ever saw her chewing all the years of her life. She never sat down at a table or partook of a particle of bread, but she wiped up with a sponge the crumbs from the tables and was satisfied with scouring pots. She was never angry at anyone, nor did she grumble or talk, either little or much, although she was maltreated, insulted, cursed, and loathed.

Now an angel appeared to Saint Piteroum, the famous anchorite dwelling at Porphyrites, and said to him: "Why do you think so much of yourself for being pious [Greek: *eulabēs*] and residing in a place such as this? Do you want to see someone more pious than yourself, a woman? Go to the women's monastery at Tabennisi and there you will find one with a band on her head. She is better than you. While being cuffed about by such a crowd she has never taken her heart off God. But you dwell here and wander about cities in your mind." And he who had never gone away left that monastery and asked the superiors to allow him to enter into the monastery of women. They admitted him, since he was well on in years and, moreover, had a great reputation. So he went in and insisted upon seeing all of them. She did not appear. Finally he said to them: "Bring them all to me, for she is missing." They told him: "We have one madwoman, a *salē,* inside the kitchen"—that is what they called the afflicted one [Greek: *paschousa*]. He told them: "Bring her to me. Let me see her." They went to call her, but she did not answer, either because she knew of the incident or because it was revealed to her. They seized her forcibly and told her: "The holy Piteroum wishes to see you"—for he was renowned. When she came he saw the rag on her head and, falling down at her feet, he said: "Bless me!" In similar manner she too fell down at his feet and said: "You bless me, lord!" All the women were amazed at this and said: "Father, take no insult. She is a madwoman, *salē.*" Piteroum then addressed all the women: "You are the madwomen, *salai*! This woman is my and your spiritual mother [Greek: *ammas*]"—so they called the spirituals—"and I pray that I may be deemed as worthy as she on the Day of Judgment." Hearing this, they fell at his feet, confessing various things—one how she had poured the leaving of her plate over her; another had beaten her with her fists; another had blistered her nose. So they confessed various and sundry outrages. After praying for them, he left. And after a few days she was unable to bear the praise and honor of the sisters, and all their apologies was so burdensome to

> her, that she left the monastery. Where she went and where she disappeared to, and how she died, nobody knows.[10]

In this story, which to us is read as a folk tale, a Byzantine version of a Cinderella story, the plot is constructed by using two basic elements: the simulated, fake madness and its concealment.[11] It is clear that one cannot exist without the other: a simulated madness cannot but be kept concealed, otherwise there is no story. However, the story is not presented as a fictional work. In contrast to folk tales, the moral agenda of hagiography is completely conditioned by its aspiration to historical authenticity; otherwise, these would not be saints' *Lives*, but fictional legends.[12] In other words, the moral function that such texts played as religious exempla defined their genre, and determined the way in which the author presented the facts. The narrative had to be presented as a *real* and *true* historical story. However, a story about someone who feigned madness but concealed it is impossible to tell without access to this person's hidden motive. This is why such narratives always include a third figure who knows, or is exposed to, the truth about the hero, and reveals it in due course to the surrounding society. This is also the case in one of the most elaborated texts dedicated to such a person to come down to us in the *Life of Symeon salos*, composed in the seventh century by Leontius, bishop of Neapolis in Cyprus.[13]

To summarize very briefly a text of around fifty folios, this is the story of a young man who becomes a fervent Christian monk and withdraws with his close friend to the desert, leaving behind his previous social life. After twenty-nine years of monastic life in the Dead Sea desert he decides to become a madman for Christ's sake. He leaves the monastery for the city, where he performs a continuous state of madness in public. Being unaware of the fact that his insanity is simulated, the inhabitants of the city think him a madman and treat him as such. This second part of the text is characterized by a literary tension that the author constructs, which confronts Symeon's conscious actions of madness with his spectators' reactions. Being unaware of his spiritual consciousness, they treat him like an ordinary madman. The reader, however, is placed in the position of the omniscient observer, and learns about Symeon's plot from the beginning. This enables the author to construct the literary tension that lies in the heart of this literary work, building it up toward the discovery of Symeon's conscious identity after his death.

In this story too, the hero is presented as a sane person whose insanity is not genuine, but deliberately assumed. His madness is not an actual mental state or illness, but a simulation, within his social and cultural context. The point of the discovery of the simulated insanity, or of the concealed spirituality, is also the point where the tension between the conscious actions of madness and the reactions of the spectators toward them is resolved. At this point the story ends. In this, hagiographies dealing with holy fools are no different from any other type of hagiography about a saint in disguise.[14] The analysis of the holy fool as a literary topos, therefore, does not pose particular problems for the modern historian. But, this is not the case for the analysis of the holy fool as a historical phenomenon.

The Holy Fool as a Historical Phenomenon

We can, of course, claim that this literature was purely fictional. No *real* holy fools existed. Such stories can then be seen as totally constructed by their authors, who had never seen a genuine holy madman or madwoman since no *real* persons feigned madness for Christ's sake. We can also avoid the question of authenticity altogether, and turn to look for the literary and philosophical roots of this literature, exploring the moral agenda of the authors who chose this literary model within the extensive production of Byzantine hagiography, the literature of saints' *Lives*.[15] However, by adopting such a strategy, we are avoiding an important historical aspect which these texts present, and which concerns the existence of holy folly not as a literary phenomenon, but also as a historical phenomenon.

Here we need to distinguish between the *reality* of people who feigned madness as a spiritual way of life on the one hand, and the way this was described and elaborated by the literature of the period on the other. It is evident that we can examine the second aspect without the first. The question is whether the first can be distinguished from the second. In other words, the question is whether we can discuss the existence of people who feigned madness when our main sources are hagiographic tales whose descriptions of historical figures are of doubtful authenticity. Did *real* people exist behind these literary characters? Did *real* sane persons consciously choose to play the mad in disguise?

To answer the question about the authenticity of holy fools, those historians who deal with the subject refer to Evagrius Scholasticus, a Christian historian of the sixth century. In his *Ecclesiastical History* he tells of the existence of this peculiar type of holy men, who "by presenting themselves deranged [Greek: *paraphoroi*], thus they fool vainglory [Greek: *kenodoxia*]."[16] Evagrius describes the acts of one of these holy madmen, Symeon, in another place in his *History*:

> Now in Emesa there lived Symeon, a man who had shed the robe of vanity to such an extent that to those who did not know he even appeared to be deranged [Greek: *paraphoros*], although he was indeed filled with all sacred wisdom and grace. This Symeon lived for the most part by himself, not allowing anyone at all an opportunity to know when and how he propitiated the divinity, nor when he held fasts or partook of food by himself. But there were times indeed when, while frequenting the main streets, he appeared to have been estranged from normality, and to be completely devoid of sense and intelligence.[17]

Thus Symeon was a true historical figure, not a fictional character invented by the hagiographer Leontius of Neapolis. Evagrius's description attests to the fact that the phenomenon of the holy fool was not a literary invention. It was grounded in Byzantine reality. Real figures were believed to practice it. This was not, however, always the case with every saint's *Life*. When it comes to the *Life of Andrew salos*, scholars tend to agree that there was no true historical figure lying behind this literary creation, but that the anonymous author based his story on the literary model of Symeon of Emesa.[18]

Although they are the most famous, Symeon and Andrew were not the only examples of Byzantine holy fools who achieved a cult in the Orthodox Church.[19] They belonged to a widespread cultural phenomenon of Orthodox Christianity whose authenticity is attested by the sources of the period. We should therefore take this phenomenon at face value. However, taking the existence of *real* holy madmen at face value proves to be a tricky business.

A Psychohistorical Approach

In searching for a way to torment themselves, holy fools were no different from other types of saints peculiar to early Christianity: anchorites (who retired to the desert), stylites (who spent long periods of their life on top of a pillar), and other types of extreme asceticism. All these types express and are dependent on expressing and portraying an abnormal pattern of behavior of self-denial. While their societies exemplified such abnormal behavior as spiritual, the modern reader tends to consider such persons as extreme eccentrics, social dropouts, or even psychotics. By doing this we avoid the social and cultural aspects of the phenomenon, and focus on the individual. Scholars who go along with this line of thought adopt a modern psychological analysis of historical phenomena. Such forms of asceticism are thus considered an abnormal psychological pattern of behavior which is grounded, at least in part, in the ascetic's mental state.[20]

Such an approach is very informative as far as the modern way of analysis of psychohistory is concerned: it reveals modern psychological classifications and shows how they can be plausibly used in historical analysis.[21] Thus young ascetic women could be considered as suffering from anorexia, while visions are considered to be caused by dementia or migraines. It is not surprising that such an approach has been adopted by psychologists and psychiatrists who have tried to apply the interpretation of their discipline to the study of history. This is the approach taken, for example, by Oliver Sacks in his interpretation of the visions of Hildegard of Bingen, or in the analysis of St. Francis's behavior as a typical kind of teenage hysteria.[22] In the case of the holy fool, this kind of reasoning will consider a person who feigns madness as a pathologically disturbed person. The sources portray the main objective of the holy fool as to be constantly despised by his society. This cannot be considered sane by modern standards, since no sane person would arrive at the conclusion that acting mad can be spiritually beneficial, and no search for humility or indeed humiliation achieved by attracting contempt could be considered sane. In fact any ascetic behavior aimed at causing bodily suffering or public humiliation is considered masochistic and abnormal by modern psychological standards.[23]

We shall get to the discipline of psychohistory below. It is sufficient to note at this stage that by focusing on the experiences of the individual, psychohistory takes the narratives of such historical texts as accurate descriptions of the mental state of historical figures and ignores the fact that the narratives it uses were constructed in order to fulfill a specific cultural function.[24] The historian, however, must acknowledge that such types of abnormality were considered holy in the society in which they occurred. Moreover, the historian needs to make this assertion the main point of investigation. In other words, historical research must treat psychopathology as a coded system.

A psychohistorical attitude, therefore, ignores an extremely important aspect of these phenomena of extreme tormented behavior, since it does not address the fact that such behavior received the approval, encouragement, and even admiration of society.[25] In other words, in their society such types of abnormal behavior were exemplified, and such figures were not considered madmen, but heroes and saints. It is thus impossible to comprehend the behavior of such persons without focusing on the way in which it was understood at the time.[26] In other words, we cannot define such persons as insane since this depends on standards of modern psychology, which are anachronistic to the society in question.[27] It is therefore essential to consider the cultural context of the holy fool phenomenon in order to decode it.

Theological and Cultural Aspects

Taking the cultural phenomenon of holy folly as the main objective of investigation evokes a number of questions: When and where did holy fools emerge? How did Christian authors treat them? What transformation did this phenomenon undergo throughout the ages? What was its theological dimension? And what was its relation to similar types of holy madness in neighboring religious environments, as well as in other cultures throughout history and in present times? All these questions stay within the scope of the discipline of history and focus on the cultural atmosphere that enabled the belief in feigning madness for a spiritual cause.[28] Since holy fools are by definition a religious phenomenon, scholars explore the theological systems which sustained this, the differences between them, and the ways in which they characterize the holy man, as well as the differences between holy fools and other fools, such as the village fool, the king's fool, and their like. Reading the holy fool as a religious phenomenon provides a means of breaking the hagiographic circle of its sources and finding the theological perception that enabled its existence. In other words, this attitude can help us find the mental context of the belief in and the existence of holy fools.[29]

Being extremely attentive to the different elements and nuances within similar phenomena, Sergey Ivanov has succeeded in reading cultural developments and ruptures in the religious productions that dealt with the phenomenon of the holy fool over more than a millennium of Greek and Russian Orthodox Christianities. Thus he has differentiated the Russian holy fool from the Byzantine. Ivanov explains the emergence of the holy fool against the background of other types of concealed sanctity of early Christianity, whose main aim was to achieve humility, while avoiding at all costs the admiration that humble behavior had inspired. Madness thus provided the "perfect" means by which people could adopt an abnormal behavior pattern which concealed their aspiration to humility. Moreover, by assuming madness, such persons attracted contempt and derision from their surroundings, and thus found the way to be in a state of constant torment. This is elaborated in the sixteenth "saying" (*mēmrā*) of the fourth century Syriac *Book of Steps* (*Liber gradum*), which describes the highest level of perfection for ascetics who go beyond the level of the fulfillment of the commandments:

> Let me describe for you an insane person [Syriac: *šāṭyā*],[30] so that when you see someone who treats himself with contempt and does not own a house or a wife and any property, not even garments besides his clothes, not food apart from a day-to-day [supply], say: "these are my [ways of life] and I should imitate them." When you see him talking in insanity [Syriac: *bešāṭyútā*] with everyone—and [if] he establishes a law for himself so that he may not become angry in order not to be found at fault, and [if] he despises the wisdom [of] the wise sage of the world and the philosopher because he is contemptuous of whatever is visible, say: "These are mine, this is the insanity/folly [Syriac: *šāṭyútā*] of the apostles." [But] when you see that he uses magic or practices divination or fornication or consults oracles or that he bows down before idols, say: "These are not mine." The fools of the world [Syriac: *saklohey d'almā*], in their foolishness [Syriac: *besaklotehon*], are not able to distinguish between whoever is dishonoring them and whoever is honoring them, and they would be talking first thing in the morning with that one who struck them in the evening. Imitate them in this way. Enter [the home of] people who are insolent to you as a fool [Syriac: *saklā*] and talk with them and honor those who honor you. Look at the fool who cannot distinguish good people from bad in this foolishness [Syriac: *beskālā*], and in the same way you should love the good and the bad while knowing them [for who they are]. When you see that he is acting foolishly, if

> someone says to him: "Go, fornicate or steal or curse," and he does so foolishly [Syriac: *besaklotehon*], do not imitate him. Because [it is] by the cunning [Syriac: *dmin ḥār'ūtā*] or worldly wisdom he will say to you: "Become a fool [Syriac: *hevei saklā*]," not by heavenly wisdom. Do not become like these cunning sages, seeing evil ones and judging them, but become like these fools, seeing [the evil ones] and disregarding their follies [Syriac: *saklotehon*]. Like a heavenly sage advise them to repent, and do not judge them like an earthly sage lest through evil ones they might die. Imitate the grace of God and treat everyone well and do not imitate him who repays everyone according to his deeds, because you are neither being [itself] nor one who is without law like him. Because if he does not establish justice for the oppressed, who will do it? Do you wish to become like him? Make for yourself a creation like him and do not become a god in his creation, lest he overthrow you as [he has overthrown] Satan.[31]

This saying constructs a model of a high level of perfection concentrated on the pure and innocent heart, total forgiveness, and love of one's neighbor, all of which will lead the believer away from society and the earthly world toward the only important combat of a true believer: the combat with Satan.[32] All the same, this saying gives a new meaning to insanity which was not in Paul's intention. It understands insanity as a form of *xeniteia*, being a *xenos*, a stranger to the world.[33] It proposes to whoever wants to be saved to become a social outcast, imitating, of course, the example of Jesus.[34] The insane, or the fool, is here a model for this purity of heart, and insanity/folly (rather than foolishness or foolery) is perceived here as a means of attaining innocence as a sense of unawareness.[35] This is the theological reasoning that leads to sanctifying people who make themselves outcasts as a form of perfection. In a word, we see here how theological legitimacy constructs the meaning of *xeniteia* as extreme social alienation and insanity.

As stated by Evagrius Scholasticus, one of the objectives of such behavior was to avoid vainglory.[36] Other texts present it as a way of humiliation and repentance. This is indicated in the fourth step, "on obedience," of John Climacus's "The Ladder of Divine Ascent," by the behavior of Antiochus the monk, who plays the madman as a means of repentance.[37] Antiochus was an honored and respected monk, who left his monastery to join a monastery in the Pontos where he could fight his vainglory by being a stranger, a *xenos*. His form of humiliation and the abuse he suffers from the other monks is presented and perceived as his way to pay off his debt to God. When he realizes in a dream that after three years he has only paid off a tenth of his debt, he decides to become a madman (Greek: *exēchon*) in order to accelerate his suffering. While not neglecting his monastic duties, as a madman he manages to repay his sin of vainglory after thirteen years (and he gets a receipt for paying off his debt, in a dream). Another example, this time from an urban environment, is Mark the fool ("of the Hippos") from Alexandria.[38] Mark was a monk who, after being "ruled by the demon of fornication for fifteen years," decides to serve Christ to redeem himself from his sin. For eight years he hangs about with madmen. He takes care of their needs out of his daily salary at the local baths or by stealing (snatching from people on the streets, specifically in contrast to the statement in the *Book of Steps*). He ridicules himself and others in the city, until Daniel of Sketis, the author of the story, publicaly discloses his true character as a holy man. It is clear that in constructing the figure of the holy fool, the authors used symptoms which were assigned to their definition of insanity and the mental perception of their society.

Taking the existence of holy fools as being grounded within a system of beliefs and mental perceptions, therefore puts the emphasis on the cultural context of this phenomenon. However, to perceive the existence of such figures only as part of a specific set of beliefs, which gave it a meaning and in which it had a specific role to play, shifts the emphasis away from the holy fool as an individual, and focuses entirely on the ways in which this figure was perceived and constructed by society, or in other words, on the cultural function that such figures fulfilled.

This perspective ignores a hidden tension within the phenomenon of the holy fool. This tension is a product of the relation between the individual who embodies the holy fool and society, and it evolves around the *true* existence of the holy fool. If feigning madness had a particular theological meaning in Orthodox Christianity, or in any other system of beliefs for that matter, it filled a specific cultural function. But was that function the main reason for the creation of the idea of holy fools? In other words, how can we know whether insane persons were not chosen to fill this cultural function to begin with? To put it differently, since this form of holiness is by definition concealed, we can never know whether such persons *really* feigned madness as a form of holiness, or whether society assigned a spiritual intention to *real* madmen.

Although holy fools are attested to exist by the sources of their time, it does not necessarily follow that they did. In other words, the question that we need to pose is the following: Were these people, who appeared to be madmen, sane persons who feigned madness as the sources tell us, or were they insane persons on whom society projected a new definition of holiness in order to fill a cultural function? Did Symeon really feign his madness? Can we really know? This appears to be a question of whether we can achieve historical certitude. However, it is a question of particular type of historical certitude.

Who Is the *Real* Madman? A Question of Ambiguity

In an article about historical certitude, Donald Logan sets out three different types of historical *in*certitude: about the existence of an event, about the authenticity of a historical document, and about human motive.[39] Each type symbolizes a different kind of relationship between historical evidence and the modern methodology that deals with its presence or absence. Historians depend both on sources and on their methods of interpretation. According to Logan's three examples, this is true in regard to the very existence of historical phenomena, the authenticity of documents about historical phenomena, as well as the causality of historical phenomena. As any historian knows, the three are connected in that they are all parts of the same methodology of the discipline of history.

These three examples are different, however, from the problem of incertitude that we face in regard to the holy fool phenomenon. Our problem here lies not with the lack of sources that could point to causality or to the motivation of these persons, but with the very question of whether the recorded phenomenon happened. The sources themselves demonstrate the incertitude over the existence of the phenomenon: "There was a certain village chief living near Emesa, and as he heard about Symeon's way of life, he said 'believe me, if I see him, I'd know whether he is a simulator (Greek: *prospoiētos*) or whether he is truly a madman (Greek: *exēchos*).'" And he goes to test Symeon, and of course fails.[40] Holy people really feigned madness as a religious way of life, the sources tell us. We, however, doubt this affirmation, but why? Our doubtfulness comes not from lack of sources, but from the way in which we formulate our analysis. We make the following assertion:

although we have concrete sources attesting to the phenomenon of sane people feigning madness for a spiritual cause, we cannot know for sure whether holy fools were *really* sane people.

But why doubt Evagrius? If we take him as a reliable source for the existence of holy fools, why doubt that they *really* feigned their madness? It is here that the main problem of interpretation lies. Evagrius is an author of the sixth century who writes within the mental settings of his time. What he saw were people who appeared mad and who became the objects of a cult as saints in disguise. Being part of the same society, Evagrius also considered them saints in disguise. We, however, by defining as part of our subject of investigation the society which believed in holy fools, come to identify a trap within our sources. The sources which describe a phenomenon lie, in the words of Lévi-Strauss, "within the same system of reference" as the phenomenon, and in fact validate and complement it.[41] This turns the description into a sort of a trap to the modern mind, which masks the very existence of the phenomenon as it is evidenced. In other words, the gap between the modern historian and his subject of investigation lies in the gap between two sets of mentality. This is not different from metaphysical phenomena attested by historical sources, whose very ontological existence is difficult to perceive by modern research. Madness, however, is not a metaphysical phenomenon, nor is simulated madness. In the way it is constructed within the phenomenon of the holy fool it presents, nevertheless, a conundrum whose nature and function we shall now examine.

Psychohistorical approaches cannot help us here since they depend on the fact that people who feigned madness intentionally for the sake of heaven *really* existed. In other words, they take such authors as historical sources for the existence of the holy fool phenomenon without taking into account that the same authors created it. Cultural historical approaches cannot help us either since they bypass the question of authenticity altogether. In fact, we can argue that the sources are masking the ontological existence of the phenomenon. Moreover, this masking appears to be inherent to the phenomenon, and corresponds to an ambiguity which this phenomenon expresses. In formulating this argument we are following in the footsteps of Shoshana Felman in her interpretation of Henry James's *The Turn of the Screw*.[42]

The Turn of the Screw novella is centered around the discovery of a letter whose author, a young governess, narrates the appearance of a ghost in the family's residence and the effects that it had on herself and the family. The letter confronts the reader with an intellectual dilemma: either to accept the existence of the ghost as *truth,* or attribute it to the governess's delirium. In his article "The Ambiguity of Henry James," Edmund Wilson chose the second perspective and applied a Freudian analysis to read the governess' character.[43] According to this approach, the governess appears a sexually repressed woman whose hidden desires lead to delirium. Wilson's analysis is thus one-sided in that it takes the novella as dealing with the difference between *real* and *unreal,* while projecting his own concept of what is *real* on the heroine's story.

Felman, on the other hand, shows how the entire novella is constructed around a multiplicity of voices which the reader is exposed to.[44] This creates an ambiguity that the reader is confronted with in the attempt to analyze and even to perceive the text. According to Felman's reading, Wilson completely ignored the fact that the literary role of the governess was constructed to serve to create ambiguity in the reader's mind. Moreover, the ambiguity not only is deliberate but also encapsulates the very subject of the novella, namely, in Felman's words, "to express the conflict which inhabits meaning."[45] By focusing on the role of the ambiguity that the author creates in the reader, Felman reveals the nature of the enigmatic character of the text: the reader's incapacity to grasp its meaning by being trapped within the story between interpretations. This situation symbolizes, in her words, "the very traps of unconsciousness."[46] The ambiguous position is not only intrinsic to the story but also essential in order to undermine the reader's consciousness. In other words, the ambiguity at the level of the story is here constructed to evoke an ambiguity at the level of its reading.[47] "The trap," as Felman calls it, is made possible by the way in which these two ambiguities relate one to another. The reader is compelled to "take sides" in order to relate to the existence of the ghost. But the author has constructed this choice in such a way that it reflects on the reader's own perception of his real world. By adopting a Freudian reading Wilson has managed to bypass the entire trap, since the psychological analysis could very well take the existence of the ghost at face value *for* the governess by making *her* consciousness *trapped.* Such a reading, which flattens the novella by ignoring its levels of ambiguity, was not James's intention, in Felman's view. She manages to reveal the "trap"—that is, the reflexive nature of the novella—by putting the emphasis not on the character of the heroine, but on the way in which the story and its ambiguity affects the reader.[48]

The holy fool phenomenon produces the same kind of "trap." It is, of course, apparent that the entire phenomenon, as portrayed by the hagiographers and the writers who described it, is constructed around the ambiguity of the fool/madman who can at any point be disclosed as *a fake* and thus holy. This ambiguity about the fool is not set at the level of the story—to the reader it is obvious that the hero is not insane. It is set at the level of the historical context which attributed such behavior to *real* people. This means that in theory any insane person could be a saint in disguise. In other words, although the reader knows from the beginning that the fool is faking insanity, since the story is told as a true historical case it creates a doubt about the perception of insanity and madmen who can be plausible holy men in disguise regardless of its actual authenticity. In other words, ambiguity about insanity and holiness is one of the effects, a deliberate effect we can argue, of this phenomenon.

The ambiguity about this phenomenon is well attested by the sources. In 692 the Byzantines held their fifth-sixth universal council in Constantinople under the emperor Justinian II. In one of its decisions the council forbade the feigning of possession by demons.[49] The decision does not refer to "madness" here by name, but to "demoniacs." Nevertheless, it is clear that it is referring to the same phenomenon.[50] Although demonic possession and medical madness are not identical, the medical literature of the period shows that they can have the same symptoms.[51] Moreover, the use of the term "demoniacs" corresponds to the objective of the Council's decision: to anathematize such behavior.

Simulation of insanity is a well-known phenomenon that exists in many societies as a means to evade social circumstance, and was also known to the Byzantines.[52] We can of course never know whether the believers simulated madness as forms of *xeniteia*, or for any other reason. Two Byzantine writers, Kekaumenos and Theodore Balsamon, give evidence that simulated madness continued to be prevalent in Byzantine society into the eleventh and twelfth centuries, and both paint a picture of ambiguity in respect to the question who is a genuine madman and who simulates madness.[53] These sorts of descriptions, like the Church's decision from 692, provide the social framework for the creation of the religious literature about the holy fool, and leave the historian in a state of vertiginous incertitude.[54] This means that the state of ambiguity of the madman and the phenomenon of the holy fool in itself affects the readers by imposing ambiguity on them as beholders of insanity in *real life* regardless of the authenticity of the actual phenomenon. This ambiguity was a real phenomenon in Byzantine society, and threatened the beholder's sense of perception of insanity.[55] To put it differently, the ambiguity of the holy fool creates an ambiguity about sanctified insanity, that is, an ambiguity between sanctity and insanity, which penetrates into the reader's perception of reality. While those reading about the holy fool do not experience ambiguity on the literary level, the holy fool's ambiguity becomes the ambiguity they experience in real life. The abnormal personality—the plausible holy madman or madwoman—thus expresses and symbolizes the ambiguity of each beholder.

This ambiguity works also in regard to the historian's own perception. The modern historian cannot know whether such persons *really* feigned their madness or whether society projected on them a form of sanctity regardless of their mental state. Moreover, this puts the historian in exactly the same state of incertitude as the society surrounding these madmen, not knowing whether a madman is *really* insane or whether he is a holy man who is faking his mental state. This "trap" we've identified is the main function of the phenomenon of holy fools. In other words, in what follows we shall see that this ambiguity is intrinsic not only to the phenomenon but also its objective and its meaning. We thus leave the level of the text in order to trace the effect that the ambiguity that it created had on the social level.

The Problem in Feigning Madness

Although the narratives that concern holy fools do not reveal an ambiguity about the heroes who are presented from the beginning as being *fake* madmen and madwomen, readers are, all the same, faced with an ambiguity in regard to the social context of this phenomenon. If the objective of these texts is to assert the existence of holy men or women in the disguise of insanity, they undermine at the same time the ability to define who is *truly* insane. If society sanctifies the existence of a fake insanity, how could it ever distinguish the *real* madman from the fake one? Thus we see that on the social level the phenomenon of the holy fool generates an ambiguity about insanity.

Once the phenomenon of the holy fool is regarded as genuine and not merely a literary construction, it undermines the capacity to differentiate the insane from the saint. Society can never know for sure whether any particular case of insanity as it appears in public is genuine.[56] The possibility that this is a holy man disguised as an insane person always exists. This also means that sanctity might be assigned to any form of abnormal behavior, including *real, authentic*—that is, unintentional—insanity. This ambiguity results in the incapacity to distinguish an *authentic* from a *fake* madman , and moreover in legitimizing this incapacity and attributing it with a meaning. The ambiguity is therefore meaningful, an integral part of the phenomenon, and derives from the fact that this literature was not written nor read as fiction, but as history, and its objective was to present the existence of a cult around such figures.

The ambiguity that we identify as embedded in the phenomenon of the holy fool at the historical social level thus leads to the following problem: if a society acknowledges the existence of holiness in the disguise of insanity, how could it ever draw a concrete line between sanity and insanity? In other words, what we see here is that the belief in the existence of the holy fool figure makes a simulated insanity an accepted norm, and renders the question who is and who is not genuinely insane impossible to discern. Moreover, once feigning madness becomes a defined form of sanctity which receives social admiration, and is institutionalized in the framework of a cult, it is legitimized and, indeed "normalized." This is the meaning of the sanctification of such social behaviors. Here we can identify a dialectics that involves society and the individual. This dialectics is constructed around the abnormal behavior of such figures and the way in which society perceives and interprets it. This is not only a question of the cultural system in which this sort of behavior "makes sense," but also a question of what effect such a sense has on society. Focusing on the question of whether such persons *really* feigned their madness, we thus shift our attention within the scope of our investigation from the holy fools themselves to the society which believed in their existence, and which created a social dynamics around the ambiguity that holy fools generate by sanctifying their behavior through such holy stories. This shift of attention originates the difference in the perception and interpretation of the phenomenon in question. This literature was written with the clear premise that sane people feigned madness for spiritual reasons. As historians, however, we read this phenomenon differently: we do not accept this premise as axiomatic. In a world of scholarship about normal and abnormal social behavior, we are aware that abnormal phenomena could have social and cultural meanings.

The ambiguity that the historian identifies represents, therefore, a social incertitude about insanity, sanity, and sanctity within the society that believed in and sanctified holy fools. Whether these were instances of pathological behavior is not important here. The main thing is that this was also an unanswerable question in their society. This incertitude means that such a society blurs the borderline between insanity and sanity by introducing a third element: sanctity. Once a hidden sanctity is believed to exist in insanity, any insane person could be a saint in disguise. Moreover, any insane person could *become* a saint in disguise. Since in this form of sanctity sanity must always be kept hidden, there would be no way of differentiating between the two. In other words, people like Evagrius could very well have attributed sanctity to *real* madmen or madwomen by judging their madness as simulated, as an enactment of a genuine holy state, thanks to their sanctification, that is, the cult that they received in their society.

A society that acknowledges the existence of holy fool can thus never know for sure whether that person is *genuinely* insane. In this, the ambiguity of the holy fool figure blurs the borderline between sanity and insanity. This is what we can term the paradox of the holy fool phenomenon: when every insane person could be a saint in disguise, no person can be considered insane with complete certitude. Kekaumenos describes this vividly when he gives advice about how should one behave when meeting a madman:

> Do not joke with a madman [Greek: *aphoronos*]; he will insult you and maybe will pull your barb; think how shameful to you. If you do let him, everyone will laugh. If you will hit him, you will be blamed and abused by everyone. The same will happen to you also with those who simulate the madman [Greek: *tois prospoioumenois to salon*]. In fact, I tell you to let them be, playing and laughing with them could be harmful. I have seen others, who laughed and played with someone like that, have killed him after playing. In any case, do not joke or hit a madman [*salos*] whoever he may be. When someone who simulates the madmen [Greek: *tou hupokrinomenou to salon*] speaks to you, hear him out, but do not consider him. Maybe he wishes to trap you through the figure of the *salos*.[57]

In fact, the only certitude that the figure of holy fools embody is that their true character cannot be disclosed. In a word, the ambiguity that their character symbolizes cannot be resolved. The problem of incertitude imbedded at the core of the phenomenon creates, moreover, another incertitude at the level of the historical analysis. In addition to the question of whether such fools *really* existed, the historian is also faced with a problem of comprehending a society in which an insane person is potentially a saint. A society whose sanity-insanity borderline is blurred loses its ability to define who is *really* insane. Moreover, once the phenomenon of the holy fool is acknowledged and legitimized, any insane person, whether *fake* or *authentic*, can in fact be considered holy.[58] In other words, the possibility that sanity is concealed under the cover of insanity and that insanity could be intentional and hence simulated, can undermine, as we shall see below, the very cause of the holy fool.

The ambiguity of this phenomenon acts, therefore, on two levels. On the one hand, it prevents the holy fool's society from knowing who is who, that is, from distinguishing an *authentic* madman or madwoman from the *fake* one. On the other hand, it does not allow the historian to establish certitude about the *authenticity* of the very phenomenon. We can answer the question why someone would make himself or herself mad for the cause of religion by contextualizing this phenomenon within the cultural and religious atmosphere of the period under examination. But, the main question concerns the holy fool as a social phenomenon; in other words, why would society choose to sanctify this sort of behavior at a cost of losing one of its most important borderlines: the border between sanity and insanity? As we have seen, the second question derives from a paradox that concerns the ambiguity of the figure of the holy fool. Although they deal with pinning down, or identifying and sanctifying, such figures, the sources paradoxically undermine any way of recognizing and identifying them. Moreover, in this they also undermine the way of identifying insanity. This is also the reason why we will not find stories about *real* madmen or madwomen who were sanctified. The sanctification in itself is a proof of the simulation of the insane state.

Psychohistory that focuses on the individual cannot helps us here since, as Joan Scott noted, it tends to reaffirm the discipline of history's concept of itself by choosing aspects of psychoanalytic theory that are least challenging to history's epistemology.[59] In the case of the holy fool we can never know whether the simulation of madness really occurred, which renders a psychological analysis of this behavior completely useless. Although sanctified insanity is indeed a psychological and a historical phenomenon, it nevertheless reveals what Scott names "the incommensurability" of history and psychoanalysis. Following Scott we shall proceed by examining the holy fool phenomenon from a historical-psychological perspective in order to illustrate what she marks as "the critical possibilities that inhere in a relationship of incommensurability" between history and psychoanalysis. As we saw, the paradox about the holy fool phenomenon does not enable us to use psychology in order to reaffirm the discipline of history's concept of itself. In fact, it does the opposite. By constructing an uncertainty about this phenomenon's ontology it renders the historian's method useless.

To Conclude

We have identified an ambiguity that the literature about insanity and holiness creates and presents to the reader. Moreover, we have concluded that as historians we are unable to decipher this ambiguity set on the level of the Byzantine reader, because we face an ambiguity of our own in regard to the authenticity of the phenomenon in question. We need to find a method that will enable us to connect as scholars to the effects that this literature had on the Byzantine reader. Yet, since we have nothing but this very literature which cannot serve as historical evidence, the question is how we can explain the meaning of this double-faced ambiguity. In what follows we shall take this as the main theme of our investigation and will put our own method of approaching historical literary texts into question. We have encountered, in the words of Michel de Certeau, a simple localization of disorder . . . an event names what cannot be understood."[60] It cannot be understood within the discipline of history. We need to look elsewhere, and in the process we will undoubtedly need to challenge the way in which historians perceives reality. We need to look for "psychic logic that will give way to the logic of history."[61] What follows is an endeavor to fit history and psychoanalysis into a two-way-street relationship. Following Felman we shall start by examining the way in which literature about the holy fool translates the story to real life.

2

Meanings of Insanity

> Literature is the theoretic discourse of historical processes. It creates the no-place where the effective operations of society get validation. Far from considering literature as an "expression" of a framework of reference, we should recognize it as an analogue to what mathematics have always been to the exact sciences: a "logical" discourse of history, the "fiction" which makes it thinkable.
>
> —Michel de Certeau, 1981

In the previous chapter we identified the paradox embedded in sanctified insanity, and found it impossible to resolve for the modern historian because it is constructed around ambiguity. The present chapter examines the social background of this phenomenon in an attempt to decipher the meaning of ambiguity that it sets around the borderline between what is normal and abnormal behavior. Our objective in the present chapter is twofold. First, we need to understand the meaning of the holy fool phenomenon for Byzantine society. Second, we need to find a way to address the ambiguity that it presents within the methodology of the field of research. In other words, in order to analyze the phenomenon in its historical context we must find a way to deal with the ambiguity it presents on both the historical and historiographical levels, that is, both for the society which is our subject of research and for our own method of analysis. Avoiding this tension would lead to an analysis focused solely on the literary, religious, or cultural aspects of the phenomenon in question.

In the previous chapter we saw that this twofold objective is conditioned by the fact that our sources conceal the ontological aspect of the phenomenon under a veil of ambiguity. We must therefore start by asking what might be the meaning of this ambiguity. If it were not for their ambiguous character, holy fools would simply have been taken to be ordinary madmen and would offer nothing to their society. However, the ambiguity embedded in this phenomenon reveals the functional character of madness itself, since it makes it impossible to establish a distinction between "fake" (simulated) and "authentic" insanity. As we shall see, it is precisely the unresolved tension around this ambiguity that makes insanity socially functional. This will require us to move in three different directions and to look for the ways in which historical, literary, and psychoanalytical analyses can unfold the meaning of creating ambiguity about insanity by attributing sanctity to it.

The Logic of History

Attempts at Explanation

The phenomenon of the holy fool has attracted a great deal of attention in recent scholarship, which has understood it in cultural, religious, theological, and social contexts.[1] The research on this topic emphasizes the social, provocative, and scandalous role of the holy fool. However, while some see this figure as part of the social structure, with a specific social role to play (like the king's fool, for instance), other see the holy fool as the perfect liminal figure of religious experience, a position which enables the fool to become, in the words of Weber, a "religious virtuoso."[2] These views are justified by Christian theology, which gives such figures the legitimacy they need, and also makes their behavior religiously meaningful: the fool becomes a special creature which in playing the "beast" manages to exist both inside and outside society, an angel present within the human being, whose role is nonetheless to touch the believers' lives and fight the evils within society as a "breaker of norms" (*antinomian*), as Guy Stroumsa puts it.[3] This approach is also developed by Andrew Thomas: the role of holy fool is to break and transform ascetic and monastic norms.[4] As liminal religious virtuosi, such figures can be extremely useful to society, but also extremely dangerous for the religious authorities.

In modern scholarship liminality has become a method of explaining the social dynamism of religion. According to this perspective, the *limes*, the borders of society, enable the rise of new social phenomena which by gaining de facto legitimacy can challenge religious authority and expand it.[5] The power that "liminal" figures have acquired on the periphery of religious experience, beside or beyond the *limes* and away from the watchful eye of the establishment, leads to a de jure change of cultural norms, and through this a change of the social structure as well.[6] In a word, liminality becomes a means of changing power relations. From this perspective holy fools are an example par excellence of this sort of liminal figure. Their liminal position as madmen expresses and embodies their particular form of alienation (*xeniteia*), and can become both theologically meaningful and socially functional. Their madness makes their sanctity particularly hard to grasp, and their ambiguity makes them immune. These religious phenomena function as a safety valve in the religious structure, rendering it elastic, flexible, and dynamic. Thus liminality is an inherent and much needed element for the functioning of the religious structure, where cultural changes appear as a reflection of social changes and vice versa. Whether we read the holy fool as a means of dynamizing monastic society or the ecclesiastical establishment, this figure represents a subversive threat to authority—any authority—and a means of changing the relations between center and periphery.

We find the response to this danger in the canons of the seventh-century ecumenical council, "the Council *in Trullo*" of 692, which aimed at suppressing such threats as "demoniac" and heretical.[7] We can also perceive the hagiography of the holy fool itself, and even the creation of this type of sanctity, as an appropriation of the dangerous phenomena of religious virtuosi by the ecclesiastical establishment, in short, as a response to the threat these phenomena express, as well as a means of appropriating them.[8] Ioan Lewis analyzed such dynamics of tension over power relation in different religious cultures, and showed them to be a central feature for the functioning of society.[9] His study, *Ecstatic Religions*, which is dedicated to the phenomenon of possession, reveals the way in which possession acts as a valve within religious societies, and offers both a means of dynamizing and changing them, as well as a means of soothing and resolving social tensions.[10] Such theories understand religion as a structure of power relations, and its different aspects as reflecting meeting points of power relations.[11] And the sanctification of such phenomena of abnormal social behavior, are understood as playing a role in such social dynamics.

Sergey Ivanov set out to examine the same question: What is it that causes society to look for sanctity in insanity? His elaborate study, which makes a firm distinction between Byzantine and Russian types of holy folly, has constructed the entire framework of the phenomenon in Byzantine society.[12] But for Ivanov too, this is first and foremost a cultural phenomenon that cannot be ontologically verified. The question whether "real" persons "really" simulated madness in order to approach the divine remains unaddressed. In fact, Ivanov is clear about this question: such persons did not exist.[13] Both Byzantine and Russian holy fools seem to be mainly the products of popular beliefs.[14] In Russian literature the village idiot represents this sort of mélange of holiness and insanity.[15] Such figures are idiots, imbeciles, but definitively not the sort of holy fools who simulate their insanity. In no way is their "authenticity" as insane or as abnormal questioned. Nevertheless, they are attributed with a role as symbols: their spiritual level, their holiness, derives from their total innocence. Since they have no reason, they can have no evil and thus are completely out of the reach of Satan. Their insanity makes their perfection total and complete.[16] Within the literary framework the historian identifies a specific literary role that the holy fools are set to play. But this is by no means the way in which the Byzantine reader perceives them. Byzantine literature makes their authenticity a matter of doubt, and their sanity concealed by a mask of insanity. Their ambiguity represents a much larger ambiguity: the ambiguity of the visible world.

Subversive Concealment

Ivanov rightly situates the Byzantine holy fool within other phenomena of concealed sanctity, which are so richly elaborated in Byzantine hagiography. Concealment of identity as a form of sanctity is a frequent hagiographic theme. One of the most famous is the woman disguised as a monk, which is mainly represented in the framework of a male monastic society.[17] The woman who conceals her sex in order to join a male environment transgresses not only every social norm, but more specifically monastic rules. Here too we are not informed whether such cases existed, or were purely figments of the imagination of monastic hagiographers. A priori, if we consider women as liminal for monastic male society, we could have found here an example of the subversive role of liminality as constructed in fictional hagiography.[18] However, the actual social role of women is here made totally irrelevant. The main thing is to render the visible world, even within a closed monastic community, uncertain, ambiguous, a field of combat.[19] In stories about monastic communities in the Egyptian desert, the figure of the cenobitic or anchorite monk or nun who simulates acts of madness expresses this very well. *The Sayings of the Desert Fathers* (*Apophthegmata Patrum*), for example, presents such persons as loners within the monastic community, but also as embodying a sort of a test for their brethren in daily life, as well as a model for imitation.[20] This can certainly join the thesis of Thomas, who attributes the role of social conscience to the *salos* in Egyptian monastic circles: provoking, dynamizing, and correcting, but at the same time preventing any feeling of self-satisfaction and personal perfection by ensuring that the borderline—the *limes*—of monastic life, whether coenobitic or anchoritic, will remain forever open.[21] Thus identifying social abnormality as a form of *xeniteia*, that is, as holiness, renders John Climacus's "The Ladder of Divine Ascent," the symbol of the fight for perfection, an infinite process. This way of stretching the ladder of perfection to infinity may have started in the monastic environment, but it certainly did not remain there.

In his *Lives of the Eastern Saints*, John of Ephesus situates this *strange* behavior of *xeniteia* within the Syrian cities, as in, for example, the story of Theophilus and Maria, who operate their holy mission under cover of two mime-actors (pimp and harlot) in the city of Amida.[22] The story is told by John, a monk who lived in the monastery of the narrator in Constantinople for seven years, and presented himself as an eyewitness:

> And they used to go about the city in that assumed garb in order to deceive the spectators, lest anyone should perceive and know what they were, and they used constantly to perform drolleries and buffooneries, being constantly in the courts of the church like strangers, jesting at the clergymen and everyone, and being boxed on their heads by everyone as mime-actors.[23]

They were a laughingstock in the city, and people used to joke with them and slap them on their heads. No one knew what happened to them at night. And since the woman was so beautiful, men were provoked by her and convinced the local governor to prostitute her. But her companion presented himself as her husband. A devout woman took her into her house; the girl did not give up her hidden mission, but begged the woman to pray that God would remove her from her sins. One night, John follows them and finds them praying, and they confess their story to him. They were a couple from Antioch who were meant to be betrothed. They heard a revelation from a holy man who directed them to "go out in an assumed garb and in strange countries, hiding the great profit of excellence which they earn, lest it be snatched from them, that they may live the spiritual life."[24] After they confess to John, they leave Amida, but are later spotted outside the city of Thella/Constantina.[25]

What these figures have in common with the holy fool is the fact that they are designated as hidden holy agents (Greek: *kruptoi douloi*, "God's hidden slaves").[26] In this story their mission is divinely revealed to the protagonist. In other forms of the "hidden slave," the protagonists themselves choose to live as secret agents of God. Besides a precarious life of wandering in accordance with the Syrian type of *xeniteia*, what such stories depict is the need of the social environment to put the visible reality into question. Such stories cannot exist, of course, without the unveiling of the disguise, and this has a specific social function which, of course, we also find in stories about holy fools. In this, such figures are tricksters par excellence.

Sanctified Insanity as a Trickster—Symeon *Salos*

The figure of the trickster has received much attention in modern scholarship, particularly in anthropology and cultural studies. Since the pioneering work of Paul Radin, many scholars have approached the subject from different angles.[27] Much of this scholarship assigns the same term, "trickster," to different figures in different societies and cultures without really paying attention to the great differences among them.[28] Many of these figures were never called tricksters outside modern scholarship. Nevertheless, many scholars do use this term, referring mainly to fictional figures who acquired a special position in distinct cultures thanks to the tricks they perform, by which they make fun of accepted norms, break taboos, and challenge and change the normal order. William Hynes has proposed the following six characteristics of a trickster: (1) possessing an ambiguous and anomalous personality; (2) deceiving and playing tricks; (3) shape-shifting; (4) inverting situations; (5) embodying messengers or imitators of the gods; and (6) presenting sacred or lewd bricolage.[29] In the seventh century, Leontius, bishop of Neapolis in Cyprus, chose the trickster framework in composing what is considered the most famous Byzantine story of a holy fool: the *Life of Symeon salos*.[30]

Much has been written on *The Life of Symeon salos*. In fact, in comparison with other texts about Byzantine saints, it undoubtedly ranks as one of the top subjects of interest to modern scholarship. The text is known from five manuscripts of the eleventh to twelfth centuries.[31] The story has three parts. After the author's declaration in the prologue that he has received the entire story from John the Deacon of Emesa, to whom Symeon confided it, he starts his story by describing the pilgrimage of two friends, Symeon and John, to Jerusalem, followed by their decision to join the monastery of Gerasimus in the Judaean desert, under the guidance of abba Nikon.[32] The second part tells how these two lived for twenty-nine years in complete solitude as grass eaters (Greek: *boskoi*) in the desert.[33] During this period, Symeon purifies himself, freeing himself from evil and attaining a state of complete inner calm, which provides him with clairvoyance.[34] In one of his ecstatic states Symeon perceives the deaths of his mother and John's wife.[35] He then decides to leave the desert in order to mock the world.[36] He goes to Jerusalem on a second pilgrimage, after which the third and last part of the text begins, in which Symeon mocks the world by playing the madman in the city of Emesa.[37]

Symeon's acts of madness are many and diverse. After his dramatic entrance into Emesa as a naked madman carrying a dead dog, he settles himself within the city, and behaves provocatively in order to scandalize the inhabitants and disturb their everyday life. His first act on a Sunday consists of throwing nuts in a church, from which he is immediately expelled. He walks around naked, defecates in public, and transgresses any norm of social and Christian behavior. This includes devouring meat and raw bacon in public.[38] He enters the women's baths, does not respect privacy, and goes inside private houses. From time to time he takes on occasional employment, but soon proves himself useless, if not dangerous. In developing the literary figure of Symeon, Leontius undoubtedly used motifs found in other stories about holy fools, and constructed a new model out of them. Derek Krueger has convincingly argued that in doing so he had the model of Diogenes the Cynic in mind.[39] Following Krueger in focusing on the author's relation to his literary hero, we shall nonetheless need to read this story as a spiritual experience, a *diēgēsis*.[40] In this we are also following Claudia Rapp's reading of the religious and theological function of such narratives (*diēgēses*).[41] Vincent Déroche has argued that the main function of the holy fool was to make others perceive their faulty behavior and repent without argumentation.[42] This is achieved by the psychological process that the figure of the holy fool generates. In fact, as Leontius presents it, Symeon's feigned madness caused a moral transformation of the city, though he had no position of authority. The main question for us is how madness can give rise to such a transformation in both the story and in real life.

At the literary level it is not difficult to see that Symeon is the trickster par excellence. His figure moves beyond the normal constraints of the body. By being as it were "without a body," the holy fool transgresses any sacred and accepted norm in daily life.[43] Symeon's objective is first of all to shock, to scandalize (Greek: *skandalein*), his beholders. He does this in both the private and public spheres, and indeed his acts clearly disturb the borderline between the two spheres. In fact, he aims to disturb any borderline: between public and private, men and women, rich and poor, masters and slaves. In this, he clearly implements literally the words of Paul (Gal. 3:28): "There is neither Jew nor Gentile, neither slave nor free, nor is there male and female, for you are all one in Christ Jesus." He disturbs the sinners and the unbelievers of the city by employing violence toward them. He makes girls cross-eyed, throws stones, and damages his employers.[44] Thus he frightens those around him. However, in order to make them change their ways, Symeon also uses magical forces. He reveals himself to them on a metaphysical level when seen conversing with angels, in dreams, or by other magical methods, all of which are intended to make others understand that his acts of violence result from their sinful actions.[45] He thus appears as the moral conscience of his surroundings. At times this message becomes explicit, as in the case of Symeon's breaking the glass vessels of a Jewish glassmaker one by one until he converts.[46] But in none of these cases does Symeon convey his message clearly. His language is opaque and subversive, and the message is expressed only through his acts of madness. Soon he becomes a one-man theater in the city. But this is a theater of ambiguities as the author portrays it.[47] People are attracted to his actions, but cannot really understand him or know who he truly is.

His prophetic qualities are eventually acknowledged. Thus he predicts which column will remain standing in a forthcoming earthquake, and which child will die in a plague. But the way he makes this known is abnormal: he wipes the columns with a cloth, and kisses the boys on their mouth.[48] The people of the city take this as part of his state of madness, and only realize in retrospect that he was prophesying. He never really allows those around him to discover his true divine character, and the fact that his madness is simulated.[49] He hangs out with possessed persons, making himself appear like one of them, and although they ask him to leave them alone, he nevertheless heals them by his prayers.[50] People even conclude that his state of madness is infectious.[51] All this leads to an ambiguity about him, which is presented to the reader at the level of the story. The conclusion of his entourage is that he is a madman of a spiritual nature. People begin to be affected by his presence and to turn to him for advice, even though they never stop treating him as a madman.[52] Each time that a miracle he performs is perceived and acknowledged, Symeon immediately acts insanely in order to cancel this impression, so that people will not doubt his state of madness.[53] This is the case, for instance, when he is falsely accused of having fornicated with another man's female slave.[54] The slave in question is pregnant, and does not contradict the accusations that Symeon is the father. He is found dancing and hitting his hand, saying that the child will not come out until she admits the true identity of the father. When the slave finally admits that Symeon is not the father, and reveals the father's identity, everyone is amazed. The family takes him for a saint (Greek: *hagios*), while others attribute his magic powers to Satan "since he is a pure madman (Greek: *epei exēchos katharos estin*)."[55] Others see him as a magician (Greek: *pharmakos*), or as a profound Gnostic.[56]

This ambiguity troubles those around him. People indeed ask themselves whether he is "truly" a madman (Greek: *alētheia estin exēchos*).[57] When a dignitary (a *protokomes*) arrives to test him, Symeon in a trickster-like manner slaps him, takes off his clothes, and proclaims: "there is no fraud here."[58] The dignitary cannot reveal him since he becomes mute.

The ambiguity about Symeon's true state remains unresolved. The author constructs this new status of ambiguity as precisely what enables Symeon to fight hidden crimes and vices and to cleanse the city of sin.[59] On the one hand, he plays and dances with prostitutes and actresses from the circus (one prostitute carries him, another spanks him).[60] On the other hand, while such acts have no effect on him, he plays the sinner, the possessed, the fool: he mimics people with deformed hips, leaps, walks on his bottom, plays a lunatic who is in trance, talks to himself. In short, it is "his favorite practice to [mimic] madness for Christ," and it is this that makes him capable of detecting and stopping sins. He sends divine punishment and accomplishes everything that he sets out to correct. Through his state of ambiguity of being—is he a holy vessel, a demonized madman, or a magician?—he can identify the sinners in the city and make them confront their sins. To preserve his ambiguity he carries out his miracles of healing through dreams.[61] The author indeed constructs his figure as "a new Lot coming invisibly (Greek: *aphanōs*) to the world as in Sodom."[62]

The analogy to Lot is significant: Symeon, like Lot in Sodom, lives in a sinful environment. Unlike the biblical Lot, however, Symeon's presence manages to transform the sinful city. Leontius brings this about by constructing the ambiguity about Symeon. In fact, this ambiguity serves to create a more general uncertainty in the city about the visible world. The author shows how Symeon's presence creates defamiliarization in his beholders, and with it a feeling of remorse about sinful acts and behavior. This ensures that the repentance Symeon causes is permanent.[63] His objective is to make people realize the existence of a hidden and divine reality: "man sees only the face, but God sees the heart. And no one can understand the actions of man without knowing his spirit."[64] The author thus uses the figure of the holy fool as means of blurring the borderline between the visible and invisible for his literary characters. The ambiguity of the holy fool makes this borderline impossible to trace.

In this way, the literary character of the holy fool enables the author to construct a social situation in which persons who put themselves in the lowest position, and are suppressed and abused by their social superiors, are put on a higher spiritual level than their abusers'. The inversion is the effect that the encounter with the hidden truth about the identity of the holy fools has on the Christian believer, and in fact on the society in general. The humiliation and repentance of the holy fools turns into the humiliation and repentance of their beholders. The Byzantine authors of such literary texts present holy fools as a means to correct society through their position as insane, as a means to make the divine presently active within society through the body of the insane. In other words, the holy fool is made here a symbol of the divine that can transform people, in a word: a *relational object*.[65] The question is how such a godly "relational object" functions not only within the story but also in real life. We shall now see that the important feature of this literary figure is to translate the story into real life, to activate this "relational object," if we will. This is done by using ambiguity.

Translating Holy Folly from the Story to Real Life

In his article dedicated to the story of a nun who feigned madness, Michel de Certeau reads her figure as a symbol of "the silence of the absolute."[66] Her body functions as a sort of a black hole (*trou sans fond*), which draws to her the sins of her entourage: Palladius calls her "the sponge of the monastery."[67] She takes upon herself whatever is missing in others, her body acting as a total negation of every aspect of social life. The story ends with the discovery of her holiness, like a true Cinderella, by the abbot who is sent to get her blessing. This discovery makes a groundbreaking crisis in the Tabennisi nunnery. In consequence, its four hundred nuns go through a process of repentance for having abused the mad nun. However, the abbot in no way reveals her true identity as a sane person who has simulated madness. He simply identifies her as holy, more holy than anyone else: "a mother to both you and me," as he says to the other nuns. Thus, through his authority, the abbot's revelation causes an inversion, both a cultural and a social one. But the heroine of this story refuses to take part in this inversion, and leaves the monastery.[68] In this way, the author manages to prolong her *xeniteia* to infinity. The story sets her as the complete negation of any norm or appropriate behavior. She does not speak, and never reveals her intention of playing an insane person. The other nuns do not repent because they acknowledge the fact that her insanity is simulated, which is never revealed. They repent because they have abused a person whose holiness is on a much higher level than their own. The fact that they were actually abusing an innocent woman is not the point here.

In a later Syriac elaboration of this story, where the heroine is named Onesima, the author devotes a much larger part of the text to her decision to simulate madness.[69] After spending forty years in the desert in complete isolation, she decides that she needs the company of others in order to be guided, corrected, and abused. In other words, she does not see herself as a *krupta doulē*, a holy hidden agent. Nor does she see herself as a vehicle of change. She seeks humiliation, which is exactly what an anchorite cannot achieve by living alone. The initiative for the general repentance of her entourage is given in both stories to divine providence. As far as the story is concerned, she insists on her public strangeness/alienation by playing the role of absolute negation. When she can no longer do this, she disappears.

Both de Certeau and Déroche show how in the story the figure of the holy fool (her body, in the words of de Certeau) is used in order to produce a change in the beholder. Déroche concentrates on the provoking character of the holy fool, and rightly emphasizes the fact that the repentance of the beholder comes with no exertion of power or authority over the believer.[70] This is for him the main quality of the holy madman. De Certeau, on the other hand, underlines the public role that this figure symbolizes as absolute otherness, the perfect stranger. At the end of the day, the unveiling of the disguise leads to repentance. But, in fact, this process deprives reason of any possibility of discerning between true and false, holy and profane, pure and polluted. He concludes that the objective of these phenomena proves here to be not a social or mental inversion, but a constant combat, a perpetual tension about interpreting reality through reason. It makes the visible invisible, instead of making the invisible visible.[71] In other words, the ambiguity of the phenomenon of the holy fool creates a disorder in the psyche of the beholder.[72] This is exactly the role that Felman identified in James's novella as we saw in the previous chapter. Such an ambiguity has a far-reaching impact, larger in its scope than merely scandalizing society. The ambiguity becomes the ambiguity of the beholder.

We see here that the personal objective of the literary character as presented by the author is by no means the objective for which the author constructs the story. While the first is to remain in a position of humiliation vis-à-vis society, the author uses this in order to generate a clash between this objective and society. The purpose of this clash is to attain an inversion of the characters' roles. Thus the discovery of the nun who feigned madness leads to her sanctification within the monastery by the nuns who abused her. This is the objective of the story: repentance of Christian society. And this objective also becomes an objective of the literary character of the holy fool. The author presents this figure as a passive character, abused and ridiculed as long as his or her sanctity is concealed, but also as an active agent of transformation for society.

As de Certeau shows, the function of holy fools is to take upon themselves (passively in the case of the nun who simulated madness, or actively in the case of Symeon and his followers) what is missing in others and in society, that is, to act as the conscience of their entourage.[73] In contrast to other types of saints, madmen do not reveal this explicitly. But through encounters with them, other people can experience exactly what their presence expresses: what they themselves are missing. Insanity makes this possible, because it is the exact negation of human structure—any structure, whether social, cultural, political, or mental. The madman and madwoman not only see what is missing, they *are* what is missing, as de Certeau tells us. Thus they need to fill this void. Here the revolutionary role of holy fools comes into play. They feel what others cannot see, and they become the vehicle for the transformation of others. This is also exemplified by another figure of Byzantine literature.

Vitalius is a secondary figure in Leontius of Neapolis's *Life of John of Cyprus*. Like Symeon he chooses to quit his life as an anchorite and to live in Alexandria in order to scandalize (Greek: *skandalein*) and transform the everyday lives and souls of the inhabitants of the city through their behavior.[74] In the words of Leontius of Neapolis, he is "approved by God to turn everyone, as David says (Ps. 15:9), according to his heart."[75] The holy fool thus becomes the means of revealing the truth about the Christian believers, and directing them to the true path. While not identified as such, the figure of Vitalius, as presented by Leontius, has all the characteristics of a holy fool who wants to mend society by a psychological transformation. His story clarifies how scandalizing Christian believers could be perceived as a means of correcting them. His first act is to prepare a list of the city's prostitutes. He then dedicates his nights and salary to paying them for a whole night, during which he keeps each of them from fornicating. However, since his mission is kept secret, he soon acquires the reputation of a great fornicator, and is consequently abused, mocked, and reproached as such. The prostitutes are the only ones who know the truth about his devotion, and share his secret. Some of them do repent and change their ways.[76] Everyone else sees him as a fornicator. He causes a general change of heart when his public message to the people of Alexandria is discovered after his death. The inscription that he leaves behind, near his body, orders Christians not to judge prematurely, prior to the coming of Christ.[77] The change of heart that the holy fool achieves in his beholders catalyzes the Christian community. It creates a psychological effect of conversion on the believers, and keeps the Christian faith in a process of constant revelation. Thus, scandalizing society by aberrant acts that seem sinful can in fact be divine, since it seeks to mend instead of to harm. One can thus never judge what one sees with one's own eyes, since there could well be an unknown truth hidden behind such acts.[78] The message is clear: there could be hidden sanctity in abnormal behavior. In this respect there is no difference between *authentic* madmen and holy fools: both reveal an alienation that becomes functional for those who surround them. In other words, the important lesson to be learned from the way in which insanity is sanctified here is that it can produce an uncanny feeling: in a word, its strangeness is contagious.

This is as far as the story is concerned. However, as both Rapp and Krueger emphasize, the main aspect of this literature is its spiritual role to both writer and reader.[79] Our main question is, therefore, what is the effect that the literary trickster embodied by the holy fool produces in real life. How does he become a religious virtuoso de facto. Theodoret of Cyrrhus explains how this works by giving the examples of the biblical prophets of Israel: God commanded Isaiah to go around naked for three years (Isa. 20:2). He commanded Jeremiah to put himself in wood and iron (Jer. 1:17, 34:1, 35:10–14), and Hosea to take a prostitute as a wife (Hosea 1:2, 3:1). Ezekiel is commanded to practice various forms of asceticism (Ezek. 4:4–6, 12:5–6):

> God commands this to attract the unbelievers by the strangeness and the paradox of the spectacle [Greek: *toi xenōi, tōi tēs theōrias paradoxōi*], so that they will listen to the divine oracles. Who would not be amazed to see a holy man walk around naked? Who would not want to understand the reason of the phenomenon? Who would not want to understand why did the prophet live with a prostitute? In this way God makes everyone

> agitated and exhorted by the strangeness and the paradox of the spectacle. Because the innovation of the spectacle makes those who believe, certain of their belief, and those who do not, change their heart—that they will be transformed by the encounter with the strangeness and paradox of the spectacle.[80]

To the modern reader such descriptions reveal the ambiguity between sanctity and insanity in the religious language, which is the subject of the present study. At the level of the story such figures are presented as tricksters par excellence. Both Byzantine readers and modern readers have no difficulty in following the theatrical situation that such figures produce within a story. Readers are aware that these individuals fool society. However, the fact that these tricksters assume a totally ordinary figure of insanity within a well-defined religious-spiritual framework moves the tricksters' situation from the literary level to real life. To Byzantine readers any madman could be a holy fool in disguise, so that any madman was a plausible trickster. Readers are thus caught up in the trickster's plausible theater of inversion. Since beholders can never really tell whether madmen are tricksters, encounters with insane persons become an ambiguous experience.[81]

This means that the state of ambiguity of the madman and the phenomenon of the holy fool in itself affect readers by imposing ambiguity on them as beholders of insanity in *real life*. This ambiguity was a real phenomenon in Byzantine society, and threatened the beholders' sense of perception of insanity, other sources tell us.[82] To put it differently, the ambiguity of the holy fool creates an ambiguity about sanctified insanity, an ambiguity between sanctity and insanity, which penetrates into readers' perceptions of reality. While those reading about the holy fool do not experience ambiguity on the literary level, the holy fool's ambiguity becomes the ambiguity they experience in real life. The abnormal personality—the plausible holy madman—thus expresses and symbolizes the ambiguity of each beholder. In this way this literature penetrates into the life of its readers and changes their consciousness. In fact, this is precisely the holy fool's objective as portrayed by the author in the story: to penetrate into the true consciousness of each and every believer, and to serve as means of transformation of consciousness by creating a zone of ambiguity. In order to understand clearly the psychological meaning of this sort of "zone of ambiguity," we need to examine its psychological effects on the beholder.

The holy fool affects believers on the individual level, and causes a psychological transformation. The question is how is this produced and to what end. Here we acknowledge the great strength of this literature that is presented as *truth* and not fiction. Byzantine literature thus found a way to translate the ambiguity about such figures from the literary level to real life by constructing ambiguity about their authenticity. This ambiguity is therefore intentional and deliberate. We need to focus here not on the phenomenon of the holy fool itself, but on the phenomenon of ambiguity that such figures projected and symbolized for their society, which could not distinguish between medical insanity, demonic insanity, and holy simulated insanity.[83] The question whether such Byzantine tales describe authentic holy fools is irrelevant in this case. Whether authentic or not, the society for which they were written believed them to be authentic. And as a consequence, society lost—Byzantine sources tell us—the ability to discern who was a *true* madman or madwoman.[84]

Whether the believers simulated such acts as forms of *xeniteia*, as a means of avoiding social constraints, or did not simulate them at all, is not something that either their society or modern scholarship can know. This is exactly the meeting point of ambiguities that this phenomenon reveals at both the level of its own society and the level of modern analysis. What is important, however, is not whether such people simulated their mental state, but the fact that their society defined such a possibility and sanctified it. Feigning a medical state lies completely within the capacities of individuals. However, when society sanctifies this, it not only legitimizes it but also turns it into a public phenomenon whose nature, objectives, and authenticity we cannot decipher. Once the idea of simulated insanity is sanctified it creates a trap whose nature and function we shall now examine. In fact, we shall see that this literature is intentionally masking the ontological aspect of the phenomenon in order to make it functional in real life. This corresponds to an ambiguity which this phenomenon expresses, and which is in fact what this phenomenon is all about. In other words, the literature we are dealing with here sets an ambiguity which readers confront and cannot decipher. In this, it manages to translate the literary trickster to a trickster in real life, and blurs the borderline between the visible and the invisible and the reader's perception of reality. But to what end?

The Psychologem of the Trickster

In a well-known essay, which he wrote as an appendix to one of Paul Radin's books, Carl Jung refers to the trickster figure as a "psychologem," which embodies the "shadow," a part of Jung's psychic structure.[85] The trickster is a collective personification of this shadow, a "collective shadow," which these stories develop and express. For Jung this is made possible because the collective shadow is an image of the shadow of the individual psychic structure: the individual shadow.[86] The individual shadow is a product of a dissociation of the ego-personality from all urges, desires, and images disagreeable to the ego-consciousness, which are therefore repressed into the unconsciousness. To Jung the personification of this inner shadow in the figure of the trickster not only acts as a psychological means of expression but also has a therapeutic meaning. It enables the psyche to acknowledge, confront, and come to terms with the inner shadow, to mobilize and submerge it in order to resolve the dissociation within the psychic structure. Albeit a threat to the conscious *self,* the shadow is not necessarily negative. Like the trickster it represents the savage, the animal, and the untamed, but also the creative, the innovative, the nonconformist, and the revolutionary in the *self.* No "self-knowledge" is possible without referring to and processing the inner psychic tension and danger that the shadow symbolizes. By embodying this shadow on the collective level, the trickster enables individuals to come to terms with their shadow within: "As in the collective, mythological form, so also the individual shadow contains within it the seed of an *enantiodromia,* of conversion into its opposite."[87] Whether or not we accept Jung's reading, we must admit that the figure and actions of the trickster have an effect on the psychological level.[88] In fact, that psychological impact is exactly the raison d'être of the trickster. In other words, the ambiguity of the phenomenon of the holy fool creates a disorder in the mind of the person who encounters him or her. The question is how can we penetrate into the psychological effect of this phenomenon and understand its meaning.

To Conclude

We came to encounter a problem in deciphering a literary creation as a historical phenomenon. How can we reveal the effect it had in real life on its readers, if all we have is literature that by constructing ambiguity masks the very ontological aspect of the phenomenon it sets out to record? It is clear that this literary creation aimed to achieve something by rendering insanity ambiguous in real life, but what? We would like to understand the effect that this ambiguity had on the Byzantine reader/beholder/society. But we cannot do that without resolving the ambiguity that we face when trying to decipher it. As historians we cannot surpass the level of the story, since stories are all we have. But maybe we are missing something in insisting on reading these stories only as the cultural creation of their society. De Certeau, Krueger, Rapp, and Felman reveal in their analysis that literature cannot be separated from the *real-life* experience of both reader and writer. The question now is how to detect and explain its psychological effect as part of our understanding of the texts. In other words, we should look for different ways to understand how the psychological process of reading about holy fools affects the psychological process of encountering them in real life. And here, Mikhail Bakhtin's analysis of "literature in great time" becomes particularly relevant.

The Logic of Literature

Between Scholarship and Literature

> A work of literature . . . is revealed primarily in the differentiated unity of the culture of the epoch in which it was created, but it cannot be closed off in this epoch: its fullness is revealed only in *great time*. . . .
>
> There exists a very strong, but one-sided and thus untrustworthy, idea that in order better to understand a foreign culture, one must enter into it, forgetting one's own, and view the world through the eyes of this foreign culture. This idea, as I said, is one-sided. . . .
>
> In the realm of culture, outsideness is a most powerful factor in understanding. It is only in the eyes of *another* culture that foreign culture reveals itself fully and profoundly (but not maximally fully, because there will be cultures that see and understand even more). A meaning

> only reveals its depths once it has encountered and come into contact with another, foreign meaning: they engage in a kind of dialogue, which surmounts the closedness and one-sidedness of these particular meanings, these cultures (Mikhail Bakhtin, 1970).[89]

What Bakhtin writes about is something that every historian, at one point or another, must experience when working on a different society, a different culture, a different era: an unintentional and unconscious dialogue is formed between the objects of research and the researchers who become themselves an object of research. Here is what Bakhtin added to his response in his notes of the same year:

> The complex event of encountering and interacting with another's word has been almost completely ignored by the corresponding human sciences (and above all by literary scholarship). Sciences of the spirit; their field of inquiry is not one but two "spirit" [*dukh*] (the studied and the person who studies, which must not be merged into one spirit). The real object of study is the interaction of "spirits" [*dukhe*]. . . .
>
> The first task is to understand the work as the author himself understood it, without exceeding the limits of his understanding. This is a very difficult problem and usually requires introducing an immense amount of material.
>
> The second task is to take advantage of one's own position of temporal and cultural outsideness. Inclusion in our (other's for the author) context.
>
> The first stage is understanding (there are two tasks here); the second stage is scholarly study (scientific description, generalization, historical localization).[90]

According to Bakhtin there can be no scholarly study which does not take into account the dialogue between two distinct cultures. This dialogue can be bridged solely by the encounter that the text produces between the scholar as an outside reader on the one hand, and the author on the other hand. What Bakhtin is proposing here is to make a distinction between studying a text as an outsider and as an insider. In other words, he is proposing we read a literary text from the vantage point of both its author and reader. His ideas gave intertextuality its present cardinal role in the study of history. Bakhtin is very clear here about the role he attributes to literature, which becomes a means of bridging the gap between cultures separated by *great time*. Readers need to get outside themselves, not only to judge and understand the context of the writer, text, and period, but also to ask how reading changes their own world. In doing this, the reader adopts the point of view of an *insider*, while reading becomes a bridge between two cultures. This is, of course, a dangerous path, since it could result in the scholar's context overshadowing the author's. However, Bakhtin insists that focusing on the dynamics of "reading the text" as a reader and as a scholar, is the only possible way to understand literature. According to him, there can be no *scholarly study* without the *understanding* of the author as a modern reader of literature, just as there can be no such *understanding* without *scholarly study*. We shall now attempt to use Bakhtin's perspective in order to make a link between the *understanding* of the author by the modern reader and *scholarly study*.

How can we penetrate into the Byzantine readers' world in order to understand the effect that stories about holy fools had on them? In other words, how can we understand the two facets of the texts about holy folly as both history and literature—on both the levels of *scholarly study* and *understanding*? In order to do this, we need to approach the subject of madness as scholars of history and as readers of literature. We now turn to the second in order to try to reveal what this phenomenon expresses to its audience and its effects on it (whether this be the audience of its own *time*, or the audience separated from it by *great time*). In other words, we need to read these texts as literature, and this means reading them not only as literature *in* their time (rather than "*of* their time") but also as literature *in* our time. In part this is what de Certeau did in his reading of the nun who feigned madness, and what Krueger did in his study of Symeon the Fool.[91] But while both these scholars remained on the literary level of the author in their readings, we shall move to the literary level of the reader. To put it differently, we shall focus not on the writer of the phenomenon of the *holy fool*, but on its reader.[92]

In order to do this we must look for the encounter between the reader and insanity and the impact that this had on the reader. We are used to reading a text within its historical context, just as we are used to the idea that the cultural context determines the reading of the text. Nonetheless, Bakhtin reminds us that as far as literature is concerned, we must also address the text on the level of the reader as insider: "The life of a concrete, determinate *other* is organized by me essentially in time (in those cases, of course, where I do not abstract his actions or his thoughts from his personality)—nor in chronological time, nor in mathematical time, but in the emotionally and axiologically ponderable time of lived life that is capable of becoming musical rhythmic time."[93] This is the powerful aesthetic of reading literature. That said, our intention here is not to develop a subjective reading of historical texts, but, just as Bakhtin is suggesting, to use the reading separated by *great time* in order to approach the reader of the author's time.

The Literary Evidence

There are numerous holy fools in the characters of Byzantine hagiographic texts. We discussed above the story of the nun who feigned madness in Palladius's *Historia Lausiaca,* who was used as the literary model for the story of Onesima (also known as Isidora).[94] We also analyzed the figure of Symeon of Emesa. Others are Andrew from Constantinople, Mark the fool "of the Hippos," as well as the obscure Paul of Corinth.[95] Both the figures of Symeon and Andrew were developed extensively by their respective hagiographers, Leontius of Neapolis and Nicephorus of Constantinople, who wrote two of the most beautiful and elaborate hagiographies in Greek literature. But holy fools also appear in other texts where they are not the main heroes of the text, but literary figures which the author employs to create a certain situation or to illustrate a certain point. This is the case, for example, in the *The Sayings of the Desert Fathers,* and in texts concerning Daniel of Sketis, *Lives of the Eastern Saints* of John of Ephesus, "The Ladder of Divine Ascent" of John Climacus, as well as "The Life of Gregentios of Taphar."[96] Déroche has identified this *topos* also in the Byzantine hagiography of Southern Italy in the central Middle Ages.[97]

Though all of these texts develop the theme of disguised holiness and simulated madness, they do not treat it in the same way. Nonetheless, what they all have in common is a very detailed description of insanity from the point of view of the person who simulates it. From this starting point, each author constructs it differently, according to his particular objective. The diversity of this literature reveals not different types of holy fools, but different motives, all of which share a common aesthetic objective which is revealed through Bakhtin's analysis of the triangular relationship between the author, the hero, and the spectator or reader. Bakhtin explains this relationship as a psychological process.

The Psychological Aspect of Literature

It is today a truism that the individual psyche is modeled on and affected by the relationships between an individual and his or her human surroundings. The development of psychology in the twentieth century was grounded in Sigmund Freud's articulation of the way in which the relation between consciousness and the unconscious is modeled according to individual drives. However, instead of implementing the psychological theories of his time in the field of literary criticism, Bakhtin has done things the other way around. He has produced his own psychological theory based on his literary analysis, and used it to develop a model very different from Freud's, where the division between conscious and unconscious has no place.[98] In Bakhtin's view, the aesthetic aspect of literature, that is, the way in which the author constructs the literary hero, and the way in which the reader perceives this and is affected by it are *relational* because they are an outgrowth of the psychological aspect of the dialogue between human beings. These ideas are laid out mainly in his essay "Author and Hero in Aesthetic Activity" and the collection of his thoughts published as "The Problem of the Text in Linguistics, Philology, and the Human Sciences: An Experiment in Philosophical Analysis."[99] Here we find Bakhtin particularly relevant to the question that we are now set to examine: What is the aesthetic significance of the literary figure of the holy fool? It is impossible to answer this question without referring to the relationship between the psychological and the aesthetic effects of literature. Here is the way Bakhtin conceptualizes this relationship:

> In order to vivify my own outward image and make it part of a concretely viewable whole, the entire architectonic of the world of my imagining must be radically restructured by introducing a totally new factor into it. This new factor that restructures the architectonic consists in my outward image being affirmed and founded in emotional and volitional terms *out* of the other and *for* the other human being.
>
> For, from within myself, there is only my own inner affirmation of myself, which I am unable to project upon my outward expressedness

> (as detached from my inner self-sensation), and that is why it confronts me as axiologically empty, lacking any affirmed foundation. Something like a transparent screen has to be inserted between my inner self-sensation (the function of my *empty* seeing) and my outwardly-volitional reaction to my outward manifestation—his possible enthusiasm, love, astonishment, or compassion for me. And looking through this screen of the other's soul (which is thus reduced to a means), I vivify my exterior and make it part of the plastic and pictorial world. . . .
>
> The point at issue here is precisely how to accomplish the task of translating myself from inner language into the language of outward expressedness and of weaving all of myself totally into the unitary plastic and pictorial fabric of life as a human being among other human beings, as a hero among other heroes.[100]

The importance of what Bakhtin writes here to the understanding of the psychological experience of the reader is tremendous. He develops this into a global psychological theory in which the aesthetic of reading is a case study for the experiencing of the *self* (otherwise impossible) through the experiencing of the *other*.[101]

In order to explain this, Bakhtin develops his two concepts of the *self*: the *I-for-myself* and the *I-for-the-other*.[102] While the first is the *self* as the self perceives it*self*, and which can only be expressed in action, the second serves as a means for the *self* to grasp it*self* through its interaction with the *other*.[103] The premise here seems to be the idea that the *self* is a dynamic entity, constantly evolving by its dialogues with *others*. Thus the psychological process of the formation of the *self* is, in Bakhtin's view, infinite—it never really ends.[104] Moreover, it is the role of literature to use and activate this process. Bakhtin constructs here an organic psychological dialogue, and asserts that the *I-for-myself* can never truly experience itself without the *I-for-the-other*.[105] Bakhtin's analysis of the relationship between the *I-for-the-other* and *I-for-myself* as a productive and dynamic psychological functioning is crucial for the theory he later developed about dialogue.

For our purpose, Bakhtin's idea about the psychological dynamics (though he does not use the term), as expressed in the dialogue between the internal and external facets of the *self* (the *I-for-myself* and the *I-for-the-other*) makes *understanding* literature an active process. In other words, when we approach a text, our *understanding* of it at the psychological level of the reader, whether conscious or not, cannot be bypassed, since it is conditioned by our functioning psychological mechanism. By employing our personal reading of a literary phenomenon, we can penetrate into its aesthetic effect. Moreover, it is our only way to reveal this effect. However, what we would like to examine here is how the psychological process of reading about holy fools affects the psychological process of encountering madness in real life. In order to do this, we shall need Donald Winnicott. Thus, to explain how the psychological mechanism that literature about holy madness activates in the reader/beholder, we need to examine both its aesthetic and psychological effects. We shall continue by analyzing the link that is established between experiencing madness as readers of literature and experiencing madness in real life. In other words, we focus here on the relation between the aesthetic of insanity in literature and in life. For this purpose we shall bring together Bakhtin, who analyzed the aesthetic of literature, and Winnicott, who perceives individual psychological processes as relational. To justify this unusual theoretical analysis let us repeat again that we are looking for a way to decipher the psychological effect that literature about sanctified insanity had in real life on the Byzantine believer. For this purpose we will indeed find Bakhtin and Winnicott complementary.[106]

Bakhtin Meets Winnicott

Interpersonal psychology and relational psychology as developed out of the British psychoanalytical school of object relations understand the human psyche as dependent on human interaction.[107] Winnicott's view occupies a cardinal place in explaining the individual psychological process as an interpersonal experience.[108] Winnicott defined the development of the *self* in babyhood as a product of the way the *other* (the mother) sees it and projects the image it has of the baby back at the child. Thus, whatever model the *self* may have, it cannot perceive itself without the images of it*self* that are projected at it by its surroundings.[109]

Winnicott focused on the early stages of the development of the infant as a formative period of the psyche. However, although the *self* is already a defined image to itself in much later stages, it is in no way independent from its surroundings. To explain this Winnicott, in his article "Ego Distortion in Terms of True and False Self," coined the pair *true self* and *false self*. While the first comes from an interpsychic experience of the world, the second is the *self* as modeled for its surroundings (this is an enlargement of Winnicott's conceptualization of the relationship between the mother/environment and the baby).[110] Such relational models of the psychological structure of the self can help us in comparing the aesthetic aspect of literature, particularly literature that concerns insanity, with the way we experience insanity in real life.

If we accept the idea that the perception of the *self* can be formed and sustained by the way in which it is acknowledged by its surroundings, we can grasp the danger that the *self* confronts in facing an insane *other*.[111] This is central to literature about insanity since the reader who confronts it in reading is affected by this encounter psychologically. Bakhtin's and Winnicott's relational psychological models will enable us to move from the position of the scholar to the position of the reader. Here we will also need to confront our own perception of insanity.

Experiencing Madness as Readers—the Aesthetic Significance of the Holy Fool

Philo describes the anti-Jewish riots in Alexandria around the year 40 A.D., aimed at ridiculing Judaean king Herod Agrippa on his visit to Egypt in these words:

> There was a certain madman [Greek: *memēnōs*] named Karabas, whose madness [*mania*] was not of the fierce and savage kind, which is dangerous both to the madmen themselves and those who approach them, but of the easy-going, gentler style. He spent day and night in the streets naked, shunning neither heat nor cold, made game of by the children and the lads who were idling about. The rioters drove the poor fellow into the gymnasium and set him up on high to be seen of all and put on his head a sheet of scroll spread out wide for a diadem, clothed the rest of his body with a rug for a royal robe, while someone who had noticed a piece of the native papyrus thrown away in the road gave it to him for his scepter. And when as in some theatrical farce he had received the insignia of kingship and had been tricked out as a king, young men carrying rods on their shoulders as spearmen stood on either side of him in imitation of a bodyguard. Then others approached him, some pretending to salute him, others to sue for justice, others to consult him on state affairs. Then from the multitudes standing round him, there rang out a tremendous shout hailing him as *marin*, which is said to be the name for

> "Lord" in Syria. For they knew that Agrippa was both a Syrian by birth and had a great piece of Syria over which he was king.[112]

Beyond constructing a vivid description, Philo gives us a clear image of the use and abuse of insanity in antiquity. Cases such as this are, unfortunately, not limited to a particular period, and attest to the cruel nature of individuals and societies. This is not the point Philo wants to make here, when blaming the anti-Jewish party in the riots between the Jewish and Greek inhabitants of Alexandria. Nevertheless, for us it is a vivid depiction of using the insane in a sort of street theater for political and social purposes in Roman Egypt two millennia ago. Of course, instances of abuse of the insane are not rare, and form part of a long and terrible history.[113] Most of us can only guess how the insane experienced being ridiculed, abused, and despised.[114] This is precisely what the figure of the holy fool experiences when entering a monastery (as with Onesima) or running about the streets simulating madness (as with Symeon). It is the ultimate form of being a "stranger"—*xenos*—to society, and the most complete form of *xeniteia*—"strangeness" or "alienation."[115] As for the literary depiction of holy fools, they achieve their religious objective once they receive such treatment. This is the case in all the stories about holy fools, who are presented as figures wishing to be despised and abused. This is being a "stranger"—*xenos*—following the example of Jesus. Strangeness, however, is two-sided, and insanity evokes this harsh reaction toward the insane person because it has a psychological effect on the beholder. This is precisely the author's intention when placing figures who simulate insanity in a social environment. The author's objective is not only to depict them as having attained such an accomplished way of life, but also to show how discovering it leads to repentance in the spectators who have abused such perfect servants of God.

This process is revealed through Bakhtin's model of the "self" as analyzed in his author-hero-beholder model, and by enlarging it through Winnicott's theory. Here we must distinguish between the reader who confronts a simulated madman as a literary figure, and the beholder who confronts a madman in real life. Facing insanity in real life, the *I-for-the-other* can never receive the image it requires in order to perceive, dialogize, and finalize it*self*. The way we perceive ourselves, as was shown above, is a product of the way others perceive us and project their perception on us. In other words, the image that the self has of it*self* is forever a product of the ways its image is projected by others, that is, it is forever relational. To Bakhtin, a person cannot really perceive it*self* other than in the field of action through the perception of others who project this actualization of the *I-for-the-other* back at the *I-for-myself.* To be altogether ignored by the other does not mean being deprived of this image: if this happens, the *self* can normally be compensated by images projected by others. But what happens when the *self* receives a false image?

This is precisely what happens when a sane person confronts insanity: the reactions the *self* receives are out of its field of reference, because they have no perceptible relationship to its own image (be it Bakhtin's *I-for-myself* or Winnicott's *true self*). A distorted image of the *self* is produced (to borrow here Winnicott's concept of "ego distortion"). But while *I-for-the-other* or the *false self* are in constant interaction or dialogue with the *I-for-myself* or *true self,* the image of the *self* projected from the insane creates a rupture between the two.[116] In other words, the encounter with insanity is lived as a true danger to the *self* of the sane person, since the difference between the internal image and the external image of it*self* is unbridgeable. Between the insane and the sane there is a failure of language. This is exactly the break in language that de Certeau and Ronald Laing speak about: when there is no language (absence of language), it does not only mean that no communication with the insane is possible, but that the dialogue between the *interior self* and the *exterior self* is cut off.[117] In this respect, abuse, ridicule, and cruelty aimed at the insane are an attempt to resolve this conflict by fighting the danger that insanity inflicts on the *self* of the person who cannot engage with the insane. The insane person is experienced as an enemy of the beholder's *self.* Abuse, alienation, ridicule, cruelty, and even death are indeed methods used to fight an enemy. When Onesima enters the nunnery, she refuses to talk.[118] Symeon, Andrew, and all the other holy fools are not satisfied with merely refraining from talking, they imitate madmen by ridiculing themselves, and also by being violent, both verbally and physically, to their surroundings. They say things which make no sense, and treat everyone they see in abnormal and incomprehensible ways.

The authors of these texts present holy fools as having the objective of becoming strangers to their audience. In doing so, they also describe the feelings holy fools evoke in those who encounter them. However, the reader is placed not at the level of those beholding the holy fool, but at the level of the holy fool. The reader knows that the insanity of the holy fool is simulated. This has a subversive effect on the reader, since the insanity thus becomes ambiguous on the ontological level. Byzantine readers encountering the holy fool as a hagiographic figure would be incapable of discerning the "holy" from the "demonized," the "simulated" from the "authentic" madman. This is because the literature we are dealing with here, hagiography, is neither written nor read as fiction, but has a religious context that renders it not only credible but also the actual truth.[119] The believer will not doubt the existence of such holy fool.

The result of the construction of simulated insanity as holy is that when the person who believes in the existence of holy insanity confronts insanity in real life, he or she becomes incapable of ending the internal conflict of the *self* which the encounter with insanity produces.[120] As historians we cannot experience this, since simulated madness does not seem part of our modern culture. But on the level of its Byzantine reader, "the book closed, the ambiguity persists," in the words of Tzvetan Todorov.[121] Or, we can even say, the ambiguity begins! Todorov defines literature that produces this sort of effect on the reader as belonging to a "fantastic-uncanny" genre, where supernatural events create a feeling of the uncanny in the reader because of their ambiguous interpretation.[122] He emphasizes the effect that the gap between the real and supernatural produces on the reader: "The probable is therefore not necessarily opposed to the fantastic: the former is a category that deals with internal coherence, with submission to the genre; the *fantastic* refers to an ambiguous perception shared by the reader and one of the characters."[123]

In religious literature, on the other hand, the gap is not there, since the supernatural is taken to be real. In modern literature "the reader remains at the point of *seems*, and never reaches certainty" with regard to the literary characters.[124] In contrast, Byzantine literature about holy fools directs the reader to feel this not with regard to literary characters, but with regard to real-life people. The uncertainty is not created on the literary level, but on the reader's ontological level. It is not the characters of Onesima, Symeon, Mark, Paul, or Andrew, whose insanity readers find uncertain, but through the identification with them, insanity in real life. If the readers have passed through the spiritual process that the author constructs for them, by experiencing and identifying with the strangeness of a holy fool, once "the book is closed," they will become incapable of deciphering the insane behavior of any madman or madwoman they encounter. Because of the psychological effect of the spiritual experience that this literature produces, an encounter with insanity will become a destabilizing experience to the reader. The internal conflict between the reader's *I-for-myself* and the *I-for-other* in Bakhtin's terms, or between *true self* and *false self* in Winnicott's terms, could not be resolved in real life. This is the aesthetic function of these narrations which are perceived by modern scholars as fiction, but were certainly not perceived as such by their contemporary readers.[125] In such a way the author employs the estrangement of his literary figure as an aesthetic device for the estrangement of the reader in real life. He translates the estrangement (*xeniteia*) of the holy fool in the story into a feeling of uncanniness of the reader.

Estrangement as an Aesthetic Device

In a letter to Romain Rolland on his seventieth birthday in 1936, Freud explained to himself the feeling of "derealization" that he experienced thirty-two years earlier on the top of the Acropolis on a trip to Athens with his younger brother:

> These derealizations are remarkable phenomena which are still little understood. They are spoken of as "sensations," but they are obviously complicated processes, attached to particular mental contents and bound up with decisions made about those contents. They arise very frequently in certain mental diseases, but they are not unknown among normal people, just as hallucinations occasionally occur in the healthy. Nevertheless they are certainly failures in functioning and, like dreams, which, in spite of their regular occurrence in healthy people, serve us as models of psychological disorder, they are abnormal structures. These phenomena are to be observed in two forms: the subject feels either that a piece of reality or that a piece of his own self is *strange to him*. In the latter case we speak of "depersonalizations"; derealizations and depersonalizations are intimately connected.[126]

Although not marked as such by Freud, this feeling of "strangeness to oneself" is closely connected to his concept of the *unheimlich* (*Das*

Unheimliche, 1919), translated into English as "the uncanny," where an image from childhood that is connected to a repressed, threatening sentiment causes it to reappear in adulthood.[127] The psyche deals with this crisis by alienating the *self* (note that Freud's "uncanny" depends on the Freudian concept of the self) and estranging it. In a word, the feeling of being *unheimlich*—"out of the familiar/one's own place," "defamiliarized"—is a psychological mechanism of defense, which in the case of Freud's memory, and according to his analysis, arose by confronting the repressed disturbing sentiments he had for his father in childhood.

Freud's concept of the uncanny has experienced tremendous and growing popularity over the last thirty years, especially in literary and cultural criticism, as a means of explaining feelings of defamiliarization, alienation, and estrangement within the framework of aestheticism, and particularly in order to explain the link between the author, the hero, and the reader or spectator.[128] I propose to understand the psychological effect of the literary figure of the holy fool against the background of these ideas about estrangement and defamiliarization. The ambiguity that the Byzantine reader was bound to feel in experiencing insanity is the product of precisely such an effect, and is related to the estrangement that it produced.

Only two years prior to the publication of Freud's *The Uncanny*, Viktor Shklovsky published his essay "Art as Device," in which he coined the term *ostranenie* as an artistic device.[129] Translated from the Russian as either "estrangement" or "defamiliarization," *ostranenie* produces a feeling of strangeness in readers or spectators, a tension that disconnects them from the familiar, aimed at stimulating them to search for new insights and new perspectives to resolve this tension that art creates. The main objective is thus not to create a feeling of alienation, but a new perspective of reality by estranging the subject from reality as perceived in the familiar way.[130] This aesthetic process acts on the psychological level of the individual or, to put it differently, creates an effect of psychological disturbance in order to change the familiar conception of things. Sean Carney explains the difference between estrangement and the uncanny through the interpretation of Bertolt Brecht's concept of *Verfremdungseffekt* (distancing effect): "The first (i.e., estranging) is a part of larger process by which we get a different consciousness and understanding, it is heuristic and therapeutic, and not merely 'alienation' or 'defamilarization.'"[131] This is precisely the incertitude that the holy fool phenomenon aimed to produce in the Byzantine reader. It achieves it by creating a feeling of estrangement that distorts the familiar. The artistic device proves to be the figure of the holy fool itself. The identification of the reader or beholder with the holy fool makes the first stand with the second, and estranges the first from the normal and accepted way of seeing things. It achieves exactly what Shklovsky defined by "estrangement" (*ostranenie*) as an artistic device, and what Brecht aimed to achieve: a new type of consciousness. The literary device is the ambiguity. Readers who follow the narrative about holy insanity forever doubt the authenticity of madmen whom they meet in real life. In other words, "once the book is closed" they are meant to experience the story in real life. The narrative invades the readers' consciousness, and transforms the way in which they experience reality. These narratives are, as Rapp explains, by no means all fiction or any type of literature we are used to.[132] The modern genre of literature which most resembles it in its effects might well be metaphysics or even pure science. Both modern science and hagiography aim to explain and to change the ways in which readers perceive the universe and their relation to it. But while the first does so with logical explanation, the second employs psychology. This is how stories about holy fools aim to change their readers' perception of ontological reality. The narrative transforms readers to beholders whenever they encounter figures of abnormal and insane behavior in their own reality. Only then could they experience the ambiguity which they confronted as readers. Naturally there will be many who will take this literature solely on the fictional level. But spiritual narratives like saints' *Lives*, as Rapp explains, mean to penetrate the psychological level of readers by translating the experience of readers into an experience of believers, in other words, a transformation of the reader's reality. In the case of holy folly, this is actualized through the psychological estrangement of the readers, in order to bring them to a different consciousness of understanding and a new perception of reality. This is the main objective of these hagiographic narratives, one that is beautifully elaborated by the author of *The Life of Andrew the Fool*.[133]

Saintly Insanity as a Metaphysical Device

Andrew is a talented "Scythian" (i.e., Slav or Bulgarian) slave, whose master, a wealthy Byzantine dignitary, admires, educates, and uses him in his household.[134] But when Christ reveals himself to him and asks him to become a fool for his sake, Andrew decides to accept.[135] His first act of madness is to sit in the middle of the night in the court by the well, to tear his clothes to pieces, and to start breaking everything around him. The conclusion of the family is clear: he has gone mad.[136] Being unwilling to part with him, his master sends him for treatment in the Church of Saint Anastasia, a well-known establishment for treatment of the insane. There he is put in chains for three months, during which time he has repeated visions, and persists in his state.[137] At the end of three months, when his state has not improved, Andrew's master liberates him, and he is finally free to roam the streets of Constantinople imitating "that amazing Symeon the ancient."[138] After this introduction, the rest of the story concerns Andrew's behavior and deeds, and describes how people react to him.

Like Symeon, Andrew walks around naked, defecates in public, and demonstrates bizarre ways of eating (unlike Symeon, he abstains from normal food and drink, drinking only from puddles).[139] He, too, is portrayed as a one-man theater of ridicule in the city, at the hippodrome, and in the forum.[140] Typical for a madman, he is despised by everyone who meets him, including beggars and stray dogs.[141] His perfect strangeness to the world is described in a manner that enables readers to empathize and even experience it.[142] This includes terrible descriptions of public humiliation and abuse (along with compassionate reactions) that lead readers to identify with the madman.

In contrast to Symeon, Andrew occasionally gives spiritual advice, which only increases the ambiguity about him: throughout the narrative we are shown that it was impossible for people to understand him. Like Symeon he takes great care to conceal his miracles. Nonetheless, metaphysical interventions are attributed to him in spite of his state, or even because of his state. In fact, people wonder about the reason for his state. Some think it is a result of magic, others of epilepsy: "only God knows the reason for his conduct."[143] Some refuse to believe it, others attribute it to his insanity, or to his being possessed by demons and hence under the influence of the devil.[144] Others are simply amazed with no explanation for the forces which they attribute to him.

Part of the reason for this growing incertitude about Andrew is the fact that certain people believe him to be a holy fool. This is the point in the story where the ambiguity that the author portrays becomes recursive, meaning that the reader confronts it on the narrative level of the story.[145] This increases the ambiguity about Andrew, and turns him to a living conundrum within the life of the city. This situation is much more elaborated here than in the *Life of Symeon salos.* If Symeon is always regarded as an authentic madman who nonetheless has some powers, in the story about Andrew the author plants the ambiguity about his true character within the story. People cannot decipher whether he is an authentic madman (whether possessed or not) or simply a holy fool.[146] But the author does not leave it at this point. In fact, presenting the ambiguity about Andrew on the level of the story has an important aesthetic function central to the author's objective: it challenges the common perception of the visible world, and provokes people to change their perception of their reality. In other words, what we see is how recognizing and acknowledging Andrew as a divine vessel overlaps with, and serves as a means of recognizing and acknowledging, the perception of the invisible world that he symbolizes. The holy fool is here a means to clear sight.

In the story about Saint Gregentios, archbishop of Taphar, most probably contemporary with *The Life of Andrew the Fool,* four holy fools appear to approve and legitimize the divine mission of the hero.[147] They are the only ones who identify him as a divine vessel. Only the fools can really see the hidden and true reality. Andrew the Fool is presented as the doorkeeper to the hidden and invisible world. Acknowledging his holiness, sanctifying him de facto, means that his beholder is of true and innocent heart, and able to accept his visions, which his life story is so full of. He demands an aesthetic inversion from his surroundings, a psychological transformation. He offers truth in illusion, which thus proves to be not an illusion at all. The holy fool is the only literary figure that can produce this transformation, because it enables his beholders to translate the estrangement from the literary to the ontological.

Much of the story about Andrew the Fool is dedicated to his visions, either in dreams or in a state of ecstasy. This starts with the first revelation of Christ, who proposes to him that he should to become a fool for his sake, and continues with spiritual voyages through Hades and Heaven, and conversations with demons, angels, saints, and Christ himself.[148] This is described as abnormal, to the point that in one of his visions Andrew asks himself whether he is not after all a true madman.[149] In this vision he finds himself in a heavenly garden, where he becomes "disembodied" (Greek: *asarkon*), and dressed in a dazzling white garment covered with precious stones. When he tries to look at the birds, his mind is carried away into ecstasy (Greek: *ho nous mou hōs eis ekstasin*), during which he loses consciousness within his vision.[150] This vision is followed by a journey through the heavens, in which Andrew follows his guide, walks on clouds, and flies.[151] His guide moves through fire, and they reach Christ sitting on his throne, who addresses Andrew.[152] The narrator constructs the description of Andrew's vision as a mystical experience, which, he confesses, sent his own, that is, the author's, soul into ecstasy, and he aims to do the same for readers.[153] In other words, the author's objective is to impose this state of ecstasy on readers.

The author portrays the ambiguity about Andrew on the level of the story. But through this literary construction of the holy fool, the ambiguity between madness and seeing the hidden truth becomes the property of every believer. This is the role that the author ascribes to his main secondary figure: Epiphanios, who believes in Andrew's holiness and experiences a vision in which he himself is taken to Hades guided by Andrew.[154] Hades is described as a place of sinners in the shape of nasty animals (beasts, dogs, crows, reptiles, snakes, vipers, dragons, and pigs) fornicating, screaming, and mocking.[155] The figure of the holy fool as the author constructs it serves as a conceptual framework in order to change the perception of reality.[156] The literary description of a fantastical imaginary world is aimed to provide readers with an emotional and psychological experience that will transform their perception of things and of themselves.

This is what the figure of the holy fool is all about: it causes an inversion of human perspective through a psychological process. The means is estrangement. And this estrangement necessitates, as we shall now see, the ambiguity of insanity. For this reason, the author leaves the ambiguity of insanity unresolved. People do indeed wonder about the holy fool's hidden knowledge (Greek: *gnōsis*), others attribute it to Satan; but no one remains indifferent to it.[157] To emphasize this, the author presents in the same story a description of a sinning deacon who has gone mad: he pulls his beard, bleats like a goat, sticks out his tongue, and barks like a dog at the men standing by his bed.[158] His insanity is divine punishment, but readers will never be able to distinguish simulated insanity from possession or authentic insanity. However, what is at stake here is not the ambiguity of insanity, but the use of this ambiguity to make beholders unable to attribute meaning to their surroundings ("only God knows the heart"; Ps. 15:9), and to make life a continuous theater of the metaphysics. To put it differently, the one-man theater that the author creates here by employing the holy fool aims to draw into itself readers not as beholders, but as participators. The ambiguity about insanity affects readers in *life*. By estranging readers in *life* it constitutes, in the words of Antonin Artaud, "a means of a true illusion."[159] The phenomenon of the holy fool proves to be nothing less than what Artaud aims at in his "Theater of Cruelty."

In the Illusion Lies the Truth

> Present-day theater is in decline, because it has lost the feeling, on the one hand of the serious, and on the other the laugh. Because it has fallen from gravity, and broken away from instant and damaging effectiveness—in short from danger. Because it has also lost the true sense of humor and the power of the physical and anarchic dissociation of laughter. Because it has broken away from the spirit of profound anarchy which is the base of any poetry. (Antonin Artaud, *Staging and Metaphysics*).[160]

What Artaud here calls "metaphysics" is "drawing extreme poetic consequences from the means of actualization."[161] This is exactly what the Byzantine author achieves by employing and actualizing the figure of the holy fool: he conveys extreme aesthetic consequences aimed at changing his readers' metaphysics. What I call "actualization" is, in a word, turning virtual reality through aesthetic means to actual reality.[162] This is what Artaud aimed to achieve in his Theater of Cruelty by constructing theater as *life* and not as a *representation* of *life*.[163]

The ambiguity of insanity that the holy fool represents enables this exact transformation of reality from the virtual to the actual field of the reader. The actualization of the invisible world is achieved through the literature about the holy fool. The holy fool is this actualization.[164] The holy fool makes the invisible world present within the city, which itself becomes a battlefield between the holy fool and Satan.[165] People see Andrew conversing with walls, fighting with air, magically changing his position from one place to the other, when he is *really* talking to angels or fighting with demons and Satan over a believer's soul.[166] Such scenes express to readers the presence of the invisible world, not the world beyond, but the actual invisible reality beyond the tangible reality—beyond the "matrix."[167] From this point of view, the stories about holy fools are no different from any other narratives about holy men. What is characteristic about them, however, is that the doorkeepers can never be truly known since they are hidden within the ambiguity of insanity that this literature constructs. In other words, unlike any other literature about magic and sanctity, literature about holy fools manages to render the presence of the invisible world forever ambiguous. The truth is presented through visions.[168] This is expressed in the section with questions and answers, where Andrew provides explanations about the infinity of time, universe, and the human soul; the creation, good and evil, angels, nature, as well as in Andrew's apocalyptic prophecy.[169] The main purpose of this is to open the eyes of the spirit (Greek: *hoi noeroi ophthalmoi*) to be enlightened by God: "He whose spiritual eyes are opened and enlightened by God, sees and perceives many things, while seeing such causes him ecstasy (Greek: *haper kai blepōn existatai*)."[170] However, since the visions are forever ambiguous (man can only feel the invisible presence of angels), the truth can never be fully actualized, only the search for it, together with its ambiguity.[171] In fact, even Andrew himself, just like all the other holy fools, disappears at death leaving a magical fragrance behind, thus making it impossible to use him for any concrete actualization of the invisible.[172]

Reading holy insanity changes the reader's reality precisely because the ambiguity of holy insanity is translated from the virtual to the actual. It outlives the story, it persists. It persists because it estranges the reader from familiar visible reality, and from familiar and visible society, thanks to the ambiguity that it plants in the reader's perception. Society appears in the literature about holy fool as a hub of constant battles between good and evil, between piety and sins. This literature does not aim to reveal a truth, but to plant a doubt in the reader. And this doubt is not only about insanity, but about the reader's own life and society, which the holy fool means to mend. This is "the double" which Artaud planted in his *The Theatre and its Double* in an evasive way. The double never appears explicitly in his essays on the theater as a subject in its own, but is present at their heart: the plague, the magic, the metaphysics, and the alchemy, all of which are neither allegories nor images of the theater, but the very *being* of the theater; they are the theater's other side, its double.[173]

Artaud wanted to restore this double to theatrical experience, and in order to make it *life,* not the *representation* of life, he used as his means the term "cruelty." The theater here is "cruel" in the sense of being in constant battle with passion and suffering, full of crises and effort; in short, the struggle of life. It thus addresses the totality of the human existence.[174] This definition of cruelty is necessary for it to become *life*: "it is through the skin that we can make metaphysics enter the minds."[175]

It is very clear that Byzantine literature about holy fools depicts them in the same way that Artaud depicts his Theater of Cruelty. It is, of course, the other way around: Artaud constructed his Theater of Cruelty according to models such as the phenomenon of the holy fool presents. Holy fools are one-man theaters. They are both actors and directors. They are also the only ones who know about their virtual theater. To their surroundings they are real life. Holy fools do exactly what Artaud wanted: they make theater into life. But they do more than that: they also make life a theater. Their very existence demolishes the distinction between life and theater, since spectators can never really know whether it is theater or life. In fact, there is no need for them to know. This literature takes theater from the level of the story to the level of the readers' reality. Through the ambiguity that it constructs, readers themselves can never know whether the madman they see is theater or life. And this is precisely the "actualization" that Artaud talks about, that turns the text into life; as quoted above, it is "the only way to make metaphysics enter minds."[176] Artaud speaks here about "mental alchemy" and about making beholders ecstatic: theater that produces trance.[177] The actualization of metaphysics in life, however, in the case of holy fools, is produced not on the level of their staging, but on the level of literary creation: it is their ambiguity in both the story and in real life—the fact that this literature *is* life—that actualizes the story about them and "makes metaphysics enter minds." In Nathan Gorelick's words, "in the illusion lies the truth."[178] For Artaud, it is only through such a psychological effect that the theater can return to its real self:

> The theater will not become itself, that is to say constitute a means of real illusion, unless it provides the spectators with a truthful precipitate of their dreams, or their taste of crime, their erotic obsessions, their savagery, their chimeras, their utopian sense of life and of things, even their cannibalism, to let themselves go not on a pretend and illusionary level,

but on an internal level. In other words, the theater must persist, by every means, in questioning not only all aspects of the objective and descriptive external world, but the internal world, i.e., of man, perceived metaphysically.[179]

We have seen so far that it is the literature about holy fools which not only constructs them as theater in the story, but also produces out of insanity a theater in real life. This literature actualizes the literary characters in the reader's life by producing in Artaud's terms a "means of real illusion." The actualization of the invisible through the holy fool becomes embedded in the beholder who confronts insanity. This is precisely how the Theater of Cruelty of the holy fool works. But the phenomenon of the holy fool is much more than Artaud's Theater of Cruelty. It aims not only to challenge the beholders and change their perception of real life, but through it to bring about change, treatment, correction, and transformation. It is Artaud's Theater of Cruelty in addition to Brecht's "distancing effect," or Shklovsky's "estrangement." And the figure of the holy fool manages to bring this about by playing on the psychological aspect of literature.

To Conclude: Insanity as Means of Change

This literature thus aims at challenging the perception of reality by generating ambiguity about insanity in the form of sanctified simulated madness. Insanity and the way readers confront it makes the perception of holiness, insanity, and through them reality, dynamic and elastic. In the following chapters we will see how the same process is generated through the figures of the ascetic and the martyr. The sanctification of such abnormal behaviors produces a mental change and transforms the perception of reality. In all these cases religion employs abnormal types of social behavior in order to create a new ontology, a new reality for a changing society. This is not only a matter of power relations and of moving the margins of society into a center. It undermines the accepted perception of reality by engaging the beholder with the abnormal, thus turning the abnormal into normal.

We have used the term "abnormality" here since Byzantine literature defines holy fools as abnormal in order to sanctify them. It is the tension between abnormality (here insanity) and sanctity that produces a psychological challenge on both the individual and collective levels. Such dynamics raise many questions. In revealing how society can employ the abnormal and the insane for its benefit, it presents a unique model of engaging with insanity. In this, it also challenges our modern conceptualization of insanity. This literature presents a new concept of insanity as a means of change. Its objective is to challenge the beholder's perception of reality in order to generate a psychological transformation. We shall now see that this challenge is well based within the perception of relational psychology. This will enable us to reveal the *psychic logic* of this ambiguity, and a new concept of insanity as a means of change. The following is an endeavor to examine sanctified insanity from the perspective of relational psychology.

The Psychic Logic

The ambiguity of the holy fool is part of the figure's role as a trickster, and functions as an aesthetic device. To understand how it facilitates change in the perception of reality through its game of ambiguity we examined the aesthetics of literature, and came to identify the uncanniness that the ambiguity about holy fools produces. In order to understand now how this uncanniness could become an instrument of psychological change at both the individual and the social levels, we shall address psychoanalytical theories which focus on the relational functioning of the self. We shall build on relational psychological models of Stephen Mitchell, and will rely on Ronald Laing's theory of object relation in order to understand the psychological relational mechanism that connects the individual to its surroundings. We shall address Philip Bromberg's and Silvia Amati Sas's conceptualization of the therapeutic process in order to explain the role that ambiguity plays (Amati Sas) in the "intrapsychic zone" (Bromberg) between patient and therapist. Such an analysis will enable us to reveal the ambiguity of sanctified insanity as a device of psychological change of both individual and society.

The Relational Matrix

Relational psychology, as it developed from interpersonal psychological theories and the object-relational British psychoanalytical school, understands the *self* in a relational/structure model instead of a Freudian drive/structure model.[180] In his social theory of the mind, Mitchell calls this model "the relational matrix."[181] The relational matrix is an interactional field that comprises self, other/object, and transactional patterns:

> We are portrayed not as a conglomerate of physically based urges, but as being shaped by and inevitably embedded within a matrix of relationships with other people, struggling both to maintain our ties to others and to differentiate ourselves from them. In this vision the basic unit of study is not the individual as a separate entity whose desires clash with an external reality, but an interactional field within which the individual arises and struggles to make contact and to articulate himself. *Desire* is experienced always *in the context of relatedness*, and it is that context which defines its meaning. Mind is composed of relational configurations. The person is comprehensible only within this tapestry of relationships, past and present.[182]

To Bromberg, the sane functioning of the individual within such a model is not integration, but the capacity to relate to the complexities of this matrix, which is simply a model that reflects the different realities that the self experiences in the relational field. "The ability to stand in the spaces between realities without losing any of them" is, to Bromberg, health: "'this is what I believe *self-acceptance* means and what *creativity* is really all about—the capacity to feel like one self while being many."[183] The meaning of the *self* within the relational matrix is the capacity to hold a matrix of its *self*.[184] "The core of the negotiation is that the *meaning* of the relationship is intersubjectively, though asymmetrically, constructed out of the patient's self-narrative and the differences from it."[185] In other words, it all depends on the individual's ability to attribute an asymmetrical meaning to intersubjective relations.

In *The Divided Self* (1960), Laing proposes a relatedness model to explain the loss of subjectivity in schizoids as a failure of discriminating and differentiating the self in its interpersonal relations. In this book Laing explains the schizoid personality, which depersonalizes others, as a defense mechanism against the danger of being depersonalized one*self*. In relational psychological terms this would be a failure to relate to a relational matrix altogether. The ability to attribute subjective meaning to one's own relational matrix is what enables a coherent and sane mind. Inability to do this prevents one from reaching a subjective meaning. We develop this discussion in order to understand how attributing sanctity to abnormal behavior functions psychologically. As we shall see, relational psychological models will enable us to compare between the therapeutic process and the process of change that such sanctification creates. The common feature is the intrapsychic zone that enables the process.

"Relational Unconsciousness" as a Device of Change

In his recent book *The Shadow of the Tsunami and the Growth of the Relational Mind* (2011), Bromberg analyzes precisely this "intrapsychic zone" that is created as part of the relational dynamics within psychological treatment (focusing on post-trauma patients). The intrapsychic zone between patient and therapist is the framework of a "relational unconscious" between the two, where the two can experience each other and each one outside their roles as patient and analyst.[186] This enables the patient to experience and process what could not be processed beforehand. As Bromberg says, since this process is relational it must pass through the relational matrix of the therapist.[187] This is the very nature of the psychoanalytical process in Bromberg's model: being relational it is shared, and must be perceived as such for a change to occur in the patient. But since this human relatedness is shared by patient and therapist, it affects the second as much as it affects the first.[188]

Bromberg defines this as a new reality created not only for the patient but also for the therapist.[189] The new reality depends on the ability of the patient to reflect on the therapist's mind experiencing his own. This also depends on the ability of the therapist to do the same thing, that is, to reflect on the patient's mind experiencing his own.[190] Bromberg names this experience of reciprocally "shared minding," which he sees as the only way of curing.[191] This process of "mentalization" is to him what therapy must aim to achieve.[192] It becomes possible only in a joint process in which rational thought is temporarily suspended (in both patient and therapist), and the gradual creation of a relational unconscious, which belongs to both persons but to neither alone, becomes possible.[193] Bromberg describes this process using a case study of his patient Martha:

> A new domain of shared space had been created between us and simultaneously, between each of our own different parts. We were both "awake" to this space and could now express in *language* the personal feelings that before could be only enacted. The fact that the cognitive processing was confusing didn't get in our way. The confusion felt more like a natural part of where we were together. It was part of what was allowing her to be with me, and me with her. It allowed me to feel personally the part of her that I had been immune to—immune because I had been dissociating the part of myself that could most relate to it affectively.[194]

This moving description vividly exemplifies how the intrapsychic space shared by both patient and therapist forces the second to change—to "be awakened" in Bromberg's words—in order for the first to change. This development of a shared therapeutic space depends on allowing the boundary between self and other to become permeable. It enables the creation of a new reality for both patient and therapist. To Bromberg, this is "the truth" that enables psychoanalysis to "provide an experience that is *perceivably* different from the patient's narrative memory."[195] It is not hard to see that this intrapsychic zone as means of change is very close to what Artaud was aiming at with his Theater of Cruelty, as we saw above. This is the role of insanity and abnormality in a religious society: to create an intrapsychic space in which relatedness can bring about a new perception of reality. To put it differently, since this relatedness is dyadic, "the insane"—a priori the patient—appears here as the therapist: a means to activate and actualize the relational matrix of the beholder in order to attain a new truth. The ambiguity about insanity and sanctity is the device to constitute the insane as the relational-object of their entourage.

The Psychological Role of Ambiguity

In her writings, psychoanalyst Amati Sas identifies the intrapsychic space between patient and therapist as a state where ambiguity is created.[196] Drawing on previous works by Argentinean psychoanalyst José Bleger, she shows how the psychic mechanism that he identifies as ambiguity-symbiosis, is enacted within therapy as a process of change. To Bleger, ambiguity is a state of undifferentiation of the ego from others ("objects").[197] Bleger gives examples of patients who project their own acts, desires, and fears on others. As a result such a person is held in a state of psychic symbiosis with the relational object (the *other*) and uses it as a depository of parts of its ego.[198] Such states of *psychic* ambiguity and symbiosis produce an inability to interpret daily experiences in reality correctly, since the borderline between subject and object, between subjectivity and objectivity, is blurred.[199] Against the background of the relational matrix model, Bleger's theory about ambiguity and symbiosis makes a great deal of sense: "ambiguity zones" in the relational matrix prevent the individual mind from constructing an asymmetrical subjective meaning, and result in an inability to discern between subjective and intersubjective realities. Bleger's identified states of ambiguity are the inability to discern, discriminate, and differentiate this meaning.

Amati Sas uses this model to explain the relational psychic dynamic that is created in therapy between the patient and the therapist. She thus understands the very foundation of psychoanalytical treatment—the transference and countertransference process—as a process in which ambiguity between patient and therapist is created and changes the perception of reality of both. This "zone of ambiguity" between the two, where the patient uses the therapist as a relational "depository" and the therapist is drawn into it and responds from this new position, is what can bring about a change: "In ambiguity (in contrast to ambivalence), the conflictual, antinomian or contradictory terms are interchangeable, because they are not yet precise, nor contrasted, nor hierarchized . . . as a consequence, the presence of ambiguity attributes to the psychic phenomena an oscillatory character of malleability, elasticity, changing adaptability, which permits an adaptation to culture, habitudes of a contextual reality and affective climate of inter- and trans-subjective relations."[200]

As we saw, the holy fool's ambiguity is transferred to other insane persons whom readers encounter in real life. The sanctification of insane behavior creates an ambiguity about every insane person and does not permit readers or beholders to really know whether they are facing a genuine insane person or a holy person whose insanity is simulated. This means that they will never know whether the insane person is "patient" or "therapist." As Sas Amati tells us, this ambiguity is a key element of therapy since it enables openness for change in the perception of reality and of one's *self*. The ambiguity about the insane that the phenomenon of sanctified insanity creates will make the sane to look for the insane in order to establish a "relatedness fabric."[201] It is a process of enactment in relational psychology, in which the sane beholder is caught in a relationship with the insane "object." The holy fool phenomenon thus turns the insane into a relational object, by producing a psychic space in which *self* (beholder) and *object* (the insane) interact.[202]

The Relational Matrix of the Insane

To Bromberg, psychoanalysis must "provide an experience that is *perceivably* different from the patient's narrative memory" in order for a change to occur in the patient.[203] This is common to all psychological theories, and serves as the raison d'être of modern psychology. But in any relatedness model, although reciprocal, the patient's side and the therapist's side are not identical. It is only the first that requires a change, while the second may or may not be changed in the process.

We saw above that an encounter with insanity is a destabilizing psychological experience, which can be lived as a threat to the beholder's psyche. From a relational psychological perspective this makes a great deal of sense, since the insane person disrupts the coherent functioning of the beholder's relational matrix by producing a zone of ambiguity that cannot be fully addressed: where the borderlines between *I* and *you*, between *real* and *unreal*, between visible and invisible are blurred. In the works of Laing and Bleger, this sort of ambiguity can be an organic product of an unhealthy development of the individual psyche, and is part of a larger interrelational mechanism. From a relational psychological perspective, social circumstances prevent the individual psyche from developing a healthy subjective relational matrix of its own. It is being held in an intersubjective relational matrix by zones of ambiguity.[204]

Contemporary relational psychotherapy does not focus on zones of ambiguity between subjective relational matrices, but proposes, instead, to resolve the contradictions within the psychological dimension of the individual and to develop a sane subjective relational matrix through the simulation of a new relational matrix in therapy, using the therapist as a relational-object device, who, according to Bromberg, must also change for the process to succeed.[205] This strategy aims at separating patients from their dependence on their given relational environment in order to create a sane independent environment. However, patients who are incapable of differentiating between themselves and their fathers, mothers, or therapists, and have a distorted perception of the world because their symbiotic relations prevent them from developing a subjective perception, reflect in their ambiguity the contradictions between their own personal relational matrix and the relational matrices of their family members.[206] To put it differently, current perspectives in relational psychology prove to be only monodimensional in pulling patients away from their environment, which such perspectives espouse as the cause of the patients' mental state.[207] However, reading the situation through a genuine relational perspective will reveal that the victims of such unhealthy constellations reflect in their mental state the unhealthiness, malfunctioning, and incoherence that exist in the relatedness fabric of their environment, or in their environment *tout court*.[208] In other words, insane persons are both products and representations, and indeed symbols, of what is wrong in their respective environments. To Laing, they carry on the back of their own psyche the scars of their relations. Thus in their insanity they reflect the insanity of the "relatedness fabric" back to their environment. They also hold the means to change it. And this is precisely what sanctified insanity produces.

The figure of the holy fool acts as a symbol of the malfunctioning of its beholders within the hagiographic story. However, the special aesthetics of this literature means that, at least in theory, it makes any real-life insane person into a symbol of his or her beholder's moral behavior as well as a vehicle for moral change. We do not aim here at situating the phenomenon of the holy fool as part of a model from a modern perspective in psychotherapy. In fact, what the phenomenon of the holy fool shows us is that insanity can be a means of change and transformation since it is a symptom of an insane environment. The insane person—any insane person—thus appears not as a mentally ill person, but as a symptom of a mentally ill environment, and moreover as its means of salvation. The ambiguity of the holy fool turns the insane person into a moral mirror of his or her beholder, and sets himself or herself as a catalyst for the beholder's relational matrix. To do that, such figures must be strong enough to divest themselves of any subjective relational matrix, which is what their *xeniteia* is all about. The figure of the holy fool is no ordinary trickster, but the moral conscience of society. As we shall see in the next two chapters it shares this position with the martyr, the ascetic, as well as with any other figure whose abnormal behavior society exemplifies. Regardless of its own objectives as a literary figure, it aims to construct insanity as a mirror in order to bring about a collective change.

PART II

ABNORMALITY AND SOCIAL CHANGE

Early Christianity versus Rabbinic Judaism

3

Abnormality and Social Change

INSANITY AND MARTYRDOM

> It is not similarity or dissimilarity of members that constitute a group but interdependence of fate.
>
> —Kurt Lewin, 1948

Throughout the previous chapters we have examined the way insanity becomes functional on both the literary and the social levels. We have used theories of literary criticism and relational psychology to penetrate into the psychological meaning of the ambiguity of the holy fool, and examined how abnormal behavior can become a means to produce a change of mentality and perception of reality.

The second part of this book continues to examine how different types of abnormal behavior were employed in early Christianity as means of social transformation. It starts in the present chapter with the disagreement about the definition of insanity, and examines the conditions of the use of abnormality in order to constitute a group by creating interdependence of fate. If modern scholarship perceives the definition of insanity as a product of the changes of mentality, the present chapter shows that regardless of the definition of insanity itself, in religious society it can also be the other way around: changes in the definition of abnormal and normal behavior can also be the engine for——mental, social, and political changes and not only their outcome.

Insanity has been defined as an physical condition as well as a social construct. The present chapter proposes to leave the definition of insanity per se aside, and instead to analyze the way in which the definition of the borderline between normality and abnormality functions within a religious society. By taking as a case study the phenomenon of the martyr, that is, the sanctification of a person who in choosing to die expresses a desire for death, the chapter reveals how abnormal behavior is used in order to invert the definition of what is normal and abnormal and produce a change of a much larger scale.

The chapter starts with a psychological and philosophical question about the definitions of insanity and the insane person. It refers to the main difference between the two and presents two major theories about insanity and the rise of psychiatry in early modern Europe. It then addresses this question by a comparative-religion historical study of the phenomenon of martyrdom in pagan, Jewish, and Christian societies in the Roman Empire. This comparison aims to define the phenomenon of martyrdom according to its social role. It shows that an individual abnormal behavior is sanctified in order to reconstruct the borderline between what is abnormal and normal as a means to define and implement a new perception of reality for society. The comparison between early Christianity and rabbinic Judaism will reveal that figures of abnormal behavior are exemplified in order to produce a change. While early Christianity defined and sanctified martyrs for this reason, rabbinic Judaism avoided it precisely in order to preclude any possibility of radical change in its mental and social settings.

Theoretical Premise: Defining Insanity

About the Definition of Insanity

No study of insanity can avoid the modern disagreement about the definition of this concept. Although psychiatry and psychology rely on lack of voluntary control as a decisive component of most psychopathologies, no unique definition of mental illness or mental disorder currently exists to explain the reason of such a lack of voluntary control.[1] The main debate concerns the nature of mental disorder and mental illness as an biological concept versus a normative concept based on value judgment or social norms of behavior.[2]

Whereas most attempts to define mental disorder have been predicated on either value or scientific criteria, psychiatrist Jerome Wakefield proposes to combine the two. He defines mental disorder as a harmful mental dysfunction, where "dysfunction" refers to the failure of an internal mechanism to perform a natural function for which it was designed, and "harmful" refers to the consequences that occur to the person because of the dysfunction and are deemed negative by sociocultural standards.[3] For Wakefield, disorder lies on the boundary between the given natural world and the constructed social world.

Another attempt to deal with this question stresses the need to distinguish causes from symptoms. Psychiatrist Paul McHugh contends that the wide array of mental health conditions tend to fall into four clusters.[4] One cluster includes diseases that produce disturbances in perception, cognition, and emotion (e.g., Alzheimer's disease, schizophrenia). Psychological symptoms arise from structural and functional pathology of the brain. The second cluster includes problems that arise when patients fall at extreme points on psychological dimensions of traits such as introversion and neuroticism. The third cluster includes behavioral patterns that have immediate positive consequences but delayed negative consequences (these do not include problems that originate in brain pathology). The fourth cluster includes problems that arise as a result of experienced events (e.g., posttraumatic stress disorder, or PTSD). Clustering psychiatric conditions according to what patients have, what they are, what they do, or what they encounter therefore helps to distinguish causes from symptoms.

A different perspective on the interaction between the biological and the social in the causation of mental illness has been proposed by psychologist Richard McNally.[5] He argues that because mental illness occurs on a spectrum of severity, mental disorder is a concept characterized by intrinsically fuzzy boundaries: the more attributes present in a given case, the more disorder-like it tends to be. It is due to this fuzziness, McNally argues, that social, political, and economic factors often prove decisive when it comes to determining whether ambiguous cases count as mental disorder.[6] Medical science alone, therefore, does not determine where we draw this boundary. In this view, mental conditions vary in the degree to which they are disorder-like. Others, however, stress that the occurrence of ambiguous cases does not undermine the concept of mental disorder as having necessary and sufficient criteria.[7] We see that these theories refer to the social context as a conclusive factor in the diagnosis of mental disease as either cause or symptom.[8]

What History Can Contribute to the Discussion

History can provide a productive field of research in revealing the social and cultural conditions that affect the definition of insanity.[9] Historical studies of insanity in different periods and cultures can reveal the compatibility and incompatibility among the biological, social, and cultural attributes of what constitutes a definition of mental disorder, and the conditions that determine its perception.[10] Here, Michel Foucault's pioneering work about the birth of modern psychiatry provides us with the best starting point to investigate the way in which insanity is defined and treated. Fifty years after its initial publication, *Histoire de la folie à l'âge classique*, in spite of the severe criticism it has received, remains the most challenging theory dealing with modern conceptualizations of the definitions of insanity and sanity.[11] In Roy Porter's words, "time has proved it by far the most penetrating work ever written on the history of madness (and, above all, the history of reason)."[12] Beyond its main thesis, which will be discussed below, the book is a testimony to our need today to conceptualize, define, and deal with insanity.[13] As both Foucault and his critics show, the importance of the study of insanity lies in the ways in which it can be situated within the historical analysis of modern society, and the way in which modern mentality was and is constructed.

Leaving aside the differences of the historical discourse about insanity, what this discourse clearly shows is that the treatment of the insane is relative to the definitions of insanity and sanity in a given society. The main disagreements are over two questions, which are naturally connected: (1) how to interpret the rise of modern psychiatry, and (2) whether the state of insanity itself is absolute or relative, that is biological or social. In spite of this disagreement, the different views, including those of Foucault's adherents and critics, share a common perspective: whatever the definition of insanity and its causes may be, the social and cultural framework that relates and corresponds to it determines the way in which the insane are perceived and treated. Both the adherents and the opponents to Foucault's theory share this view and understand the rise of modern psychiatry as a change in the perception of insanity, which is analyzed as a part of a much broader development in the perception of reason and knowledge in general.

Foucault on Insanity

Foucault traces the origins of the early modern change in the perception of insanity back to Descartes, and explains it as a product of the new conceptualization of reason as a method destined to appropriate all knowledge. Without summarizing it here, his thesis clearly demonstrates how abnormal behavior is perceived to cover the spectrum of a new definition of "unreason"—*déraison*. This is in view of the new means by which reason, that is, rational reasoning, becomes defined in early modern Europe as the unique method of attaining and applying knowledge. Once reason equals knowledge, any other forms of perception, other than through reason, are by definition irrational and are thus rendered illegitimate.

Attributing insanity to different, that is, irrational, forms of perception, serves here as a means not only of making them illegitimate but also, according to Foucault, of appropriating them and submitting them to a new form of "rational reason" by conceptualizing them as insane. In a word, reason could not have developed the way it has in early modern Europe without alienating any unreasonable (irrational) behavior as "insane." "The great confinement," the incarceration of all alienated persons—*les aliénés*—throughout the seventeenth and eighteenth centuries, the nucleus of Foucault's argument, stemmed from the new modern equation between the two borderlines, reason/unreason and sanity/insanity, and served to express the triumph of the first (reason = sanity) over the second (unreason = insanity). It served as a practical means of appropriating madness by shutting it away from society, which thus became a "sane" society. Not only was reason henceforth defined as sanity of the mind, but sanity of the mind was defined as reason. The consequence was, in Foucault's own words, that madness in "the age of reason" came to cover the entire spectrum of *déraison*—"unreason"—and its essence.[14]

What interested Foucault was in fact the way reason had become a way of exerting power by appropriating any form of unreason. Pathology was, to Foucault, the means created by rationality for this appropriation. Madness, once defined as unreason, that is, the failure to reason and the failure to perceive reality through reason, constitutes for him the example par excellence. In order to submit, conquer, and appropriate unreason, Foucault explains that reason had to conceptualize unreason in moral terms. Pathology proved to be a necessary means to this end. Its development served, according to Foucault, to define the incapacity of the mind to think in compliance with reason as a product of the passions of the body, and hence a disease defined in moral terms. The definition of madness as a disease proved to be a social and cultural construct as well: a pathological change affects the mind which dwells in the brain and causes a mental change. This mental change originates in a moral flaw and causes a false perception of reality.[15] Any form of unreason was defined as a false perception of reality, while the inability to perceive through reason was declared a disease.

This thesis, which was severely criticized as a misreading of the writings of the French psychiatrists of the turn of the eighteenth and nineteenth centuries (see below), must be understood in view of Foucault's main objective. He was looking to understand the asylum and the new psychiatric treatment of the nineteenth century as forms of exerting power over the insane and of subduing them. The moral aspect, once proven, served in order to confine the insane to an asylum in a way similar to that whereby criminals were confined to prison. Society's fear of the insane was henceforth formulated and perceived in the same terms as its fear of criminals. This fits very well with the perception of madness as a social construct, a product of morality, whose treatment must therefore also become a moral process. Confinement thus proves, according to Foucault's reading, to be a moral means, and the asylum the place both of defending the society of the sane from the insane, and of a moral rehabilitation of the insane. Moreover, psychiatry, even psychoanalysis for that matter, can thus be perceived as the ultimate moral victory of modern reason.

A Different Perspective

Part of the opposition to Foucault's ideas must be understood as a moral objection to the question of what constitutes modern knowledge. The most challenging and thought-provoking criticism of his book is the historical analysis of psychiatric evolution by Marcel Gauchet and Gladys Swain, which in spite of its magnitude and importance has not been translated fully into English to this day.[16] Growing out of Swain's earlier works on the history of psychiatry, this book is large in both its scope and content. Moreover, it provides a counter-reading to Foucault's book, which can no longer be read without it. Together with the works of William Bynum and Roy Porter, it provides the most extensive research on the history of modern psychiatry. We shall not analyze the findings of Gauchet and Swain here. Nevertheless, we will see that they too, though opposing Foucault's reading, understand the definition of madness as a product of the social and indeed political structure in which it is perceived.

La pratique de l'esprit humain: L'insitution asilaire et la révolution démocratique, published in English in an abbreviated form as *Madness and Democracy: The Modern Psychiatric Universe*, takes as a starting point the same main prepositions as Foucault's book, that is, the fact that there is a correlation between the way in which madness is defined and the social and political attitude toward the insane. However, it takes as its objective not the analysis of power relations as a product of a new modern mentality, but the analysis of the body of writings of the first modern psychiatrists working in the age of the French Revolution. Gauchet and Swain's main concern is the relation between modern psychiatry and the idea of modern democracy. A thorough analysis of the first modern works on psychiatry by Daquin, Pinel, Bichat, Cabanis, Esquirol, and others, against the background of the invention of a new practice of psychiatry, reveals here a thesis completely contrary to Foucault's. It was precisely the same creation of "reason," argue Gauchet and Swain, that enabled the application of a new system of the understanding of madness in order to cure it.

Gauchet and Swain take the new mentality in which the reign of reason has no limits, not in order to explain Foucault's alienation and incarceration of unreason away from this reign, but as a means to understand it. However, here too, we observe, madness had to be completely appropriated by reason. In order to be "understood" it needed to be perceived, conceptualized, and hence "seized" by reason. But from this point onward, the authors diverge greatly from Foucault. They underline the identification of madness mostly with mania, which made madness a temporary state (attributed with chronicity), comprised within the science of medicine, and thus curable.[17]

Just as in Foucault's analysis, so here too the perception of the place of the insane member of society needed to be backed up by a moral justification.[18] In contrast to Foucault, Gauchet and Swain attribute the moral aspect to the cure, rather than to the science of pathology. They show how the definition of pathology as an organic passion of the body led to disconnecting the morality of the insane from their state of insanity.[19] This perspective created a need to decipher the symptoms, and interpret them in relation to the passions. The results were new methods of cure.[20]

Thus the understanding, the "reasoning" of madness, resulted in its perception as a curable state, which was the asylum's main purpose. The asylum appears not as the expression of alienation and confinement of *déraison*, as Foucault would have it, but as a product of the new way in which madness is seen, and the desire to cure it. The asylum corresponds to the need to detach the insane from their environment, and provide an organization adaptable to their requirements, where they can be treated and be cured. Gauchet and Swain reveal how the asylums of the early French Republic functioned as mental hospitals and provided conditions for healing the insane following Pinel's (1745–1826) assertion that there is no madman who cannot be cured.[21] In a word, "modern reason" (*la raison modern*) was not developed to exclude the insane, but with the need and the intention to reintegrate them within society. Moreover, the asylum as a place to cure the insane is here perceived as the only way of making them independent. The cure of the insane thus means their rehabilitation as active sane members of society, but also an affirmation of the capacity of human beings to change their social and political circumstances via a mental change.

The mental change that was introduced in the republican era and redefined the relation between persons, in the authors' view, also changed the medical relationship between the physician and the patient. It enabled the physician to transform 'the other,' the patient, an individual in whom the illness resides, into an object of investigation, by detaching the patient from the person who examines him, with the sole objective of liberating the patient. Here the conclusion of the authors is very different from Foucault's: the perception of this 'other' was not a triumphant measure of power of possession but, on the contrary, a perception that a subject who is not master of himself is not free in relation to all other members of society.[22] The perception of the cure as the reinstatement of the insane within the democratic discourse is both a product and an affirmation of the republican discourse. The main moral treatment, which a century later would be formulated in psychoanalytical terms, consisted more than anything else in the development of a method whereby the alienated person could perceive himself as a person.[23] This was exactly what liberation meant in the age of revolution.

Gauchet and Swain thus show that the new perception of the man as a subject of science came about together with the new perception of the man as an independent, sovereign individual, both legally and politically. This is quite the opposite of Foucault's analysis. Insanity was perceived in "the age of reason" as a crisis in the new category of the individual's sovereignty, and not as method of exacting sovereignty over the insane. The asylum appears here as a means toward the social and political liberation and integration of the "other." Foucault's "great confinement" is hereby declared "nothing more and nothing less than a 'modern myth.'"[24]

A Relative Definition of Insanity?

In his preface to the new edition of the book, published in 2007, Gauchet goes even further than defining Foucault's conceptualization of insanity in mythic terms. He questions the very perception of insanity as a construct, which to his mind replaces "real insanity" (*folie réelle*) with imagined insanity (*folie imaginée*), a sole creation of "reason." Foucault's very reading of insanity as a social construct is here demonstrated to be extremely dangerous: if the way in which insanity is defined is completely dependent on the way in which sanity/reason is defined, there is no real medical state of insanity. In other words, and although never declared as such by Foucault, insanity cannot be at the same time both an organic, that is, physical and medical, state and a mental state. The objection that Gauchet raises to Foucault's analysis is whether insanity can really be considered a relative concept.

This is a serious attack on Foucault's reading, and one to which he could not reply. Having been written in 2007, it might, nevertheless, reflect a reading of Foucault in an anti-postmodern perspective. It is important to understand that the entire debate concerns the question of defining insanity through either a positivistic or a relativistic perspective. Modern Western society has constructed the *Diagnostic and Statistical*

Manual of Mental Disorders (*DSM*) to provide a range of mental and organic combinations. But is this not simply a way of avoiding the question of whether insanity is a relative or an absolute term? Is insanity really a combination of the mental and physical aspects, both an absolute and relative phenomenon, or is this definition merely a reflection of contemporary thought? Such an attitude could be extremely dangerous, as Gauchet tells us, mainly because it could reduce insanity to nothing more than a cultural construct.[25] In what follows we shall leave aside the contemporary definition of insanity in favor of the ways in which society establishes such a definition, and the circumstances, conditions, and objectives of such a process.

Change of Mentality = Change in the Definition of Insanity

An excellent example of this sort of correlation between the definition of insanity and the social and mental structure that maintains it is found in the comparative study by Catherine Clément and Sudhir Kakar of two simultaneous parallel phenomena of abnormal behavior at the end of the nineteenth century: two mystic figures, a woman in France and a man in Bengal, who seem to share identical symptoms of abnormal mystic behavior.[26] The first is hospitalized at La Salpêtrière hospital, while the second is venerated as a saint. Whatever "organic condition" they might have shared, the comparative study clearly shows that the way in which this condition is perceived and responded to by society depends on the cultural and mental language in which it is defined.

The difference between nineteenth-century France and nineteenth-century Bengal produced two very different receptions of what appears to be the same phenomenon. It is, in the words of Clément, the story of two systems of faith that correspond to two systems of cure.[27] While the visions of Ramakrishna have meaning in his society, those of Madeleine *la Bouc* ("the Goat") are found completely outside any collective tradition that could have attributed a structure to them.[28] Nineteenth-century France did not recognize a mystic structure because it did not need one. It declared it not only meaningless but also insane. By comparing the behavior of a series of French women incarcerated in a mental hospital with the language of Indian mysticism, Clément argues that the series of deeds and norms defined as symptoms of mad behavior by nineteenth-century French society appeared to be guided by a decoded mystical system, meaningless to modern French mentality but full of meaning in its contemporaneous Bengal.[29] Gauchet would certainly find this rejection of psychiatric norms dangerous. But whether or not we subscribe to such a relativistic perspective, we cannot but agree that abnormal, "mad," behavior is perceived as such according to the prevalent mental and cultural norms and society's means of conceptualizing it, regardless of how we would define it today using our modern *DSM* conventions, and regardless of its "real" causes and state. According to the same approach, the *DSM* corresponds nicely with our contemporary mental definition of the psychological sphere. If we put aside the positivistic versus relativistic debate, we are nevertheless bound to conclude that a change in mental and cultural norms goes hand in hand with a change in the way in which insanity is perceived and treated.

In addition, it is important to note that the way in which insanity is perceived also corresponds to the way in which the insane are treated. Whether analyzed as a way of alienating insanity by confining it and exerting power over it (Foucault and his followers), or as a means of curing and reintegrating it (Gauchet and Swain), in both cases the new ways in which the insane person is perceived and treated are read as a product of the social and political changes of the era. In other words, modern research into its historiographical and philosophical trends has revealed the correlation between the way in which insanity is perceived and the mental context which defines it. A behavior is perceived and defined as abnormal in relation to what is considered to be normal and abnormal within the system that defines it, whether its nature is organic, mental, or social.

For our purpose, which concerns the relation between insanity and sanctity, we can avoid the question about the nature of insanity in favor of the question about the way in which it is perceived. We can conclude that insanity is thus conceptualized and defined in a way that conforms to a given mental and social setting. This is the most productive contribution of Foucault's analysis. As much as his relativistic approach can be criticized (if he was ever a true relativist), there is no doubt that he paved the way to analyzing insanity in relation to its place within the mental structure in which it is defined.[30] This also means that a change of mentality entails a change in the perception of normal or abnormal behavior. This is all the more important if the change occurs in the way in which reason is defined. No one will contest this attitude, which is now deeply rooted in the modern perception of history as modeled and influenced by the trend of the *histoire des mentalités*.

In what follows we shall see that the change in the perception of what constitutes normal/reasonable or abnormal/unreasonable behavior not only is a product of a mental change, but can also serve as a means of achieving it. Whatever ways we use to define insanity today, the question is whether a change in the mental structure could not only be projected onto the insane, but also read in and through them. In this way, phenomena of abnormal behavior acquire a social function, and could serve as a means for society to implement a new perception of reality. Neither Foucault nor his most severe critics address such a perception of the relation between society and the way in which it perceives abnormal behavior. According to both of them, the changes in the ways in which insanity is defined and treated are conditioned and determined by the changes in the mental, social, and cultural settings, whether or not they refer to insanity as an organic state. The present chapter will show that this relation could also be defined the other way around, meaning that a change in the definition of what is normal and abnormal could act as a means of producing a change of mentality and a new perception of reality.

There seems to be no better example to illustrate how abnormal behavior is used as a means to implement a change in the perception of reality than the figure of the martyr. If the perception of reality is used as a criterion to define and identify the insane, we shall see that martyrs have an important role in enabling their societies to produce a change of mentality and perception of reality.

Insanity and Martyrdom

A Different Kind of Abnormality—the Martyr

The martyr, needless to say, has received much attention in modern scholarship, whether in the framework of Christian antiquity, medieval religions, or in modern and even in present times. We are used to attribute the term "martyr" to historical or contemporary figures who have sacrificed their life for their beliefs. These could also be nonreligious beliefs, though the term is highly loaded with religious connotations.

The Greek etymological origin of the term, *martus*, means "witness." It was first used by the early Christians in the sense of a person who died for a cause. It came to designate those particular Christian believers who were executed during the Roman persecutions for bearing witness to the true God by refusing to participate in the Roman pagan imperial cults. What exactly were they bearing witness to is never explained explicitly in early Christian *martyrologies*—as the texts that recorded them are named—beyond their nomination as "witnesses of the God" (Greek: *martures tou theou*).[31] The term was transliterated into Latin in early Christian Latin texts, generally avoiding the Latin equivalent, *testis*. The corresponding Syriac term is *sāhdā* (*sāhdûtā*—testimony/witnessing).[32] Its equivalent Arabic term—*šahīd*—was later used in Islam to designate the believers who died in the battle of their religion. The comparable Hebrew term—dying for the sanctification of God's name (Hebrew: "dying for *kiddush hašem*")—is different in its meaning and has no relation to bearing witness. As we shall see this difference is telling with regard to the political function of the phenomenon of dying for one's beliefs.

Today, however, both the Greek and the Arabic terms—martyr and *šahīd* (pronounced sha-hid)—are used ubiquitously to mean anyone who has died a heroic death. What a heroic death is, of course, is a matter of opinion, and reflects the perspective of whoever uses the term. It ranges from persons who valued their ideals over their lives, persons who were killed and had no choice in the matter, persons who died in battle, as well as persons who died while killing others. In all cases the term refers to figures whose death has become a symbol. It is beyond the scope of the current study to sum up or reduce the different types of historical and social phenomena that are termed martyrdom today into a single model. Nevertheless, we shall focus on two aspects related to the phenomenon of martyrs and their sanctification: its social function and its significance in challenging the boundary between normal and abnormal behavior, and through it the perception of reality. As we saw above, it is the relationship between these two aspects which interests us.

As far as the sanity-insanity boundary is concerned, although martyrs who voluntarily killed themselves or killed others may be occasionally referred to by outside viewers as exhibiting insane behavior, they are not considered insane by the society which grants them the title of martyr, mainly because it is normally required that they would be conscious of their cause of death. Of course, this does not rule out the possibility of a psychological analysis of their behavior, especially if we define it as a "pathological desire for death."[33] Such an attitude was taken by Ruth Stein in her analysis of the letter left by Muhammad Atta in his car on September 11, 2001.[34] Muhammad Atta was a suicidal killer terrorist who considered himself, and is also considered by a few others, a martyr. It is not our intention to compare here people who kill themselves for their beliefs with people whose beliefs also include the killing of others. It is, however, necessary to understand what perspective considers them to be martyrs.[35]

In her article "Evil as Love and as Liberation," Stein reveals the tight bond between the two opposing facets of an act of massacre and self-massacre that was done out of religious conviction. The act of violence defines the figure, whether we consider him a martyr or a terrorist, within a context of a sacred war. But, as Stein argues, it also has an inverse psychological and mental effect through which the killer expresses his love of his father-God by sacrificing himself together with the persons whom he kills. A priori the suicidal act is an act of agency, but on the other hand it has an inverse effect on the psyche by a negation of the self and by its complete immersion within its love for a father figure—God. As Stein explains, the violence is necessary because love must be expressed through a self-negating act.[36] The sacrifice is henceforth the sacrifice of the self.[37] Stein also focuses on the social and psychological aspect that inverts this ultimate act of self-destruction into an act of liberation. But whatever the psychological social context of such an act may be, it is defined and enacted within a specific religious and political context. This context gives the killer a sense of righteousness and enables any act of killing to be termed "a sacred act." This inversion of meaning seems to be, as we shall see, a defining feature of the martyr.

In what follows we will focus on the reason why abnormal behavior of self-denial that ends with death came to be sanctified by society through its definition as martyrdom. The violent death also marks the martyr's crime, since martyrs are not only those who die for their beliefs, but also those whose actions are considered a crime by their opponents, since they are always defined in the framework of a conflict. In fact, their main function, as we shall see, is to define a conflict by an inversion of meaning. In other words, the martyr is defined as a figure of abnormality in order to invert social norms and change the social settings in the framework of a new perception of reality. To do this we shall take a comparative-religion study, focusing on the period in history during which the concept of martyrdom as we perceive it today was formed: the period of the Roman persecutions.[38] In the center of this examination we will compare how two contemporaneous religions, early Christianity and rabbinic Judaism, defined and commemorated their opposition to Roman rule. We shall see that while early Christianity constructed the model of the martyr as a means of change, rabbinic Judaism whose objectives, in contrast, were aimed at suppressing any possibility of change, avoided the creation of such a model. At the end of this chapter, we will be able to define the abnormality of the figure of the martyr according to the social function of a saint, as a means of implementing a mental and political change.

Martyrs Confronting Roman Persecutions

Much research has been dedicated to the subject of the Roman persecutions. Christians, however, were not the only group that was violently harassed by the Roman authorities during the first centuries A.D. Two other groups recorded the maltreatment they received from the Roman government in the form of the heroic behavior by historical figures. The first were Jews who expressed their resistance to Roman rule in the Jewish revolts against the Roman state in the second century (A.D. 66–74, 115–117, 132–136), and were consequently executed. The second were members of the Alexandrian pagan elite whose political struggle against Roman rule has come down to us on papyri from rural Egypt. In modern scholarship the descriptions of their trials and executions received the name *Acta Alexandrinorum*—"The Acts of the Alexandrians." All three cases of resistance to Roman rule were recorded simultaneously during the period known as Late Antiquity, from the second to the sixth centuries. All three portray cases of the heroic death of historical figures resisting Roman rule. But as we shall see, only one case, the Christian martyr, was constructed in order to challenge the definition of normality and abnormality and implement a new perception of reality for a new society. This is exactly what the comparison to the other contemporaneous cases, the Jewish and Alexandrian "martyrs," reveals. Comparative religion proves here to be a powerful tool to decipher the role of abnormality as a defining feature of the martyr, and to reveal the condition for its creation and sanctification as a means of change.

In his book *Martyrdom and Rome,* Glen Bowersock demonstrates the phenomenon of the Christian martyrs to be grounded within the Roman civic life. Bowersock makes it clear that the new phenomenon of women and men who give their lives publically for a cause is dependent on a certain political culture. In other words, martyrdom does not appear without a context within which it can be perceived and understood. What is interesting for our purpose is the fact that during the same period three different phenomena of what we can name in Roman terms "noble death" took place.[39] The common feature of all three was the fact that the Roman perception of noble death was not attributed to them by the Roman authorities who executed them. Although their battles and rivalry were defined by and grounded within the Roman political culture, they were perceived by the Roman authorities as criminals and were charged with high treason (Latin: *maiestas*).[40]

Three preliminary facts should be underlined concerning these three groups and the texts that they produced. First, most of these texts were not grouped together until modern times. Second, the *Acta Alexandrinorum,* "the Pagan acts," refer to events of the first and second centuries A.D., and record the earliest of the events involving any of the three groups.[41] The Jewish texts refer to prominent Jews who were executed for high treason in the first half of the second century, while the earliest of the *Acts of the Christian Martyrs* refer to the persecutions of the mid-second, but mostly of the third and the beginning of the fourth centuries. Third, unlike the Jewish and Christian texts, the pagan acts have not come down to us through a textual tradition, but were found on papyri whose discovery was completely accidental. We can only speculate about the scale of their circulation, and we cannot know whether similar texts were written in other Roman provinces to commemorate the deeds of political leaders who expressed similar resistance to the Roman rule.

Put together, what these texts do show is not only the large scale of the resistance to Roman rule in the provinces, but also the echo and promotion that this resistance received. Our main concern, however, will not be given to the political anti-Roman aspect, but to the social, cultural, and mental aspects of the phenomena. We shall focus on the meaning of the differences between the ways in which these political figures were commemorated as heroes in order to understand what changes of mentality their remembrance and cult as saints produced in their respective societies. But first, we should address their classical archetypes.

Any historian who deals with martyrdom in antiquity normally chooses to start with Socrates's execution. *The Apology* of Plato does not need to be repeated here. Socrates is the ultimate example of a person who was executed for beliefs and actions that he refused to renounce, and his historical significance is mainly thanks to both. Classical literature is full of other cases, both individual and collective, which were constructed according to the same model of "a noble death."[42] The example of Socrates is still the most famous of them all, and was as famous in antiquity. In fact, it was adopted as model by both pagan and Christian authors.[43] However, an earlier prototype, with a literary rather than historical origin, seems to have been largely overlooked by the scholarship about martyrdom: the figure of Antigone.[44]

Sophocles's tragedy was written and performed probably around the fifties of the fifth century B.C., a few decades prior to Socrates drinking his cup of poison. It concerns an individual who defies the new law of the city of Thebes, promulgated by the king, by insisting on performing the funeral rites of the gods for her brother, considered a traitor by the Theban government. The play turns on the question of loyalty to earthly or heavenly laws: the political or the religious sphere. It was written in the heyday of Athenian rule, before its descent into the Peloponnesian War. The play is relevant to our purpose because it seems one of the earliest examples of a voluntary death defined within a rivalry between two sets of norms of conduct: earthly and heavenly, temporal and eternal. Three hundred years or more later we find the same kind of rivalry articulated through the voluntary death of a group of people as a political act in 2 Maccabees. These were Jews who refuted the anti-Jewish persecutions of Seleucid rule in Judaea and preferred their own or their children's death over the violation of the biblical commandments. The Maccabean example of dying for a cause is important because it formulates the political struggle of the Hasmoneans against the Seleucid king in religious terms.[45] Thus it sets up a confrontation between loyalty to an earthly king and loyalty to the heavenly God in order to justify a political revolt.[46]

The combat of the early Christian martyrs will be articulated, as we shall see, exactly in the same manner. In fact, of the three types of what can be termed "anti-Roman martyrdom," the Christian combat is the only one to be modeled in this way. In the *Acta Alexandrinorum*, or *Alexandrian Acts*, the combat is completely an earthly one, while in the Jewish rabbinic texts that record anti-Roman struggle no combat whatsoever is articulated between the heavenly and earthly spheres. The following comparative study will show that the figure of the martyr is constructed and sanctified as a means to express a combat between two opposing systems of thought, or in fact between two opposing perceptions of reality, in the objective of a political inversion.

The Acts of the Alexandrians: Articulation of a "National Combat"

Herbert Musurillo named the accounts of the Alexandrians who were executed by the Roman emperors *The Acts of the Pagan Martyrs*.[47] This appellation is no longer used in present-day scholarship. His edition lists eleven documents along with ten fragments which record the battle of the Alexandrian elite against Roman imperial rule in the first and second centuries A.D. This list has since been enlarged and complemented by other findings, and comprises today over seventy related documents and fragments, according to the rich appendix of Andrew Harker's *Loyalty and Dissidence in Roman Egypt*.[48] None of these texts has come down to us from Alexandria. They are all copies that circulated in the rural and urban Egyptian provinces. They narrate the confrontation between prominent Alexandrian figures and the Roman imperial authorities. Some of the texts record Alexandrian delegations to Rome during the reign of Gaius and Claudius. Others are presented as records of interviews or minutes of trials for high treason that end in the executions of the Alexandrians. They all underline the bravery of the Alexandrian leaders who defy imperial rule in Egypt.

In one of the most elaborated texts, Appian, a gymnasiarch, is tried by the emperor for accusing the Roman authorities of tax exploitation of the local population (300 percent on the price of wheat).[49] Appian defies the emperor for being tyrannical, and contextualizes his own execution within the framework of the history of Roman-Egyptian political relations since the time of Caesar and Cleopatra.[50] The text clearly refers to a local Alexandrian "national" concept in developing its anti-Roman dissidence, which was, according to Harker, what these texts were all about.

The literature of the *Alexandrian Acts* must have been much richer and more varied than what has come down to us.[51] It was clearly used to construct a historical aspect to the Alexandrian combat against the Romans, no doubt in order to articulate it in local and/or "national" terms. The extent of the seventy complete and fragmentary documents identified by Harker and their chronological range over the first six centuries A.D. demonstrates the importance of their circulation as a means of recording these deeds in order to create and implement a local political consciousness.[52]

Harker has argued that the background for the political conflicts in Alexandria was the tension between the Jewish and pagan populations under Roman rule in the city. Both communities sent embassies to Rome in the 40s of the first century to deal with these tensions.[53] In the "Acts of Isidoros and Lampon" for example, the trial and execution of these two figures by Claudius is presented as part of the favorable attitude of this emperor toward the Jewish population.[54] Two documents depict similar situations where prominent Alexandrian leaders confront the Roman emperor in Rome, objecting to his favorable attitude toward the Alexandrian Jews, and are consequently executed.[55] The first cites Trajan, while in the second, attributed today to Hadrian's reign, the name of the Roman emperor has not survived. The interesting thing about these two texts is that both Trajan and Hadrian, if the second document did indeed originally refer to him, were famous for the measures they took against Jewish populations. Trajan crushed the Jewish revolts of 115–117 in the Diaspora, and Hadrian subdued Judaea in 135–136. Although the *Alexandrian Acts* are presented as contemporary, they were copied and edited after the events depicted, which means that at the time of their circulation the Roman suppression of the Jewish revolts was a known fact. In spite of this, they are constructed according to the model of a similar text from the reign of Claudius, which had depicted a Roman attitude favorable to the Jewish population at the expense of the pagan political elite.[56]

This fits Harker's main thesis that these texts were composed to represent a "national combat" of the pagan Alexandrian elite against Roman rule in Egypt. The local Jewish population was hence a local competitor over the embodiment of resistance to Roman rule, and thus had to be represented as the antithesis of the pagan Alexandrians, that is, as favorable to the Romans. In other words, the *Alexandrian Acts* portray dissidence from Roman rule that seems to be constructed in reference to the Jewish uprising. If we elaborate more on the idea of the "national" concept that the authors of these texts wanted to evoke in their readers, it is clear that an attack on the relationship between the local Jewish population and the Roman rulers was necessary. But the interesting thing is that these texts portray competition between the pagan and dissident Jewish populations in Alexandria over the active antagonism to the Romans. This is very similar to another competition against Roman rule that took place in the same period, which involved the Jewish and Christian populations.

The Jewish Rabbinic Texts: The Need for a Religious Sphere

In *Dying for God: Martyrdom and the Creation of Christianity and Judaism*, Daniel Boyarin argues that during this period Jews and Christians were defining themselves by competing in their active antagonism to Roman rule. The anecdotes in the rabbinic literature about the Jewish heroes who sanctified God's name in the period of the Roman persecutions is here taken not only as equivalents to the early Christian martyrologies, but also as having a significant part in their motivation and vice versa. The social and cultural dynamic that Boyarin describes resembles the one expressed in the *Alexandrian Acts*: in order to articulate a sense of togetherness, a group's cultural creation needs to portray its uniqueness in comparison with another group.

But where does this leave the martyr? It is a matter of debate whether the political heroes of the *Alexandrian Acts* could indeed be termed martyrs. Undoubtedly this depends on our definition of the word, which we shall come back to below. The pagan Alexandrian elite did not confront Roman rule in the religious dimension. Religion is not mentioned in the texts that have survived, and the conflict is articulated solely as a political one.[57] This raises the question of whether political rebels can be considered as martyrs at all, since they do not attest to a different faith—a different set of laws. In fact, the Alexandrian-Roman conflict could hardly be articulated in religious terms since the Alexandrian rebels were pagans. This is not the case as far as the rabbinic texts are concerned. As we saw above, the martyrdom described in 2 Maccabees (and later in 4 Maccabees) is a combination of a political cause defined in religious terms. However, the Jewish sense of martyrdom as it developed later in rabbinic circles put the emphasis not on the political cause, but on the religious faith. The political circumstances are normally ignored. Historically the conflict was indeed political, but in the stories it is articulated in religious terms and within a religious framework with no reference to the political context. As far as Jewish tradition is concerned, dying for the faith was not a new concept. It was formulated, however, in the Roman period as a new term of "dying for sanctifying God's name" (Hebrew: *kiddush hašem*).

There are biblical examples of Israelites who were willing to sacrifice their lives, or the lives of others, for their cause.[58] The most famous one is the binding of Isaac (seen later by Christians as the *topos* of the crucifixion). Another example is Samson's suicide among the Philistines. And yet another is the story about Hananiah, Mishael, and Azariah (Shadrach, Meshach, and Abednego) who are thrown into a fiery furnace by Nebuchadnezzar for refusing to worship the Babylonian deity, but are miraculously saved by God (Dan. 3). None of these examples were termed in Hebrew as "dying for sanctifying God's name." The same is also true in the case of the Maccabean martyrs as they are depicted in 2 and 4 Maccabees.[59] Whether the relevant chapters of 2 Maccabees were written in the second century B.C. or later, they do not in any way employ the terms "witness" or "dying for sanctifying God's name.

Although the expression "you shall not profane the name of my sacredness" (Hebrew: *lo teḥalelu et šem kodši*) is used in the Bible to refer to obedience to God's commandments, it is not used in the positive meaning of "sanctifying my name" apart from Isaiah 29:23. It is in the *Tosefta,* a collection of second-century A.D. halakha,[60] that the expression is used in reference to putting one's own life in God's hands.[61] The *Tosefta* mentions that in time of persecution (Hebrew: *shmad*) one should give his or her life for even the slightest percept, and bases this on a citation from Leviticus 22:32 ("You shall not profane my holy name that I may be sanctified among the children of Israel").[62] In midrash *Sifra Leviticus* (second–third centuries) we find the following take on the same Leviticus 22:32: "Yield yourself [interpreted as "your life"] to sanctify my name."[63] This command concludes the anecdote about the exemplary behavior of Pappus and his brother Lulianus (Julianus) who were executed by the Romans. The execution of the two brothers is mentioned anecdotally in both the Babylonian and Palestinian Talmuds as well as in the midrashic literature, and is contextualized in different ways.[64] Some of the anecdotes about Pappus and Lulianus are not set within a historical context. The more historical anecdotes place their execution in the reign of Trajan, probably as part of the revolt of 117, but no political context is given.[65] The two brothers certainly predate the Bar Kokhva revolt and are not numbered among *Aseret Harugei Malkhut* ("The Ten Slain by the Kingdom"): ten tannaitic sages who were executed by the Roman state. The executions of the ten sages are normally narrated separately in numerous stories throughout the rabbinic literature. All ten executions were grouped in midrashim from Byzantine Palestine, to which we shall return below. In modern English scholarship this regrouping is named "The Story of the Ten Martyrs." Just as scholars have named the *Alexandrian Acts*, here too the Christian term of "witness" was borrowed by modern scholarship and attributed to a common phenomenon of heroic death. The common element of the rabbinic stories about the ten rabbis is the Roman suppression of the Judaean revolts of 132–136, although the political circumstances are hardly discussed.[66] In fact two of the ten—Rabbi Ishma'el the High Priest and Rabbi Shim'on ben Gamliel—are men of the first century who died in the Judaean war.

Indeed, some of the stories about these rabbis, both individual and collective stories, ignore the Roman persecutions altogether. The issue in several of them, in particular those centering on Rabbi Akiva, is the believer's devotion and love for God, expressed in the process of dying for him.[67] Other stories emphasize God's satisfaction with this human sacrifice.[68] Others, however, do highlight the acts of defying the Roman suppression of Jewish activities, teaching, and studying of the Torah in particular.[69] Naturally they were all modified and edited to support the arguments for which they were used by the different compilers and editors of the rabbinic texts.

In contrast to the *Alexandrian Acts* and the *Acts of the Christian Martyrs*, the main objective of these rabbinic stories was not to commemorate the resistance that these figures expressed against the Roman rule. Historical circumstances are hardly ever mentioned here. We therefore cannot easily term them "Acts." However, what they do demonstrate is the circulation of stories within the rabbinic literature about figures of Jewish rabbis of the first and second centuries who were persecuted by the Roman government. Undoubtedly they were all considered heroes. The main question is in what ways they were portrayed as such, and to what end.[70] As we shall now see, the three groups present in their narratives three distinct perspectives to construct their collective memory.

If the *Alexandrian Acts* were written from a completely Roman political and cultural perspective, the rabbinic stories about "those slain by the kingdom" are, as Boyarin has shown, all about the devotion to and love of God.[71] It is because of their devotion that these heroes are tortured and executed. Such a representation turns the political combat against the Roman state into a religious Jewish manifesto, where there is no need to record and commemorate the historical circumstances. This is all the more so if the objective of the rabbis were to damp down the political struggle against the Roman state. The rabbinical elite would not necessarily subscribe, in the period following the revolt, to the very act of revolting. In a word, sanctifying God's name here seems to be a means of constructing the memory of the revolts in religious, instead of political, terms and to turn the anti-Roman political objective into a love-of-God goal. This is in contrast to the way in which Christian martyrologies form their concept of dying for God.

Whence Martyrologies?

In contrast to both the Jewish and the Alexandrian texts, their contemporary Christian texts that record the trials and executions of the Christian martyrs have come down to us through a long tradition of cult and text. Some, indeed, are stories, summaries, or developments which are given in the writings of the Church Fathers.[72] Others, however, have independent manuscript traditions.[73] They vary greatly in terms of the historical circumstances they present, the descriptions they provide, and the literary characteristics they exhibit. Nevertheless, they all share a common structure: a trial of persons identified as Christian, who refuse to obey the imperial command and participate in the imperial sacrifice, and who are consequently executed publically, often after undergoing harsh torture. The trial, which differentiates these acts from the rabbinic stories, enable the authors to depict the confrontation between the martyr and the representative of the Roman ruler, often the local proconsul, within a political framework, making it a public matter.[74] In contrast to the Alexandrian texts, which keep the confrontation against Roman rule on an earthly political level, the trial in the Christian texts symbolizes a metaphysical confrontation: between the Christian God, represented by the martyr, and the empty Roman beliefs, which are represented by the Roman proconsul or his equivalent.[75] As far as the Roman emperor is concerned, the martyr stands trial for violating the imperial law of conduct. But as far as the martyr is concerned, it is the Christian confession of God which stands trial, and it is for the martyr to confess (Greek: *homologizein*) to his or her God by witnessing (Greek: *marturein*) on God's behalf.[76] This is in contrast to the rabbinic texts, which turn on the sanctification of God's name.[77]

The question of the authenticity of the early Christian martyrologies cannot normally be resolved. The authenticity of some is far from certain, while others have been demonstrated to contain a strongly authentic nucleus.[78] Some were written in the form of an epistle by the martyrs themselves or by the local Christian community, which was sent by one Christian community to another to inform them of the heroic death of some of its members, or its bishop or other leader.[79] These epistles, which circulated among Christians and reached the Church Fathers were later compiled and integrated into their writings.[80]

We have seen that, whether Christian, Jewish, or pagan, these persons whose society considered them as having died for a cause, were commemorated by texts and stories. The circulation of these texts and the commemoration of their protagonists enabled their heroic death to be turned into a symbol that served as a public identifier for their communities.[81] In their book *The Martyr's Conviction*, sociologists Eugene and Anita Weiner focus on the theme of the martyr's motive as a social construct. They analyze the way in which "social movements socialize their members to both profess the martyr motive and then sustain this motive until the act of self-sacrifice."[82] This provides a symbol of conviction for a newly created society, which is the martyr's social function. The main question, however, is what kind of symbol, and what kind of conviction. To put it differently, the question is whether such figures of heroic death symbolized the same phenomenon and conviction in the same ideals to each of their respective communities.

Boyarin has argued that for both the Christian and the Jewish communities the martyrs symbolized their active antagonism to Roman rule. This is also true as far as the *Alexandrian Acts* are concerned. Often this antagonism was realized also in reference to the contention of another group. However, within each group this anti-Roman contention was expressed in different terms in order to symbolize quite a different kind of battle. Among the three battles only one kind, the anti-Roman Christian battle, necessitated the figure of the martyr. It is essential to analyze the ways in which the deeds of such figures were recorded in order to perceive the meaning that their respective communities attributed to their acts. Both Jewish and Christian late-antique writings provide much information about the ways in which the memory of these heroic deeds was constructed and about their objectives. They reveal very different approaches. The Jewish equivalents to the compilations of the acts of Christian martyrs are the midrashim which were written about the ten sages. Here we find for the first time a regrouping of the stories about their executions, which gave them the respective title *Aseret Harugei Malkhut*—"The Ten Slain by the Kingdom."[83] This regrouping appears in the following midrashim: *Midrash Canticles, Midrash Lamentations Rabbah, Midrash Psalms, Midrash Proverbs, Heikhalot Rabbati,* late-antique piyyutim, and the late (probably medieval) *Midrash Eleh Ezkerah*—"These I shall commemorate' (paraphrasing Ps. 42:5 and *Midrash Lamentation Rabbah* 1)."[84]

First, it should be noted that the list of ten sages varies from version to version. The most prominent appear in all versions, but there are others (and not always the same ones) who appear in only a few of the versions.[85] Moreover, the form of the narrative represents an open and flexible literary structure, in which historical circumstances are often ignored.[86] As we shall see, the absence of historical circumstances in most of the anecdotes about "The Ten Slain by the Kingdom" is indeed intentional and meaningful, and works in contrast to the figure of the Christian martyr.

The story that serves as a framework in *Midrash Canticles, Heikhalot Rabbati,* and *Midrash Eleh Ezkerah,* and is also mentioned in *Midrash Proverbs,* relates to the executions of the ten sages as the atonement of the ten tribes of Israel for the sale of Joseph into slavery by his ten brothers in Genesis 37.[87] To summarize briefly the framework story of *Midrash Eleh Ezkherah*: since the destruction of the Temple is not lamented by the Children of Israel who are satisfied with their sages, God makes the Roman emperor study the Torah in order to teach a moral lesson to the post-Temple generation. The Roman emperor, whose name is not mentioned, reads the Torah and gets to the sale of Joseph by his brothers. He then calls the ten sages of the generation and asks them about the punishment for a crime like this. When they reply that the sale of a free Israelite by another Israelite is a capital crime, the emperor declares that the ten must be executed to pay for the crime of Joseph's ten brothers. This verdict is followed by Rabbi Ishmaʿel's, one of the ten figures, mystical ascent to heaven to verify whether this is a verdict from heaven or from earth (in which case it could be diverted by the sages). In the course of his journey to heaven, he encounters angels and learns about the heavenly decision. He sees the divine altar on which pious sages' souls are being sacrificed daily. He and the other nine sages accept this sacrifice gladly. The midrash then describes the execution of each of the five couples of sages, borrowing references from the earlier rabbinic stories.[88]

In "From Individual Guilt to Collective Sin," the second chapter of *From Martyr to Mystic*, Raʿannan Boustan warns that because Jewish and Christian martyrologies developed in cultural proximity, research on them "run[s] the risk of becoming overly general."[89] This leads him to contextualize what he calls "The Story of the Ten Martyrs" within a rabbinic literary framework. He meticulously demonstrates how two traditions were merged into one story: the atonement for the sale of Joseph and the mystical ascent to heaven of Rabbi Ishmaʿel. He identifies the first in Byzantine Palestine piyyutim and midrashim, which were already connected at that time to the Jewish day of atonement, Yom Kippur.[90] He identifies the second in mystic traditions about Rabbi Ishmaʿel.[91] He explains the combination of the two through the figure of Rabbi Ishmaʿel as high priest, whose function was to provide collective atonement.[92] This brilliant analysis moreover inverts what was until now the acceptable order of composition. The nucleus of *Midrash Eleh Ezkhera* is here demonstrated to be a post-Talmudic Byzantine Palestinian creation, contextualized as part of the development of a mystical tradition of which *Heikhalot Rabbati* is another creation.

This midrashic development provides a clear interpretation of the phenomenon of martyrdom in the post-Talmudic Jewish theological context: the act of execution of the ten sages provides collective atonement and is understood within a growing mystic discourse, but in the process deprives the ten figures of any choice or decision in their fate. They are not God's agents, but the sacrifice of his people, and they will get their reward in the afterlife. In no way does the rabbinic literature allow the sage an option of choosing between being loyal or disloyal to

God, or loyal or disloyal to the earthly ruler. In fact, no confrontation between the earthly and heavenly rulers is expressed here. This tallies with the contextualization of this story within a mystic discourse, but also eliminates any possible confrontation between the sages and the Roman authorities. In *Midrash Eleh Ezkhera* as well as in *Midrash Canticles* the Roman emperor, who is depicted as a sage himself, is God's agent no less than the ten sages whom he executes.

Although *Midrash Eleh Ezkhera* is considered a later midrash, its frame story linking the idea of collective atonement to a mystical discourse is shown by Boustan to be a creation of rabbinic Byzantine Palestine. A priori this midrashic framework story seems an equivalent literary development to the cycles of Christian martyrs, a truly Jewish martyrological compilation. In reality, it has nothing to do with the term. The execution of the ten sages has a meaning, but its meaning must be understood within an internal Jewish theological system,[93] and in no way does it reflect, support, or adhere to an earthly battle against the kingdom of Rome. In fact, the rabbinic anecdotes and stories about the ten sages divorce their execution from any historical context, the context of the Jewish revolts in particular. Their death reassures the continuation of Jewish life as before. In other words, it suppresses any desire for a political change by constructing a nonpolitical memory to historical events.[94]

The sages who died in sanctifying God's name are contextualized within a mystical framework and gets their reward in the afterlife. This becomes the meaning of the historical event of their death. The story regroups sages from different generations. The compact version of all ten figures narrows down any possible repetitive political impact. It prevents individual cults and individual memories of these historical figures. Moreover, it blocks the historical memory of the ten sages within a single chronological framework and within the limits of a literary and theological context. The mystical sphere dominates all other spheres.[95] If the sages are indeed God's agents, they prove to be passive agents. They are absorbed in the heavenly sphere, but do not implement any change on earth. This, in fact, is clear from the other rabbinic stories about those "Slain by the Kingdom," leave *Heikhalot Rabbati*, which as a general rule avoid the political circumstances of the sages' executions.[96]

The absence of an anti-Roman agenda is all the more visible against the background of the Christian martyrologies. By eliminating any anti-Roman battle, this specific midrashic frame-story prevents the ten sages' executions from becoming a catalyst for a political and also a mental change. It is what differentiates these figures from their contemporary Christian martyrs, and also the reason why they are not portrayed as figures of abnormal behavior. This also tallies with the fragmentary characteristics of the Talmudic stories about the Jewish "martyrs," and portrays a complete contrast to the perspective that constitutes the Christian martyr. We can argue about the meaning of the terms "martyr" and "martyrology" when there is no earthly battle to fight. In any case we are bound to agree that the martyr's battle is defined and is used as a key element in order to implement a change as will now be shown.

It is not a coincidence that we have so far avoided calling the ten sages "martyrs." Indeed, we shall contest this attribution by going back to the original meaning of the term as it was formed and crystallized in early Christian doctrine. As we shall now see, what forms martyrs is the mental and social framework that supports and uses them. By attributing a term to cultures that did not use it we are ignoring one of the most important aspects about these cultures: the differences between them, that is, the uniqueness of the way in which each one of them developed. Moreover, by focusing too much on resemblances in order to show a common cultural language we also preclude any ability to understand the social function of the phenomenon in question.[97] We shall now go back to the early Christian authors in order to examine how they constructed the concept of the martyr within the doctrine that they created and implemented. We will then be able to connect this construction to the main question that this chapter set out to examine: how can abnormal behavior be employed in order to generate and implement a change in the perception of reality.

The texts examined so far—the *Alexandrian Acts*, rabbinical stories and cycles, as well as Christian martyrologies—are mostly posterior to the events that they narrate. They thus reflect the way in which each group wanted to record the events in view of its objectives in a Roman Empire that was already in the process of Christianization. However, in order to examine the way in which the figure of the martyr was constructed in "real time," we have Christian sources alone, written in the period of persecutions. This is a methodological observation that must be taken into consideration in any comparison between sources of the different religious groups in question.

The Martyr Figure as an Inverter

The first Christian apologies of the second century, by Aristides and Justin Martyr, scarcely pay any attention to the phenomenon of martyrdom. Whether Aristides's text was written under Hadrian or Antoninus Pius, it predates the martyrdom of Polycarp of Smyrna (155 A.D.) which is considered the first martyrology.[98] Justin Martyr's *Apology* is directed to Antoninus Pius, and also cites a letter of Hadrian which was sent to Minicius Fundanus, proconsul in Asia 123/124.[99] The letter encourages the inhabitants of the province to appear before the tribunal in person if they can support their accusations against the Christians of transgressing the laws of the Roman Empire.[100] In the second part of his *Apology*, Justin refers to a trial conducted against Christians in Rome under Antoninus Pius.[101] Justin's main point is not to narrate martyrologies, or commemorate the death of the martyrs, but simply to appeal to the emperor against the condemnation of Christians. In fact, he does not use the term "martyr" in relation to the Christian believers. When he does use the term, it refers not to a certain Christian believer, but to God, who is "a witness to the innocence of the accused Christians."[102] The execution is not described as an act of confession of the believer who is being executed (as it will develop later). In fact, there is nothing positive about it. It is an act done without a cause.[103] Justin's two Apologies are a defense treatise for Christians, describing their cause as a battle against the evil demons of this world. However, in this battle against evil, the Christians who are executed have no particular role. Their suffering and their execution are simply a mistaken judgment on the part of the Roman state. It will be the theologians of the third century who will change the meaning of "witness" from God witnessing to the innocence of his faithful, to the faithful witnessing his confession (Matt. 10:32–33).

The Christian authors of the end of the second century to the beginning of the third century—Clement, Tertullian, and Origen—developed a new political perspective to articulate the experience of the Christians who were executed by the state. In this perspective, the figure of the martyr is constructed as a combination of two elements: confession of Christian faith together with the idea of battle over earthly rule. We find this combination at the heart of all Christian martyrologies, and it is this which sets them apart from both Jewish and pagan texts about persons who die for a cause.

The extent of the Roman persecutions against Christians before the Decian persecutions is a matter of debate.[104] However whatever their real extent was, the persecutions caused a wide-ranging echo thanks to the way they were recorded and formulated by the authors of their period. Along with this, the Christian authors also constructed the idea of the Christian martyr, by making death meaningful for the victims themselves, as well as for all Christians. We can see the seeds of this construction in Ignatius of Antioch's epistle to the Romans, in which he expresses his desire to die for Christ.[105]

In his *Stromata,* written probably during the reign of Septimius Severus (193–211), Clement refers to Christian martyrs at length. He devotes part of his account to modeling a theological meaning for a martyr's execution. In fact, the suffering of the executed Christian believers was a subject of theological dispute in the second century. According to the Gnostic Basilidis of Alexandria, Christians were condemned to execution to atone for sins in their souls' previous lives.[106] As Bowersock has shown, in the fourth book of his *Stromata* Clement refers directly to these views, and constructs a new theological perspective on victims of Roman persecutions.[107] He equates the victim with the perfect and accomplished (Greek: *teleiōtis*) man whose execution is the accomplishment of his salvation (Greek: *teleiōsis tēs sōtērias*).[108] The victim has accomplished not life, but rather love for God.[109] We also find here the meaning that Clement gives to the term "martyr": the confession (Greek: *homologia*) toward God is a testimony of faith/acknowledgment (Greek: *marturia,* a *gnōstikis marturia*).[110] In their execution, martyrs embody the act of confession of their belief in the framework of divine wisdom (Greek: *hē theia sophia.*)[111] Moreover, this ultimate sacrifice, a "glorious purification," separates the martyrs' soul from their body, and since heaven is the place of the soul, this act of accomplishment establishes the martyrs in the highest religious position, which will make them the judges of the nations and the rulers of all people.[112]

In the *Stromata,* Clement does not deal with the persecutions at all. He is mainly concerned with establishing a theological reasoning and causation to explain the execution of Christian believers. His views are similar to the ones we find in later rabbinical texts about Jewish sages whose executions express their devotion and ultimate love for God, with one difference: their act of confession is not formulated as a testimony to divine wisdom. Both Tertullian and Origen developed this point in order to turn the execution of the Christian from a private act of an individual believer to a public act for and on behalf of Christianity.

Written probably around the same years, Tertullian's *Apology* is innovative in both its rhetoric and objective. Using the strategy of a defense treatise on Christian practice, Tertullian turns his text into an open attack on the anti-Christian persecutors and against the Roman system of belief: "It is you, then, who are the danger to mankind, it is you who bring upon us public misfortunes—you, by your contempt for God and your worship of statues."[113] While from the Roman point of view, Christians who refuse to participate in the public imperial cult were criminals just like other criminals, for Tertullian the criminal is whoever refuses to become a Christian.[114] This perspective enables him to formulate the persecutions in Christian terms as a battle for the Christian faith against Roman rule. In this battle, the martyrs, the Christian soldiers, enable the Christians to multiply.[115] "There is a rivalry [Latin: *aemulatio*] between God's ways and man's; we are condemned by you, we are acquitted by God."[116] And, a few sentences beforehand, Tertullian states what has become the most famous sentence about Christian martyrs: "we multiply whenever we are mown down by you; the blood of Christians is seed."[117]

Tertullian has not only turned the martyr into a soldier, he has managed to make a metaphysical battle from the trials and executions of criminals of the state. The objective of the Christians is not only salvation through the conversion of others; it is a victory over the enemy: the Roman state. The Christians' innocence no longer suffices to articulate their situation.[118] They must also fight and conquer Roman concepts of criminality. This becomes apparent in Tertullian's epistle *Ad nations* ("To the Nations") written apparently at the same time. The "nations" are the inhabitants of the Roman Empire who adhere to Roman rule, and insist on denying the Christian God. Tertullian turns the attack of the Roman authorities against the Christians, and their execution, into a universal battle between two sets of beliefs. In other words, he uses the persecutions in order to articulate Paul's teachings within the political context of the end of the second century and portray the Christian new perception of reality. This epistle and his *Apology* turn the persecutions into a universal battle. The martyrs are soldiers in the war over the order of the earthly world, the Roman Empire.

This battle explains the joy and satisfaction of the condemned

Christians who go to their death.[119] It is not clear whether the Christians who were sentenced to death really greeted their fate with joy (the fact that we possess letters of exhortation points to the opposite). It is, however, certain that this was the impression the Christian writers wanted to establish. Tertullian sets this out in his writings because it enables him to formulate the Roman persecutions as a war, and the executed Christians as soldiers in that war, not criminals. In other words, the inversion of the attitude toward death is necessary in order to construct a larger inversion: turning the passive Christians into active combatants, combatants against the Roman state. In this Ephesians 6:10–18 is transformed from a battle against the devil to a battle against the Romans.[120] This is how a new perception of reality is realized. And this is in contrast to the way the dying for the Jewish God is portrayed in rabbinical texts. In this way Christian authors reacted to the Roman persecutions, and set out a theological and political perspective that turned the execution of a Christian from the private act of an individual believer to a public act, meaningful to all Christians by transforming the reality of the Roman world into a Christian world. In order for the Christians who faced execution to perceive the significance of their death, Christian authors addressed them directly.

Both Tertullian and Origen wrote texts addressed to Christians who faced execution. In contrast to Tertullian's short epistle, *Ad martyras* ("To the Martyrs"), Origen's *Eis marturion* ("To testimony," translated into the Latin as *exhortatio ad martyrium*) is a relatively long and elaborate text.[121] While Tertullian is mainly concerned with inspiring courage in Christians who face death, Origen presents a full theological treatise on the martyr's situation. The two texts reveal the difficult and desperate state of the Christians who faced execution. In both cases, the author's main objective is to invert the role of the believer from a passive victim into an active combatant. Love of God is just one element that these authors use. The emphasis is nevertheless given to the justification and necessity of the execution. Although this could be seen as an act of self-conviction by a person who is in a completely passive state, we should note that neither Tertullian nor Origen faced execution when they wrote about martyrdom.

Tertullian's main point is to convince the condemned believers that their execution is a necessary means of fighting for the Christian faith. This becomes explicit in Origen's treatise, which constructs an image of a universal war of the Christian God whose martyrs are his soldiers. Origen brings citations from the Old and New Testaments in order to present this war and the battle of the "witness," that is, the martyr, as not only courageous and meaningful to the martyrs themselves but also to Christianity in general.[122] A martyr's death is the ultimate sacrifice, and the expression of this figure's love and unity with God through confession. However, the act also has meaning for the entire community of Christians, because through it they can prevail and triumph over the Roman state. Here we find a complete inversion of roles: death becomes a means for the victory of the entire community. It is no longer the atonement of Christ for the salvation of humanity, but resistance to the persecutions and the fight for God as a means to the victory of the Christian faith and God over the earthly domain: "The martyrs in Christ together despoil the sovereignties and the powers, and they participate in his triumph as fellows of his sufferings, thus they share the braveries of his sufferings which include triumphing over the sovereignties and the powers. These you soon see conquered and overpowered."[123] Clement had already noted that according to Heraclites and Plato, heroes are those who die in battle.[124] In fact, both Tertullian's and Origen's discourses are reminiscent of Pericles's funeral oration as was articulated by Thucydides, rather than any of the rabbinical texts cited above.[125] Moreover, Tertullian and Origen make this a battle between heaven and earth. Persecution does not simply mean testing Christians' faith and love of God, but is used here to produce both a mental and a political change—in short, a change in the perception of reality, and in fact a change of reality.

The construction of the figure of the martyr who goes willingly and joyfully to his or her death as a token of victory is employed by the Church Fathers in order to implement the mental change that Paul talked about. A recurrent theme in both theological and hagiographical writings about martyrs is the way in which their refusal to participate in the Roman imperial cult is perceived as madness (Latin: *insania*; Greek: *mania/aponoia*).[126] The main point of these writings was to implement a new set of principles that would also enable a change in the political sphere (the Greek term *aponoia* also means "rebellion"). This is also the reason why they adopt 2 Maccabees as a model.[127]

In "To testimony" (*Eis marturion*), Origen employs anecdotes about religious perseverance from 2 Maccabees in order to construct an exemplary model for the Christian martyrs.[128] Similar examples are used in later rabbinic texts, in *Midrash Lamentations Rabbah* in particular, though they are not used there as exemplary figures for the Jews who were killed by the kingdom in the persecutions that followed the Judaean revolts.[129] Rather, they serve as symbols of the destruction of Israel, and the Temple in particular. They thus take their place in the lamentations on the destruction.[130] In the Christian discourse they are used, in contrast, to exhort revolt.

The adoption of the Maccabean martyrs (El'azar the priest, and the mother and her seven sons in 2 Macc. 6–7) by Christianity as protomartyrs is well known and has received much attention in modern scholarship.[131] They were the subject of homilies by the Church Fathers.[132] They were also subject of hagiographers, who used them as prototypes. This is, for instance, the case with the martyrdom of Sophia and her three infant daughters, a Syriac text that was constructed exactly along the line of the Maccabean mother and her seven sons.[133] The Maccabean prototype of the martyr fitted Christian objectives extremely well, but not only because of the similar political context of the Seleucid persecutions. The intention of the author of 2 Maccabees was to justify the Hasmonean revolt in the eyes of the Egyptian Diaspora. In order to secure the support of Egyptian Jewry, they needed to justify their revolt not only against Seleucid rule in Judaea, but also against the Jewish priestly dynasty from which they had usurped the high priesthood.[134]

In both 2 Maccabees and the Christian martyrologies, the figure of the martyr serves as a means of creating a religious conflict in order to put a much broader conflict into the political domain. The martyr thus allows the formulation of the political conflict in religious terms. This battle is portrayed as a battle between heaven and earth, which legitimizes the revolt and usurpation. This is apparent in the writings of the Church Fathers and in Christian martyrologies, but in other writings as well.[135]

Just as 2 Maccabees presents persecuted Jews who died for their belief in order to secure support for the revolt, the Roman persecutions of the Christian martyrs enabled the creation of a political agenda for Christian religious believers. In other words, the presentation of Jews who stand up against the Seleucid persecutions and are consequently executed, turns the Maccabees into soldiers for the Jewish faith on behalf of all Jews.[136] In the same manner, the Christian martyrs are not just soldiers in God's battle against Roman rule, they are presented as soldiers for all Christians. Moreover, the portrayal of martyrs as combatants in a metaphysical moral battle cannot leave the spectators indifferent. If they do not become their supporters in this battle, they remain their rivals. In other words, the figure of soldier-martyrs turns their execution into a battle for everyone. This sort of depiction of the martyrs' battle along with the representation of their reactions to the persecution as abnormal and extraordinary behavior was a key element in creating a Christian mentality of revolt, and in turning the religious community into a politically combating entity. This is made apparent in the *Didascalia Apostolorum*.

Whether written in the 30s of the third century or later, the *Didascalia Apostolorum* can be contextualized as part of the persecutions of Maximinus the Thracian (starting from the year 235) or Decius's persecutions (starting from the year 250).[137] Two chapters (19 and 20) concern martyrdom, and both are directed to all Christians, and not specifically to the martyrs themselves.[138] The terms that the text uses are the Syriac equivalent to the Greek words for witness and witnessing: *sāhdā* and *sāhdútā*, respectively. Although these are often translated as "martyr" and "martyrdom," the Syriac text stays loyal to the original meaning of the terms, and keeps the sense of juridical witnessing of the confession in God (see below for the terminological development). Besides a short paragraph of exhortation, chapter 19 is directed not to the martyrs themselves, but to Christian believers who are called to not deny the martyrs, but to support them in any possible way. They are asked to bribe the guards, if possible, in order to ease the conditions of the condemned believers, and make use of their possessions to redeem them from bonds: "And you shall not be ashamed to go to them when they are in prison. And when you do these things, you shall inherit everlasting life, for you become sharers in their testimony/witnessing [Syriac: *sāhdútā*]."[139] Indeed, any believer is requested to consider the Christian who is condemned for his belief as a holy witness (Syriac: *sāhdā kadíšā*): "An angel of God, or God upon earth, one who is spiritually clothed with the Holy Spirit of God . . . and has renewed again the witness [Syriac: *sāhdútā*] of the passion."[140] In order to eliminate the fear of joining the martyrs in their fate, the chapter adds: "Yet if we be called to witness, let us confess when we are interrogated, and when we suffer let us endure, and when we are afflicted let us rejoice, and when we are persecuted let us not be wearied. For by acting thus, not only shall we save ourselves from the Gehenna, but we shall also teach those who are young in the faith, and the hearers to act thus—and they shall live before God."[141] This allows the author to link the act of witnessing to the idea of resurrection, which is the subject of the following chapter. Just like Christ, through his or her execution the martyr serves as a token for the idea of resurrection.[142] At the same time the act of witnessing "for his [God's] name" (Syriac: *meṭil šmeh*) absolves the martyr's sins and enables the resurrection of the witness him- or herself who is forgiven.[143]

Martyrs thus symbolize the passage from life to death, but also the opposite passage from death back to life. They embody Christian belief and Christian perspective, but in this, also the identity of the Christian community in forming its war agenda against earthly Roman rule. The development of the idea of the martyr and martyrdom in general is thus an inseparable part of early Christian doctrine to which acts of martyrdom provide an affirmation.

We find the apogee of this development in the idea of the martyr as part of Christian doctrine in the writings of Cyprian (d. 258). Several of his epistles are addressed to Christians who were imprisoned either before or after their trial, during the persecutions under Decius.[144] In all of these writings, Cyprian inspires courage in them and exhorts them to stand firmly on their confession in Christ, thus demonstrating, just as in the exhortations of Tertullian and Origen, how much this was needed. His exhortations are read in the spirit and tradition of Greco-Roman speeches before a battle.[145] Nevertheless, to convince his addressees, who are about to be passively executed, that they are in fact facing a battle, he emphasizes their divine role in fighting God's war on behalf of all the Christians on earth, along with their personal benefit in the afterlife. In his treatise addressed to Fortunatus as exhortation (Latin: *in exhortatione*), he sets out the objective of this war: putting an end to the worship of idols. This, he writes, is God's plan.[146] The martyrs are thus fighting to achieve this goal which, although divine, must be fought for and achieved on earth, in order to change the Roman Empire. The battle between God and the idolaters is here articulated, in a similar way to the way in which it is set out by Origen, as a battle against Satan.

This theological and political construct of the martyr is a development of the Christian authors of the second and third centuries, who respond to the persecutions as an advantage for creating a combatant

Christianity. It is in contrast to the way in which the rabbinic writers dealt with the same subject. Whether in staying within the limits of the idea of the love of God, sacrifice, and atonement, they rejected any political contextualization of the executions because they rejected the very idea of revolt. This is also the case in regard to the most famous and often cited rabbinic story of "martyrdom": the death of Rabbi Akiva as narrated in the Babylonian Talmud (*Berakhot* 61b). Rabbi Akiva transgresses publicly and intentionally the Roman prohibition on studying the Torah, and is caught, tortured, and executed. Although the anti-Roman provocation is noted, it does not form the core of the story. The provocation serves here as a means of producing an anti-Christian debate about conversion to Christianity and the study of Torah, rather than an anti-Roman agenda.[147] In fact, in the period in which this story was compiled, the Roman state was indeed already Christian. And though Rabbi Akiva is publicly challenging Roman regulations, the Babylonian Talmud does not portray him either as a means of combat, triumphing over Roman rule, or as a means of conversion.[148]

In contrast, the idea of the Christian martyr as it was created and articulated by theologians and hagiographers (and by authors who were both) made martyrdom a collective experience of Christianity in the objective of changing the Roman reality. This enabled them to create the idea of a combatant Christianity, and to use it to implement universal change, a change which was not only social and mental, but also political. Whether Roman persecutions were myth or constructed as a myth,[149] it is important to understand the figure of the martyr as an inverter: a symbol of clash with the state, its values, its norms, its mentality, and its reality, in order to conquer and invert them. This is, to conclude, the objective and the essence of the martyr. The experience of the "witness" as it was formulated by early Christian authors was used as an identifier for a new society which formulated its raison d'être through its war with the state, and the negation of its norms and values. This is apparent from the way the Greek verb *marturein*—"witnessing"—entered the Latin.

The use of the Greek terms *martus*, *matrturion*, and *marturein* is ubiquitously translated as "martyr," "martyrdom," and "to experience/suffer martyrdom." However, although modern translations have given the term a passive meaning, the verb *marturein* stays in the Greek texts in the active form: to witness or testify.[150] The medial and passive forms of the verb (to call for testimony and to be ascribed with testimony, respectively) are not used in the early Christian Greek martyrologies, which keep the original active meaning of the terms, testifying and bearing witness.[151] In fact, the terms "martyrdom" and "martyrology" were not known to these authors, who named the texts they had written about martyrs: *marturia*, "testimonies" in Greek, and *passiones*, "passions" in Latin.[152] In using the passive meaning of "to suffer martyrdom" as a translation of the Greek *marturein*, modern scholars and translators have adopted the Latin use of the Greek term. The Greek term appears in its passive form only in the Latin martyrologies, which normally avoid the equivalent Latin verb *testari*, and create a new Greek form by Latinizing the verb *marturein* as a Latin passive verb: *martyrizari*.[153] The Latin passive form *testari* means "to testify."[154] The Latinization of the Greek verb is an indication of a new meaning that the Christian authors wanted to convey, in order to reflect not the act of the testimony itself, but the act of giving testimony through persecution, torture, and execution, that is, in order to construct the new phenomenon of becoming a martyr.[155] In Latin, it appears in Tertullian's writings to and about martyrs.[156] This also enabled Christian authors to apply the Maccabean prototypes which had nothing to do with testimony and witnessing, but which they have "martyrized," in the meaning of modeling them in the image of their own "witnesses."

The Martyr Figure as a Means of Creating a Christian Society

It is well known that the early martyrologies were not usually composed by contemporary authors, although they are presented as such. This has led scholars to doubt their authenticity. Modern scholarship tends to agree that although some do contain an authentic nucleus, most of the martyrologies were assembled and compiled in a later period.[157] Candida Moss has recently revealed the elasticity of the construction of the Christian martyr figure. By focusing on different geographical settings, she has shown how different Christian authors have simultaneously constructed and used martyrdom in different ways.[158] We can enlarge the scope of this analysis to non-Christian environments. As stated above, Christian environments were not different from Jewish and Alexandrian in constructing the memory of historical figures who died a heroic death.[159] The Christian authors, nonetheless, were different from both their Jewish and pagan contemporaries in conceptualizing, constructing, and using the martyr as a figure of inversion. The objective was to generate an inversion of a bigger scale: an inversion of not only the mental and social but also the political framework of the Roman Empire.[160] This is what distinguished the Christian martyr as a catalyst of change from the rabbi who also welcomes his tortures and death "for the Name," but was not aimed at fighting the Roman state in order to invert its values.

The Christian battle with the Roman state by and large came to an end at the beginning of the fourth century with the Edict of Milan, if not earlier.[161] Signed in 313 by Constantine and Licinius, this edict legitimized the Christian cult within the Roman Empire. Although the persecution of Christians was mostly over after the beginning of the fourth century,[162] the Christian martyr was a recurrent theme in the writings of Christian authors of the fourth to sixth centuries. Writing within a Christian Roman Empire, the Church Fathers continued to develop, elaborate, and use the figure of the martyr. The fourth to the fifth centuries in particular witnessed the creation of homilies, sermons, and hagiographies about the early martyrs. The figure of the martyr was now used not only to symbolize the battle against the demonic pagans in retrospect of the victory over the pagan emperors, but also to set new forms of conduct and beliefs for the emerging Christian society. We find the figure of the martyr used as a symbol of a broad mental transformation in the writings of the authors of this period.

This new rhetorical use is already apparent in the beginning of the fourth century in the writings of Lactantius. Chapter five, "On justice" (*De iustitia*), of his *Divine Institutes* is written precisely in the moment of change under the reign of Constantine, when persecutions seem to be over but still fresh in the author's mind.[163] In the beginning of the book, Lactantius states that his objective is to convince the unfaithful of the holy and true wisdom. Both Tertullian and Cyprian, he writes, failed in this objective because they did not have the capacity or the rhetorical means to produce such a mental change. Unlike them, he declares himself set to construct new concepts, not to respond to accusations.[164] Lactantius focuses on justice in order to link God's divine moral conduct to the earthly domain.[165] The persecuted martyr is the just man who symbolizes not only the conflict between two sets of moral values, but the option of inversion of moral justice on earth. Lactantius connects the sense of justice in human law directly to Christian morality, and uses the martyr as the instrument for the mental transformation that he sets to establish.[166] The most essential virtues inherent to justice, Lactantius explains, are piety and equality (Latin: *pietas, aequitas*) since both are divine, emanating from God.[167] The persecutions produced virtues of patience and innocence (embodied by the martyrs).[168] They increased the numbers of the faithful. Lactantius's dichotomy between persecuted and persecutors is a key rhetorical element in implementing an inversion of meaning. The martyrs' battle enables him to define a new juridical rationality for the emerging Byzantine state. He models the historical memory of the persecutions and the Christian martyrs who resisted them in the objective of constructing a new political agenda. Implementing a new concept of justice for the state means changing the values and norms of the current juridical system as well as replacing the "persecutors" themselves, that is, those responsible for the persecutions within the Roman legal system.

In the fourth to sixth centuries we also see how martyrdom acquires a new rhetorical function, and is used in many homilies, sermons, and hagiographies in order to implement a new mentality and new norms of conduct.[169] Gus George Christo has dedicated his study to the perception of martyrdom in the writings of John Chrysostom, and Carol Straw has shown the way in which Augustine and Gregory the Great reworked the meanings of martyr and martyrdom in their writings.[170] Both studies make it clear that the concept of martyrdom underwent substantial changes over the period of the four centuries between the second and the sixth.

While still referring to martyrdom by death as an imitation of Christ's suffering and sacrifice, John Chrysostom's homilies construct the figure of the martyr as a saint who has a place in heaven as an intercessor between the Christian believer and God. This theological and social role is connected to the endurance of the martyr's soul, an exemplary model for every believer. Chrysostom turns the martyr's battle against the Roman imperial government into a battle against Satan and the demonic world. Although both Origen and Cyprian had already drawn this equivalence between the Roman persecutions and demonic forces, Chrysostom attributes the idea of the persecutions to a satanic initiative aimed at destroying the Christian faith.[171] Formed as a symbol of the triumph of Christianity over the pagan empire, martyrdom now becomes an emblem of its triumph against Satan. This enables Christian authors to present any battle against the demonic forces as in line with the martyrdom of the second and third centuries. Moreover, it enables Chrysostom to develop the idea of martyrdom by association. Believers, who associate themselves with the martyr, either by imitation, veneration, or service, can thus become living martyrs themselves, who have triumphed over the devil.[172] Martyrdom proves here to be a means of portraying a new perception of reality that Christian authors want to convey to believers.

Gregory of Nazianzus also uses the battle of the martyr as a model for any battle for the Christian way of life on earth.[173] He uses the veneration of the martyrs' tombs in order to translate their battle into a battle of every Christian against the passions of the body.[174] The same is also true for Evagrius Ponticus. The collection of the chapters about asceticism, attributed to his disciples, use the idea of the martyr who fights the devil.[175] The martyr's battle is transformed in the teaching of his disciples into a symbol of the "martyrdom within" of every Christian, the battle against the passions of the body, and the sins that they entail.[176] In this, they apply the concept of the "martyr" as a combatant for new type of morality to "the battle within," which had already been done a generation beforehand by Lactantius.[177]

Having acquired metaphorical meanings, martyrdom became a universal experience, open to every Christian. In fact, as Jerome presents it, "the martyrdom within" is not only a recommended way of life, but obligatory in order to vanquish the devil's power which the passions of the body express.[178] In this, John Chrysostom, Evagrius Ponticus, and Jerome are not unique. Basil the Great, Gregory of Nyssa, and indeed Eusebius himself reworked the term "martyr" along the same sort of lines. It is important to understand the creation of martyrologies as an integral part of the same movement: the construction of a mentality, a new perception of reality, and a system of cultural conduct for the newly created Christian society. As Straw has revealed, this process is constantly fluctuating according to the different needs of the Church Fathers at different periods. Focusing on Gregory the Great's homilies, she shows a parallel development in the Latin West, here too in implementing a new way to perceive and experience reality within a metaphysic Christian framework.[179]

Inversion of Normal and Abnormal Norms

Martyrdom seems to have a dynamic definition which changes in view of the social, cultural, and political needs of the society. This is, of course, not surprising in view of the fact that the figure of the martyr is constructed with the purpose of creating a model. In this, the pagan Alexandrian, the rabbinical Jewish, and the early Christian victims, who were all executed by the Roman authorities, were identical. However, only one group portrayed their victims as agents whose behavior defied the acceptable Roman norms of conduct—the Christians. We saw that this was done in order to define the conflict against the Roman state in new terms, and to give it a broader metaphysical meaning. This was required not only in order to survive the persecutions, but also in order to turn them into a victorious and creative experience, which was essential if Christian belief was to prevail. The martyrs symbolized not only the conflict but also the inversion of roles—from victim to conqueror—through the act of witnessing of faith. The importance of the act of witnessing cannot be overstated. It expresses the change of mentality that the martyrs introduced and symbolized, and which set them apart from the Jews and the pagans who died in their revolts against Roman rule. However, as far as the early Christian martyrs were concerned, there was a political dimension to this change of mentality. This meant using the conflict that the martyrs symbolized in their bodies and their deaths as a means to bring about a political inversion. The martyr became a means to define a group in the political sphere by implementing a change of mentality in the religious sphere. There was no other way to bring this about but by inverting what were considered normal and abnormal norms of conduct.

Josephus emphasized throughout his *Jewish War* the willingness of Jews to die for the Law.[180] He chose to end his book with the outcome of the six hundred fanatical Sicarii who escaped to Egypt and Cyrene and tried to provoke the local population to revolt against the Roman government. Fearing any Roman repression, the heads of the local Jewish communities in Alexandria turned them in. Josephus's report ends with their torture and execution, describing their refusal, including even the small children, to accept Caesar's authority.[181] Josephus here expresses the very essence of the martyr whose act is considered both bravery and folly.[182] Naturally, this description reflects Josephus's own judgment, as well as the fact that he was writing for Roman readers. Nevertheless, the scene of the public execution of hundreds of believers who refused to subscribe to imperial authority, and whose behavior and judgment is considered bravery from one perspective and madness from the other, will become prevalent in Christian martyrologies.[183] Josephus attributes madness to them because of their incapacity to be reasonable and comply. The Sicarii's revolt in Egypt failed. Moreover, no group used them as model to implement a political change. They did not become martyrs. In other words, no one continued with the line of inversion that Josephus had laid out so clearly. Unlike the Christians, their abnormality was not used as a means for social change by any community.

The Church Fathers, on the other hand, personified their aspirations for a political change by constructing the martyr as a figure of inversion. While the Jewish sages who were executed by the Roman state symbolized collective atonement and mystical love for God, the Christian martyrs were constructed as inverters, catalysts of a mental and political change, as a means for both defining a new perception of the reality and implementing it. The writings of the post-Nicene Church Fathers show that the martyrs continued to fulfill this function as a vehicle for any cultural or mental change on the Christian agenda.[184] The martyr, who became the symbol of the Christian victory over the pagan authorities, was turned by the post-Nicene Church Fathers into the emblem of the war against, and the triumph over, the satanic passions of the body. In this the figure of the martyr personified the mental change that was demanded from every believer. It is not accidental that this change was formulated in relation to the passions of the body, since overcoming the sufferings of the body is what symbolized the martyr's triumph.

To Conclude: Between the Martyr's Function and the Definition of Insanity

Going back to the interpretations of what constitutes insanity in "the age of reason," we saw that both Foucault, on the one hand, and Gauchet and Swain, on the other hand, identified the change in the definition of what constituted insanity in the way in which the passions of the body were perceived. For all three scholars, the incapacity of the mind to think in compliance with reason was defined as a product of the passions of the body. However, Foucault reads the definition of insanity as related to a product of a pathological change which causes a mental change and a moral flaw. In contrast, for Gauchet and Swain the definition of pathology referred to an organic state of the body, and allowed the separation of the disease from any moral aspect related to the mind. If we look into the way in which both theories position what could be termed the moral aspect of the perception of insanity, to put it very bluntly, we can see that the two diverge on the following question: whether the separation between passions of the body and mind, pathology and mental reasoning, has attributed a moral flaw to the state of insanity (Foucault) or, on the contrary, has liberated it from any moral aspect (Gauchet and Swain). In both interpretations this was a product of the new moral and mental norms of society. With the martyr, we see the inverse movement.

What is so remarkable about the martyr is the fact that this figure was constructed as a moral emblem in order to enable the inversion of the moral aspect for the entire society: what seemed to be abnormal behavior—*aponia*, an act of madness—was not in fact perceived as abnormal. On the contrary, this abnormal behavior was constructed as heroic because such a construction inverted moral norms. Martyrologies were written to exemplify a social abnormal behavior, which the authors wished to present as new norms of conduct. Just like Josephus, the Christian authors used "madness" (*mania, aponoia*) and "folly" (*mōria, mōrainein*) as rhetorical means to conceptualize the martyrs' abnormality.[185] Through their resistance to their immoral persecutors, martyrs portrayed a new perception of reality and personified the inversion that the Christian mentality aimed to achieve. Setting the martyrs' moral abnormality as an alternative to immoral normality enabled Christians to establish the abnormality of the martyrs' behavior as the norm, and to thereby implement the new perception of reality that they constructed. Once this was achieved, the same was also possible for any norms that Christianity needed to establish.

The figure of the Christian martyr shows the social need that calls for an abnormal model of an "inverting figure." The execution of the Sicarii as narrated by Josephus is extremely telling in this respect. The Sicarii were not perceived as martyrs because no social movement was there to construct and make use of their torture and death and to sanctify it. Since it was not put to use, their execution was "testimony" (i.e., martyrdom) for no one. In other words, it could not become functional, and hence did not acquire any meaning.

The term "martyr" therefore marks the sanctification of an abnormal behavior as intentional and courageous. Abnormal behavior is, of course, not the same thing as insanity. However, the challenge that Christian authors introduced to the definition of the normal-abnormal borderline of their period, by attributing a moral aspect to it through the figure of the martyr, set it in a social dimension that was also relevant to the definition of the sanity-insanity borderline. In other words, once abnormal behavior was defined in the social dimension as moral, and normal behavior as immoral, such a perspective could be expanded to any type of abnormal behavior. Those figures who portray abnormal behavior are sanctified, that is, they are marked as social models, because society finds in them a means to define and implement a new set of norms for a new perception of reality. In the case of the martyr of early Christianity, we can even say that the abnormal behavior of a desire for death was a construct of the authors themselves. In this, society chose to sanctify such acts of abnormality in order to define and implement new norms and settings. The link between social abnormality and social change proves here to be central. In contrast, rabbinic Judaism was not interested in the transformation of the world and the implementing a new perception of reality, but wished to maintain its political and religious status quo. For this reason martyrdom, death for a political cause, was not needed. We do not see rabbinic figures used as symbols of political inversion through their abnormal behavior, since there was no need or desire for inversion.

In a word, those figures who portray abnormal behavior are sanctified, are marked as social models because society finds in them a means to define and implement a new set of norms. In the next chapter, we continue to examine this idea in another type of social abnormality that society employs through sanctification, and which can be also considered pathological: asceticism.

4

Socializing Nature

THE ASCETIC TOTEM

The center of the first scheme of nature is not the individual, it is society.

—Émile Durkheim and Marcel Mauss, 1902

In the last chapter we examined the abnormal behavior of the martyr, his desire to die for a cause in voluntary death, as a deviant means of inverting the moral values and norms of social conduct. Our question was whether a process of mental change could be not only the cause of development in the definition of what is normal and abnormal, but also its consequence. Or to put it differently, whether society could use figures who challenge the borderlines of normality by their behavior in order to implement a broader change of mentality necessary for any religious movement.

The present chapter examines another example of sanctified deviancy: asceticism. The origin of the term is the Greek word *askēsis*: exercise, training, or practice. It was one of the terms used in early Christianity to refer to forms of corporal abstinence that require training of the body.[1] The core of the ascetic's experience consists of acts of self-denial and corporal torments inflicted on one's own body. Asceticism has received much attention from modern scholarship from the nineteenth century on. The rise of the scientific fields of psychiatry and psychology in particular, prompted scholars to focus on the pathology of people who withdraw from society, confine themselves, and starve themselves, and to define such behaviors as masochistic and pathological. In this chapter we shall examine the abnormal behavior embedded in the phenomenon of asceticism from an anthropological point of view in order to understand its social function. In what follows we will use an anthropological theory (of Philippe Descola) and a sociological theory (of Peter Berger) as premises, and will argue for their relevance to the study of deviancy in the religious experience. We will then apply this, in the second part of the chapter, to a historical study of asceticism in early Christianity and rabbinic Judaism. Here too, a comparative-religion approach will reveal two different social rationales in defining and using abnormal behavior that consists of corporal self-torments. Asceticism became an important topic of research because of its importance as a historical movement as well as its psychological abnormality. The scholarship has addressed what seemed to be two contradictory aspects. In the present chapter we will see that the ascetic figure became such a motor for historical development precisely because of its abnormality.

Theoretical Premise: Nature as Culture

Asceticism as a Social Phenomenon

Asceticism was part of a much larger movement in the history of Christianity, which included monasticism (from the Greek *monos*—"alone") and anachoretism (Greek: *anachōrēsis*—"retreat," *anachōrizein*—"to withdraw or retreat"). Withdrawing from society into the desert or wilderness (Greek: *erēmos*) to live as a hermit and a monk (Greek: *erēmitēs*—"of the wild or desert," *monachos*—"alone"), required a constant battle against the passions of the body and unwanted thoughts. Both of these were attributed to demons and Satan (cf. Jesus's battle against Satan in the desert). In order to overcome such dangers, both body and mind became a subject of constant exercise, with the objective of reforming the self.[2] The origin of Christian asceticism is traditionally attributed to third- to fourth-century Egypt. By the fifth to sixth centuries it was a widespread phenomenon throughout the Near East, a major cultural and social movement which attracted writing by Christian authors, and had a far-reaching influence on the structure of Christian societies.

In 1995, Vincent L. Wimbush and Richard Valantasis edited and published a large volume of collected essays dedicated to asceticism. Without attempting to define it in a general and embracing manner, this project comprised the different fields and research directions taken over two decades to analyze the phenomenon of asceticism.[3] This publication reveals that the way we define the phenomenon is largely dependent on the way we interpret it, whether as pathology, a way of living, a philosophy, a mental state, or mental disturbance. The different approaches in this publication also reveal that the phenomenon of asceticism cannot be defined in an exclusive manner, since it acts as a combination of all these aspects.

Scholarship of the last fifteen years has predominately focused on the individual experience of asceticism, in order to understand the ascetic's state of mind, moral justification, practices, and abnormal behavior (food restriction, self-confinement, social withdrawal), as well as on the ascetic's psychological state.[4] In what follows, we shall analyze the ways in which these different aspects intertwine, offering a new meaning for society. In this, we will follow in the large footsteps of what is acknowledged as a masterpiece of historical study, Peter Brown's *The Body and Society: Men, Women, and Sexual Renunciation in Early Christianity*. Published in 1988, this book has provided a touchstone for the study of the early Christian attitude toward and practice of the body. It has acquired this status because it focused on the vast mental change that ascetic behavior led to in Christian society, thanks to both Christian practitioners and the Church Fathers, who constructed a new discourse of asceticism in their writings. Here, as in some of his other studies, Brown shifts the attention from the individual whose behavior we tend to define as the phenomenon in question, to society and the way it constructs and manages the individual's behavior. The phenomenon of asceticism appears to have a cultural objective that gives it a meaning, defines it, and justifies it. In what follows we will focus on the reason why abnormal behavior involving self-torments and self-denial came to be defined by society as asceticism. For this approach, too, Brown's studies have paved the way, specifically his seminal 1971 article, "The Rise and Function of the Holy Man in Late Antiquity." Although this study was not necessarily concerned with the ascetic as such, but with the general phenomenon of the holy man, it did concentrate on examples of Syrian ascetics who became in their time symbols of the divine.

As in his later study on the body, Brown's focus in this article is on the phenomenon of the holy man as a cultural construct that serves a social and political function, more than on the individual experience and the practice. The ascetic is given these social functions because they exist independently of the ascetic figure, and because the political and social figures who used to fill them are no longer available. Holiness acts here in the service of the social and political, and is defined by such. Since "The Rise and Function of the Holy Man" does not focus on ascetics, it does not treat the question of why ascetics in particular are called to fill this void. Brown's *The Body and Society* shows that ascetic behavior is part of a larger cultural and intellectual movement. However, beyond the scope of research on asceticism, these two studies show Brown's perspective in which holiness is analyzed first and foremost as a social and cultural construct.

In what follows we will see that holiness was specifically attributed to ascetics because of their abnormal behavior. Thus, although we are following Brown's lead, our conclusion will be different: ascetics were not chosen and sanctified as a means of social stabilization, but of social transformation. The ascetic's "pathology" in modern terms, allowed the linkage of the relationship between man and culture to nature. It was the ascetic's abnormality, his "pathological behavior," which made the ascetic into a *dynamic totem* for society. We shall use the term "totem" in this chapter to show that the function of ascetics was to connect the natural and cosmological with the social. In this, they enabled society to form a new culture through and with nature. Their dynamic character was expressed in their being employed to produce social, mental, and psychological changes, hence we can call them here "dynamic totems." It is first essential to explain the meaning of "totem," a term which has nearly disappeared from the scientific discourse of the last decades.[5]

The Saint as a Dynamic Religious Totem

The concept of a totem, or more precisely its application to "primitive societies," was predominant in anthropological and psychological discourses of the first half of the twentieth century. It was subsequently shown by Claude Lévi-Strauss to be nothing more than an intellectual myth. "Totemism" appears in his studies of the 1950s and 1960s first of all as an "intellectual means" to differentiate "savage" from "scientific" ("nonsavage") societies, a "totemic illusion" (*l'illusion totémique*).[6] The purpose of the present chapter is not to prove the contrary. In fact, we are in debt to Lévi-Strauss for unveiling the false separation between "savage" and "nonsavage," "static" and "dynamic" societies. What we would like to show in the present chapter is that one way for a society to introduce changes in its structure and definitions involves the creation and use of totems to connect society to nature. This was the role of the abnormal behavior, or the "'pathology," of asceticism: it enabled society to redefine its relation to nature, and through this to redefine itself.

In using the term "totem" we shall not refer to the idea that certain groups of people establish a cultural link with certain animal species as means of social classification. Nor shall we refer to Philippe Descola's concept of continuity between humans and different kinds of nonhuman species as part of their ontological perspective.[7] We shall refer to the social functionality of those figures who personify a link between culture and nature. We use the term "totem," not "symbol," "saint," "hero," and so on, because the social functionality of the ascetic was defined in terms of both culture and nature. In fact, the main meaning of ascetics' activities is to link the two together into one coherent system, hence the term "totem." In *Les formes élémentaires de la vie religieuse: Le système totémique en Australie* (*The Elementary Forms of Religious Life*), Émile Durkheim used totemism to show that the backbone of social identities, social behavior, and social perception is religion.[8] He showed how rites, especially those which ensure the reproduction of the totemic specie, are constructed so that moral efficacy produces physical efficacy. We shall not define the totem in this chapter in the same manner, but as a figure that enables relationships between man and nature, and man and culture. We can certainly remark here on an affinity to Durkheim's functionalism. In both cases the totem's function is to connect the moral with the physical aspects of a living society. Moreover, in this the totem acts, and is also defined, with reference to the psychological dimension. In the words of Lévi-Strauss: "The totemic relation cannot be found in the actual nature of the totem, but in the associations which it evokes for the spirit. . . . It appears not as a cultural phenomenon, but as a natural result of natural conditions . . . and hence a product of the psychological and biological dimensions, and not the ethnological."[9]

Totemism, as defined by Lévi-Strauss, is a systematic organization that equates the social with the structure of the psyche through the ways man relates to nature.[10] Lévi-Strauss has shown that the function of the totem is not to separate groups, but to express the way in which a group portrays itself vis-à-vis nature. In his theory therefore, the relationships of man and nature, and man and culture, do not necessarily form a whole. We shall not argue the opposite, but we shall see that in the period of changes under examination, asceticism enabled the creation of new totems which served exactly to link these two relationships. This is not to say that such totems exist in any given society, but that they are functional to societies as means of creating a change in structure. This was the case in the Jewish and Christian environments of the Byzantine Near East, which defined and used asceticism in order to socialize nature.

Socializing Nature

> Each specific form of cultural conceptualization also introduces sets of rules governing the use and appropriation of nature, evaluations of technical systems, and beliefs about the structure of the cosmos, the hierarchy of being, and the very principles by which living things function.[11]

In this statement, Philippe Descola articulates a new perspective in anthropological thought about the culture-nature dualism which dominated the discourse of the social sciences throughout the twentieth century:

In the twenty-first century it has become a given that nature is also a social construct.[12] However, this is not Descola's point. In his studies Descola undermines the dichotomy between nature and culture by showing that nature could be not only part of culture but also, through the social, culture itself. He has established a new perspective in which the ways people relate to nature define their social and cultural relationships.

This is especially revelatory in his book about the Achuar, the last of the Jivaro peoples in the Upper Amazon.[13] In this study, Descola analyzes, as he says, "the relations between humans and their environment from the standpoint of the dynamic interactions between the techniques used in socializing nature and the symbolic systems that organize them."[14] The socialization of nature is indeed at the core of this study. But the socialization of nature does not appear here to be a cultural process that forms a society at the expense of the relationship between man and nature. On the contrary, nature and the different ways in which man relates to it are demonstrated to be essential means of establishing and sustaining the entire Achuar social system. Indeed, Descola shows how each and every fragment of social life is defined and affirmed through its relationship to nature. The book reveals Achuar social life as a universal system that derives its meanings both from the ways in which it relates to nature and the ways in which nature relates to it. Ecology—the relations between a community of living organisms and its environment—is, in the case of the Achuar, the way in which they perceive and define their society. Nature not only forms part of *the social*, but is also the structure that maintains and affirms it. This is what Descola calls "socializing nature."

No similarity can be found between "our naturism" (the idea of nature existing independently of human action), and the Achuar's cosmos: a continuum between human beings and natural being. The Achuar managed to establish this perception of the cosmos as their society by specifying the modes of communication that humans can establish with each of its component parts.[15] This combines the social and the natural into a single system. In fact, what the study of the Achuar's perception of the cosmos reveals is that there is no distinction between the social and the natural. What we may term as "natural" is what gives the Achuar a social meaning and a sense of themselves within their surroundings. Thus nature appears to be a system of social meanings, without which the Achuar have no existence as a society.[16]

One example will illustrate this: gardening and hunting. Agriculture, or the use of plants for nourishment, as well as the use of animals, are not separate from the role that every member holds in society in the Achuar perspective.[17] Moreover, the relationship between humans and the plants they grow and the animals they hunt is defined as a social relationship, and is backed by an animistic perception in which both plants and animals (though not all of them) have souls.[18] This anthropopsychic perception acts on the ecological level and enables the Achuar to communicate with their surrounding and nature as their proper society through a system of myths, dreams, and magic chants. Naturally, this is not unique to the Achuar. However, Descola's analysis reveals that the

Achuar's system is a method not only of exploiting and relating to nature but also of relating to and communicating among humans, that is, as culture. Thus, once the garden is perceived as a consanguineal world, it affects the entire system of human relations. This is also apparent, to give a second example, from the way in which the Achuar, as river dwellers, perceive their place within the conduct of the cosmos. The water world appears as the mediating space par excellence for much of Achuar social life: movement, fishing, and sexual and marital connections. Copulating in the water of the river, for instance, makes part of the water cycle of the universe, and hence is perceived not only as affecting the spirits of the fish, but also as having a direct cause on the balance of the water cycle of the universe for both its regulation and disorder (i.e., river water, rainwater, floods, and drought).[19]

"Socializing nature," therefore, does not mean creating a new society with nature, but perceiving nature as one's own and only society. What links man to nature is shown by Descola to form *the social*. The particularity and uniqueness of this approach do not need to be emphasized. Its implications for anthropological, ecological, and sociological theories are far-reaching: a system of references of humans to nature enables humans to be in communication with both nature and humankind.[20] The feeling of being one with nature thus derives from the reciprocity that the Achuar establish between the social, ecological, and biological aspects of their life. In fact, from this perspective, biology and society are not two distinct aspects of life, but form a single whole.

This perception of a universal society—universal in the sense of embracing both humans and nature—gives the feeling of being one with nature. In what follows we shall see how asceticism precisely serves this end: to embed in the believer a strong sense of being one with the nature. In a word, this socialization of nature was what the pathology of asceticism aimed to do. The question of why inexplicable or abnormal individual behavior becomes meaningful to society is what the present chapter, and in fact the entire book, is about.

The Sacred Canopy and Collective Asceticism

In his *Sacred Canopy: Elements of a Sociological Theory*, Peter Berger focused on the dialectics between the social and the theological or metaphysical, and argued that the second is defined in order to support the first. He calls this "theodicy," which is not a justification of God's actions, but is defined in sociological, anthropological, and psychological terms. Theodicy, to Berger, is the idea that phenomena which are outside the social and the perception of the natural order can be attributed with significance that is meaningful for both the social order and individual psychology.[21] In other words, theodicy is the moral justification of society in cosmological/metaphysical terms.

Berger's theory about the sociological aspect of religion defines society and the act of socialization as a product of human activity that enables individuals to perceive themselves in relation to the world by "externalizing themselves."[22] Social reality, according to this perspective, is consciousness. All cosmic phenomena that are not defined within the framework of this consciousness and social reality are "covered" and are referred to by the religious sphere. By applying the concept of sanctity, religion connects the cosmic to the social. Theodicy, as Berger defines it, enables sanctification, and thus socializes external cosmic phenomena. Without going into the second part of his book—"Historical Elements"—where his objective was to explain the process of secularization, which he later renounced, we shall use here Berger's concept of theodicy. We shall see that it is an essential element of socialization, which can draw light on the functionality of asceticism. The abnormal behavior of the ascetic appears to be the most powerful tool of theodicy in the period under examination. But we should start first with the question of theodicy itself.

In the first chapter of his book, "Religion and World-Construction," Berger sets out the theoretical premises of his conceptualization of the social need for religion. According to his social reading, a social reality equals consciousness because it creates a universal structure for the human being by establishing a *nomos*, a conduct protocol, which at its basis is social. But the very existence of such a *nomos* of social reality will always be threatened by inexplicable *anomic* phenomena. Thus there will always be tension between the *nomos* and the chaos of the world. Religion responds to this tension by legitimating *anomic* phenomena through the notion of sacredness. By preventing a state of *anomie*, the concept of the sacred enables human beings to relate to the cosmic dimension of life. To put it simply: religion enables individuals to externalize themselves in relation to *anomic* phenomena by creating a *nomic* cosmic context. This objective of religion is both social and psychological.

Religion gives a social aspect to the chaos through the psychological effect of the sacred on the individual. The concept of theodicy that Berger uses here is the means of achieving this, since it enables the individual to integrate the *anomic* chaotic experiences in his or her life into the *nomos*—their socially structured context. Legitimating these experiences means creating a socialized (i.e., "sacred") context for them. Theodicy thus provides "an extended sheltering canopy of the *nomos*," and is "rooted in the characteristics of human *sociation*."[23]

Berger's theodicy also has a psychological effect on the individual level. Not only does it legitimate the individual *anomic* experiences, it also creates an individual bond between humans and their surroundings by contextualizing *anomic* experiences (dreams, calamities, deaths, etc.) within a sacred space (i.e., "the sacred canopy"). In this way, an individual's perception of the world acts on the psychological level, but at the same time is connected to the processes (of externalization, objectivation, and internalization according to Berger) that form the phenomenon of society. In the second part of this chapter we shall see that asceticism produces exactly the same effect. By defining a particular abnormal human behavior as "asceticism," that is, as a way to reform society, this abnormality or social deviancy, whether or not we call it insane behavior, is sanctified and legitimized in order to form a system of theodicy. In the period under examination, Jewish and Christian communities developed parallel concepts of ascetic practices precisely to this end.

Collective and Individual Asceticism

Collective Asceticism: A Rabbinic Ritual

Mishnah Ta'anit is a short tractate in *Seder Mo'ed* (the order of Special Days), whose subject is establishing rules of conduct in times of drought. There is no need to emphasize here the cardinal place of the water supply in any economy, all the more so when agriculture forms its largest part. Tractate *Ta'anit* regulates the Jewish protocol for dealing with natural calamities by prayers, fasts, and torments of the body. Literally, the term *ta'anit* is derived from the root *'a-n-h*—"to torment"—in its reflexive form, hence the act of tormenting oneself.[24] Two preliminary facts should be underlined: First, the Mishnah is the first rabbinic codification of regulations of Jewish rituals in the post-Temple era, and it offers the earliest protocol that we have for Jewish conduct in times of drought. Second, the basis of tractate *Ta'anit* is the concept that natural disasters are inflicted as punishment by God, who requires repentance and atonement from men.[25]

Jewish *ta'anit*, or fasting and tormenting the body, and Christian forms of asceticism are not identical. The first are defined as public provisional practices, that is, as rituals, while the second are a way of life for believers. Nevertheless, both Jewish and Christian practices of self-denying torments of the body, whether or not we call them ascetic, are defined as atonement or repentance. The idea of repentance, atonement, and reformation of human conduct through torments of the body is what private and public, individual and collective, provisional and permanent forms of asceticism have in common. This is the core of the phenomenon of asceticism. It is what transforms it from pathological masochism, madness, or social abnormal behavior into a socially accepted norm that provides society with a means to relate, connect, and control the chaos of nature. This is Berger's concept of theodicy.

Whereas in the Second Temple period the practice of sacrifice was the epiphany of Jewish cult, the rabbis of the post-Temple second century had to deal with the question of how to construct a new cult with no temple at its center. Naturally, sacrifice was the established norm in antiquity to connect to the gods, in order to thank, implore, or appease them. The ancient Jewish cult set at its center the connection to the Jewish God through the temple, in particular the Temple at Jerusalem. This developed into a religious system over a period of nearly six hundred years, from Cyrus the Great to Vespasian. In this respect, the Jewish cult was no different from any other religious cult in antiquity. However, the destruction of the Temple in 70 A.D. during the Judaean War left the Jewish cult with no focus and practically no ritual. There was a need to find alternative ways of connecting to the Jewish God.[26] There were prayer houses, as well as other forms of Jewish cult.[27] And there was also Jewish law and customs: the Torah—the *nomos* of the Jews (Greek: *ho nomos tōn ioudaiōn*). In the first century B.C. and the first century A.D., this *nomos* was the center of intellectual activities that put its theoretical aspects into practice. It was this concept of *nomos* as a product of intellectual activity that was chosen by the rabbis of the second century to replace the cult of the temple; in a word, creating *nomos* (both law and code of conduct and customs) as ritual. The result was the development of sets of regulations for any aspect of Jewish life, implementing the Torah in everyday life by interpretation. These regulations were compiled in the Mishnah under Rabbi Yehudah haNasi toward the end of the second century A.D.

As for *ta'anit,* public fasting and the infliction of torments on the body in times of trouble, at its basis we find the concept of self-denial as repentance. Biblical stories about the Flood and Sodom and Gomorrah in Genesis serve as a touchstone of the perception of calamities as moral punishment. The Hebrew Bible also constructs a method of reformation and repentance through the definition of the Day of Atonement—Yom Kippur.[28] The Mishnah has used these ideas to construct a public ritual of self-torment—*ta'anit*—a collective ascetic practice.[29]

Mishnah Ta'anit sets up the ritual of public asceticism and defines the circumstances in which the rabbis need to decree a *ta'anit*—a period of acts of self-torment that are performed as a collective ritual of the community. The tractate is divided into four chapters. The first deals with the question of when to say prayers for rain, and when the rituals of *ta'anit* should start if no rains come. This chapter also determines the increases in the rhythm of fasting and other bodily torments as winter proceeds with no rain. The second chapter deals with the ritual itself. This includes a public exposure of the ark of the Torah, public prayers, and blessings. The third chapter deals with the question of what constitutes natural disasters and their circumstances. Here we also find an expansion on the definition of disaster to include disasters caused by humans and ways of dealing with disasters. The fourth chapter gives a specific protocol for prayer in times of *ta'anit,* and also specifies memorial days of *ta'anit.*

This tractate aims at constructing a system of theodicy that enables the new post-Temple Jewish society to replace the rites around the Temple with a new method of perceiving, relating to, and managing the chaos of nature. This is the process of objectivation that Berger has defined: relating to abstract phenomena in a concrete way, and turning them into tangible objects by attributing them with a social context. We can certainly define this as asceticism because, just as in Christian practices, theodicy is formed by and through the practice of torments of the body, whether as atonement, repentance, self-reformation, self-transformation, or a mystical encounter with the divine.

After setting the exact timing for the prayer for rain, the Mishnah determines the specific day in autumn that marks the beginning of the order of fasting if no rain comes.[30] As winter advances without rain, the order of prayers and fasting becomes more and more strict, and is determined by the rabbinical authorities (Hebrew: *beith din*) for the entire public. Self-torments include fasting; the prohibition of working, washing, bathing, and oiling; the wearing of leather sandals; and sexual intercourse.[31] If nothing helps ("if these have passed and were not *answered*"), the entire social life is changed. People reduce all activities, business transactions, construction projects, planting, betrothals, and weddings: "and they should reduce their greetings one to another, as men who are reproached by God."[32] This is a clear indication that disasters are perceived as God's punishment for human conduct: earthquake and plague also constitute a reason for public asceticism.[33] The reason for decreeing a *ta'anit* is to demonstrate public repentance. As for rain, if public fasting does not help and rain does not come, the torments of the body continue until harvesttime, when they should stop. Thus if after a completely dry winter, rain appears only after the month of Nisan has ended (harvest), this is a sign of a curse from God.[34]

While the first chapter of the tractate concerns prayers, individual fasting, and self-torments, together with the way everyday life is affected by the *ta'anit*, the second chapter describes public rituals headed by the rabbinical authorities (the Nasi and the head of the juridical court), where "the ark" (of the Torah scrolls) is taken out into the city's main street. There are public acts of mourning, blowing of the rams' horns, and then twenty-four blessings are said, the Eighteen of everyday, with the addition of six blessings of mourning. After each one of the last seven,[35] the spokesperson adds, "He who *answered* [Hebrew: *'anah*] Abraham on Mount Moriah will *answer* [Hebrew: *ya'aneh*] you and hear your cry on this day" followed by a blessing; "He who answered [Hebrew: *ya'aneh*] our fathers on the shore of the Red Sea will *answer* [Hebrew: *ya'aneh*] you and hear your cry on this day"; and so on, evoking biblical figures whom God answered and helped.

A priori, there is nothing particular in reciting blessings so that God may answer prayers for rain in time of drought. However, the Mishnah here links together torment of the body and the act of imploring God. By using the same Hebrew root *'a-n-h*, "to torment," in its second meaning "to answer," the Mishnah brilliantly connects God's answer to the torment of the body. Thus the term *ta'anit* is not simply torment of the body, but torment of the body in order to receive God's forgiveness (i.e., God's *answering*) through repentance and prayer.[36] The linguistic means serves here to make *ta‘anit* not only *torments* of the body, but also the call for God to *answer* them. In this way public asceticism is defined as a rabbinic ritual of the second century.[37]

The objective of the entire ritual is to amend the balance of nature, which is perceived in relation to man, that is, the balance between man and nature. This balance can be lost through human unlawfulness, but can also be restored through human self-torments (Hebrew: *ta‘anit*, from the root *‘a-n-h*) which are perceived as repentance, when God *answers* them.[38] This balance between man and nature is defined and is managed within the framework of the relation between the entire community and God. As a consequence, the process of repentance to restore this balance is collective and public. Everything is collective, not only the repentance through asceticism but also the unlawfulness and its blame.

It is important to note that a few centuries later, both the Palestinian and the Babylonian Talmuds connected the imbalance in nature directly to its cause, the collective sin of lawlessness, by using the term *‘avon*—"unlawfulness." In the Palestinian Talmud rain comes down to earth for grace and suffering (Hebrew: *ḥesed* and *issurin*), but stops because of four types of sin (Hebrew: *‘avon*): idolatry, incest, murder, and refusal to give alms after alms have been declared.[39] In the Babylonian Talmud Rabbi Yehoshu‘a ben Levi is quoted in regard to the need to take the ark out during public fasting "so that we should be despised for our sinful act" (Hebrew: *venitbazeh be‘avoneinu*).[40] The Hebrew term for sin—*‘avon*—is translated as *anomia* in the Septuagint (Gen. 19:15, Job 7:21). And this brings us back to Berger's theory of theodicy as a mechanism to provide answers for anomic phenomena. What he meant as anomic were natural phenomena that cannot be controlled and maintained by human reasoning (and hence are outside the human *nomos*). It is as if Rabbi Yehoshu‘a ben Levi was pointing to Berger's words by saying that according to the theodicy set by *Mishnah Ta‘anit*, the *nomos* is divine. Anomic phenomena therefore are caused by human transgression of this *nomos*.[41]

The interesting thing about Rabbi Yehoshu‘a's explanation is that it collectivizes the sin: it is "our sin" (Hebrew: *‘avoneinu*) and not "our sins" in the plural, hence it marks a common blame shared by society.[42] The fact that both the sin and repentance are collective makes the psychological level of the individual's relation to God part of society through the collective ritual. Collective asceticism as a public ritual serves here as means of implementing a new Jewish theodicy that replaces the theodicy of temple rites.[43] The psychological aspect of the religious experience appears here as collective. Similarly, we shall see an equivalent development of a Christian means to control nature by implementing a new theodicy of asceticism also through the idea of penitence.

From Private Asceticism to Public Reformation

In an innovative reading of early Christian authors, Elizabeth Clark has shown that Christian asceticism developed as means of interpretation of biblical rituals that were no longer applicable.[44] Christian asceticism thus appears as a parallel development to the Mishnah with the same objective: the creation of a new means of maintaining the social functionality of the rites of the Temple. However, in contrast to the Mishnah, Christian methods of dealing with the replacement of temple rites are much less straightforward. In the second century Christians did not have a figure equivalent to Rabbi Yehudah haNasi who could impose juridical authority, and their means of defining new norms of conducts did not include issuing a collective *nomos*. As Clark writes, today it is largely accepted that asceticism was growing in popularity among Christians before the fourth century, in the first to the third centuries.[45] However, it is important to note that what we define today as asceticism, or early Christian asceticism, comprises a number of different practices: sexual abstinence, social withdrawal, renunciation of the temporal world and its characteristics, fasting and other corporal types of self-denial, as well as corporal self-torments with the objective of subduing any passion of the body. What is common to all is a denial of what is considered common and normal social behavior marked as "temporal and corporal." In a word, the objective of denying temporality and corporality is to attain the divine, which is extemporal, spiritual, and incorporeal. At the basis of this lies the notion that the relationship of humans to their body has a direct effect on the relationship of humans to God, and hence God to humans. We find this rationale of fasting and other self-torments in both rabbinic Judaism and early Christianity.[46]

Arthur Vööbus, Richard Finn, and Elizabeth Clark reveal in their studies the theoretical and theological setting of the phenomenon of asceticism within the Christian framework, which they trace to the Christian writers of the second and third centuries.[47] This concerns mainly fasting, sexual abstinence, and attributing the state of virginity with a spiritual meaning.[48] It was the Christian authors of the second and third centuries who made this connection through the reading of the body of the Christian believer as holy, a symbol of God's temple that needs to be preserved as pure.[49] This idea attributed a spiritual meaning to any act of self-denial. Like the phenomenon of martyrdom, defining self-denying behavior within a religious framework sanctified it, by imbuing this behavior with a meaning for all believers. Investigating whether Christian asceticism developed first as a practice or as a theology will lead us, of course, to a vicious circle. This is not necessarily due to lack of evidence for the period in question, but mainly to the fact that such forms of self-denial could not have been treated as "ascetic" without the development of a corresponding religious theoretical framework.[50]

Asceticism is often perceived as a clear manifestation of the negation of the cultural by means of a new connection between man and nature. The fact that it is often equated with withdrawal from society—anchoretism (Greek: *anachōrēsis*)—follows the same line of thought. The descriptions of individuals who left everything they possessed in order to live as solitary hermits in the desert present them as living the life of animals, in caves and the open air, in solitude. They do not work, but wander about and eat whatever they can find in a manner similar to wild animals: grass, roots, and herbs (hence the name "browsers"—Greek: *boskoi*—attributed to some of them).[51] They dress in rags and straw, or go around naked, and inflict severe punishments on their bodies. A priori, such behavior avoids the cultural through a return to nature. The diet of the ascetic is based on raw vegetables and roots (hence avoiding any culinary culture).[52] Ascetics also often reject any kind of man-made clothing, whether of linen or skin. Moreover, the sources often describe them in the desert wandering about, and in a similar way to animals.[53]

However, although the encounter with nature, and the animal kingdom of the wilderness in particular, is an integral part in the description of the everyday life of ascetics or anchorites, they are not described as being part of wild nature. The ascetics do not loose their identity in nature. On the contrary, through their practices (Greek: *askēses*) in the wild they gain a new identity and are able to control nature.[54] Fasting, self-denial, abstinence, and mastery of the animal kingdom are all manifestations of the ascetic's triumph over nature, whether it is a part of universal nature or a passion of the body.[55] The practices of self-denial enable the ascetic to eliminate the very separation that we make today between the two "natures"—human nature and the nature of the universe—which are the two aspects of the same "corporal and terrestrial nature."[56] The elimination of this separation is the elimination of the very idea of "naturism," that is, the idea of nature existing independently of human action. As we shall see, this elimination is at the heart of the phenomenon of asceticism. It enables ascetics, and through them society, to control the balance of nature through miracles.

Ascetic *anachōrēsis* is not an anticultural pro-nature movement. It is an act of denial of all aspects of human nature, both cultural and biological. This leads ascetics to leave the cultural sphere as well as their own corporal nature in order to get to the spiritual aspect of nature, where there is no distinction between man and nature.[57] Ascetics manage to achieve this by denying their own corporal nature, and because their acts of self-denial are perceived as repentance.[58] Mastery over wild animals manifests a new order of universal nature.[59] The emblematic connection between repentance and nature lies, of course, in the story of the Fall and its Christian interpretations. "In the beginning," Adam was meant to be one with nature, both inseparable from it and master of it, but his sin made him loose this position.[60] The ascetic anchorite process aims to enable man to move in exactly the opposite direction.[61] The way of life of the ascetic or anchorite is hence not defined in contrast to the cultural, but in contrast to the separation between man and nature. To this end, the wilderness (Greek: *erēmos*) becomes essential.

The fact that anthropology and psychology have defined the cultural as a negation of the natural may and should be put into question.[62] In fact, the study of asceticism from the perspective of the man-nature-society relationship provides means to challenge this premise.[63] Moreover, in order to change the cultural, asceticism shows us, man transforms his relationship to nature. The mélange between anchoretism and asceticism enables individuals to combine the negations of both cultural and social (by withdrawal from society) and human nature (by negating and hence mastering the corporality of human existence). As we shall now see, anchoritism could well have been a step against both the social and the cultural (outside normality and outside reason). But hagiographic narratives define it precisely as a means of producing a new culture and a new society—thus providing it with both social and cultural reasoning. Anchorites manage to fill this function through their mastery of the balance of nature, that is, through their ability to perform miracles.

What Is a Miracle?

Normally defined as a divine intervention in nature, the miracle is beyond the scope of the present study.[64] It is, however, vital to understand the functionality of attributing such divine interventions to human beings, and specifically to ascetics, in the religious communities in question. In the sixth book of his long poem *De rerum natura*, Titus Lucretius Carus (c. 99–55 B.C.) discusses at length natural phenomena as part of the perception that he introduces for understanding nature and its elements. Rains, thunder, lightening, storms, and floods are all results of the dynamics between the elements.[65] Lucretius does not talk about balance and imbalance in nature, but explains creation, transformation, and death according to laws of causality about substance and particles. He is clearly advancing his theory against a religious perception when he says:

> and so with all else that men see happening in earth and sky, when they are often held in suspense with affrighted wits, and abase their spirits through fear of the gods, keeping their spirits through fear of the gods, keeping them crushed to the earth; because their ignorance of causes compels them to refer events to the domination of the gods, and to yield them the place of kings.[66]

In his holistic theory of physics, Lucretius draws heavily on Epicurus. Humans are thus one element in nature, composed from the same particles as the world that surrounds them.[67] Their existence and disappearance change nothing in the global mechanism of the cosmos. On the contrary, their own course of living keeps to the same laws of causality of nature, "nature's rationale" (*naturae ratio*).[68] Such a theory of nature was not built on notions of theodicy, but in opposition to such notions, and was not aimed at the psychological aspect of human beings. Lucretius did not set out a method for individuals to externalize themselves as part of this theory.[69] It is important to note that this is precisely the reason why a theory of the universe that ignores the social cannot become a religion. "Socializing of nature," to employ Descola's central term, perceives human beings not merely as "a part of nature," but as "a part of the society of nature." Man is thus involved in a dynamic relationship with nature in the sense that he is influenced by it in accordance with the way in which he influences it. And this is the social medium which the ascetic achieves through miracles. This is also why we here call this medium totemic. In order to show this we must examine the conditions that turn the miracle worker into a totem. But first, how do we define what a miracle worker is?

A Pagan Miracle Worker: Philostratus's *Apollonius of Tyana*

In the beginning of the third century, the sophist Philostratus was commissioned by the empress Julia Domna (d. 217), wife of Septimius Severus, to record the life and deeds of Apollonius of Tyana, a pagan miracle worker who had lived a century and a half earlier.[70] This text, which has survived in twenty-five manuscripts, is often cited as a pagan version of stories about Jesus. Philostratus tells us that he based his narrative on the writings of Damis, Apollonius's companion and disciple, as well as on the letters of Apollonius, and the legends that circulated in the cities through which he had passed.[71] He presents a vivid and colorful narration of Apollonius's life, beginning with his childhood in Tyana in Asia Minor. Through eight books the reader follows the travels of Apollonius around the inhabited world, the meetings and exchanges that he conducted with other philosophers, as well as the development of his reputation as a miracle worker throughout the Roman world.

It is important to note that the two main features which Philostratus attributes to Apollonius in his narration are inseparable: the control that Apollonius acquires over nature which enables him to perform miracles or wonders (Greek: *thaumata*) is directly connected to his philosophy. Just like Pythagoras, writes Philostratus, Apollonius's philosophy allowed him to converse with the gods and acquire a wisdom which gave him access to divine knowledge.[72] This was the reason for his supernatural capacities and actions, which were not, Philostratus emphasizes, a product of magic.[73] The distinction that Philostratus makes between divine wisdom and magic is essential to the framework that he sets out for his narration: Apollonius is described in a way that enables his biographer to restore his audience's faith in philosophy as a way of living, and to restore the ancient rites of the gods. He portrays Apollonius as a wandering philosopher, not as a sorcerer, and this is because his main objective is to use the figure of Apollonius to crafting a narrative about the power of the sophist way of living and its importance for social and political life. In other words, Philostratus's aim is to construct a theodicy of pagan philosophy. His theodicy appears as a competitor to the Christian theodicies (the plural form will be explained below) which were crystallizing in his time throughout the Roman Empire. With this end in mind, miracles were essential.

At the basis of Apollonius's capacities and his status as a miracle worker is the idea that the gods are just (Greek: *dikaioi*).[74] This concept connects his philosophy to nature and defines it as a theodicy. The sense of morality in philosophy as the just way of life for human beings following the rules of divine wisdom gives a framework to the story. The author uses it all through his narrative by confronting Pythagoras's philosophy with the different types of wisdom known in his time (in Persia, India, and the Egyptian desert). Faithful to the sophist tradition, Apollonius's behavior is characterized by modesty and "asceticism," that is, abstinence as a way of living. The Greek verb *askeisthai* is used several times to mean "practicing," including the time when Apollonius is described as "practicing [Greek: *askēthentēn*] silence" for five years.[75] His voluntary silence brings him not only internal calm but also the ability to restore calmness to society. Philostratus presents Apollonius's abstinence from speaking as a means of ending the famine in Pamphylia.[76] Apollonius also avoids sacrificing and eating animals, and does not wear any clothing made of animal skin or hair.[77] This derives from his great knowledge about the animal kingdom, which is described in the second part of the first book. He refuses to make animals act "against their nature."[78] His practices, which are the result of his moral conduct and are attuned to the gods' will and nature, provide him with the ability to perform miracles and to foresee the future.[79] In this way he foresees earthquakes and is able to stop them. His reputation as a man who can fight calamities makes him an important figure, who is invited to cities in turmoil.[80] The terms "holy," "saint," or "man of god" are not used by Philostratus in relation to Apollonius. Apollonius is not venerated as a god, nor does he attain the position or cult of a prophet, but he is called on and is employed ad hoc to rescue cities in different parts of the Empire.[81] He also performs miracles of healing and resurrection.[82]

Returning to Berger's idea of theodicy, Philostratus builds a sense of theodicy through Apollonius's function of correcting the morals of public behavior.[83] But amending morality by restoring faith in the gods—which he does through public speeches and miracles—does not change the social or cultural order. New communities do not crystallize as a result of his teaching and actions. In fact, Philostratus describes Apollonius as a symbol of a public moral conscience. He is mainly engaged in passing moral judgment on social matters and imperial politics.[84] He has no social function.

In the sixth book of the *Life of Apollonius of Tyana*, the protagonist on his way from Egypt to Ethiopia arrives in the land of the "naked men."[85] These men live in the Egyptian desert in the Thebaid under the open sky.[86] Their sanctuaries are scattered over the hills. They form one community (Greek: *koinon*), and worship the Nile, seeing it as both earth and water.[87] They relate to nature by their way of living in the open wilderness, as well as through their miracles.[88] And they have their own philosophy. They persuade Apollonius to join them after explaining their particular way of living:

> But from our wisdom you will hear that it is right to sleep on the bare ground, to be seen toiling in nakedness, as we do, to think nothing welcome or pleasant that has come to you without toil, not to be boastful or seekers of vanity, and also to avoid dream visions that lift you from the earth. If you make the choice of Heracles and show an iron will, not dishonoring the truth or avoiding the simplicity of nature, you can say that you have caught many lions, exterminated a Hydra, a Geryon, and a Nessus, and all of Heracles' conquests.[89]

What is significant about the description of the "naked men," apart from the resemblance to the lives of Christian anchorites of the fourth to sixth centuries, is their social function. They serve as a religious and juridical authority.[90] Thus Apollonius meets a man from Memphis, who travels all the way from Lower Egypt to the Thebaid to meet them, so that they can absolve and purify him from the impurity of an unintentional killing he had committed.[91]

Philostratus attributes Apollonius with wisdom and control over nature, which enable him to restore the moral conduct of the Empire. In this, he places Apollonius in a long Greek intellectual tradition of the "divine man" (Greek: *theios anthrōpos*), of the pious philosopher (combining in his time Platonic metaphysics and the Pythagorean way of life).[92] Unlike other Pagan "divine men" Apollonius indeed performs miracles.[93] However, his social function ends there. The construction of Apollonius as a sophist miracle worker does not imply a new concept of nature or a new society.

In contrast to the sophist miracle worker, Christianity and Judaism construct the miracle and the miracle worker as a means of social and psychological transformation. As argued above, the capacity to intervene in the course of nature is not only connected to but also conditioned by the ability to triumph over corporal or terrestrial nature. The triumph over corporal and terrestrial nature means implementing a new concept of nature for society, according to which calamities are punishment from God. We see this at the core of both *Mishnah Ta'anit* and Christian asceticism. In both cases, and contrary to *The Life of Apollonius of Tyana*, asceticism serves as a means of repentance. A priori, *Mishnah Ta'anit* sets out a public form of repentance, while Christian asceticism is personal and performed in private. Nevertheless, the Christian authors of the fourth to fifth centuries construct the ascetic figure as a medium for achieving balance in nature, a divine balance, through the transformation of both man and society. In this, the ascetic acts as a dynamic totem which enables society to redefine itself by the psychological effect that the ascetic has on other individuals. Ascetic saints are therefore as much a public phenomenon as their contemporary Jewish ascetic rituals. All the miracles that are attributed to the ascetic, whether they concern natural disasters, human-made calamities, clairvoyance, or healing; whether they are performed on behalf of individuals, the public, or the saints themselves—they are all there to set up a new form of theodicy for the newly crystallizing religious communities of the Near East. The miracle thus appears as a means of implementing a new set of beliefs on the social level, in order to reconstruct society.

Both Christian ascetics and *Mishnah Ta'anit* set up new structures for new societies. In Egypt, in Syria, and in Palestine, the ascetics came to play this part through their cult. Their unique, bizarre, and abnormal way of life appeared at first as a manifestation of the negation of their own social lives, and secondly, served as a magnet for people who wished to transform their personal lives as well as their environment. These two features turn the eccentric withdrawers, the social dropouts, and abnormal figures into "anchorites," "ascetics," and "saints." We can define this process as "theodicizing society," using Berger's concept of theodicy as attributing meaning to phenomena that are outside the social and the perception of the natural order, with the objective of transforming the social order and the individual psychological dimension. This process is what transforms pure magic into "miracle"—miracle in the sense of a means of implementing and assessing a theodicy. The process of "theodicizing society" took on different forms in different regions of the Near East. In what follows, we will focus on two distinct Christian models: the Egyptian and the Syrian, and compare these with two distinct Jewish models that developed in Palestine and Mesopotamia.

Egypt: The Anchorite Totem and the Desert

The Greek term *anachōrētēs* (from *anachōrizein*—"to withdraw or retreat") is primarily attributed in fourth-century papyri to a person who has retreated from society, to whom one prays to get help in both spiritual and economic matters.[94] It reveals a specific social function to the meaning of the term, and the circumstances in which it was employed. The very act of "being an anchorite" meant gaining social legitimacy as a holy person. It also expressed the social need for this legitimacy. The hagiographic literature of the time is very telling in revealing this need, which is matched by the ascetic anchorite's capacity to manipulate nature in order to restore it to its rightful course. The correspondence and letters addressed to ascetics in the fourth through sixth centuries reveal these ascetics as intercessors and spiritual fathers, around whom new communities of believers took shape.[95] This is manifested in the prayers addressed to them from members of these communities. Hagiographic literature conveys important evidence in its objective to institutionalize the veneration of ascetic anchorite figures.[96] Moreover, the process of the institutionalization of such figures produces not only a cult but also the cultural and psychological transformation of the believer.[97]

The literature about the Desert Fathers describes the men who approach the anchorite as people in transition. They do not stay the same after their encounter, nor does their society. It is the miracle that ensures the believer's transformation. The gift of miracles is not given to any beholder. It is a product of divine grace and bestowed only upon worthy people who have already completed a process of self-transformation.[98] This process guarantees the activation and expression of a new theodicy that links man to nature. The hagiographic texts thus appear not as literature belonging to a particular genre, but as a vehicle for implementing a change. It is our most significant evidence revealing the social agenda of the creation of the anchorite movement. It was created as a result of the individual ascetics who withdrew to the desert. The prayers and the requests for blessing were a product of this literature's great achievement.[99]

The *Sayings of the Desert Fathers*, the *Life of Antony* by Bishop Athanasios of Alexandria, the "Life of Paul of Thebes" by Jerome, the *History of the Monks in Egypt*, the *Lives* and works of Pachomius and his disciples, and the *Lausiac History* by Palladius are all creations of the late fourth and fifth centuries, which describe the retreat of Christian individuals away from society into the wilderness of the Egyptian desert.[100] It is notable that new communities of believers mushroomed around ascetic anchorite figures who withdrew to the Egyptian desert. These new communities were the nucleus of the coenobitic and semi-coenobitic monasteries.[101] However, the anchorites also drew adherents from both city and village. *The Sayings of the Desert Fathers* (*Apophthegmata patrum*) is perhaps unique in focusing primarily on recording the legends about the anchorites for their own use. The *Lives*, together with compilations such as *A History of the Monks in Egypt* (*Historia monachorum in Aegypto*) and the *Lausiac History* by Palladius, focus, in contrast, on the encounter between the anchorites and the believers who approach them (among whom are the authors of these works themselves). They depict the spiritual transformation of the believer who accesses the anchorite as a means of connecting with nature, and through it, with the new society of believers.[102]

In this way, the anchorites managed to transform both individuals and society. They were the vehicle to repentance, thanks to their immediate link to nature, and because nature came to be perceived as a spiritual sphere. They could foresee the future for everyone. But their clairvoyance was due to their ability to read the moral quality of every human being.[103] This is why they could predict the future. Their use of their supernatural powers is solely a result of the new theodicy that they manifest and apply. Their power appears as a means of implementing it in the social life of both village and city. This is exactly what differentiated them from pagan miracle workers such as Apollonius of Tyana. When Apollonius rescues a city from calamity, heals a person, or prophesies, he does it through his own powers, without reference to his objects.[104] The ascetics and anchorites, in contrast, use their power in order to transform the believers by implementing a new concept of relation between man and nature, a new theodicy whose representatives and living proofs they are. The main objective here is transformation through repentance or conversion. We see this in the acts of conversion of pagan villages, or the repentance of Christian believers from the city who approach the anchorites.[105] In both cases, the ascetic's power over nature carries through a new way to connect the individual to the cosmos.[106] This is, of course, a direct continuation of the Gospels. However, contrary to the Gospels, the motor of change is defined here as asceticism. This justifies the control over nature. "Asceticism" here equals "totemism," since the ascetic's function is totemic: it enables the individual believer to become one with nature through a new society of believers.

The result was the transformation of Christian societies in Egypt during the course of the fourth and fifth centuries. This comprised the foundation of numerous monasteries both near the cities and in the wilderness, along with the mental and psychological transformation that the process of Christianization required. With the Edict of Milan of 313, Christianity became a legitimate Roman religion. The Christianization of the Roman Empire was a process that had both public and private aspects. On the public level, laws were issued and institutions were founded in a process that lasted for several centuries. On the private level, a new sense of society needed to be attained in and for every individual. In Egypt this was done by employing the desert as a place of transformation.[107]

This transformation was essential for the individual, as well as for the public. This is evident from the letters and prayers addressed to the anchorite fathers, and also from the narratives which were composed about them, where the objective was precisely to set up the figure of the anchorite as an essential element in both public and private life by acting as its medium or totem. This is why Anthony acquired such an important position: his cult demonstrated that he was essential for Christian social life in Egypt. Neither Clement nor Origen were able to achieve a movement of transformation like this, because they could not provide the psychological effect that a direct link to nature offered. The greatness of the figure of the anchorites in Egypt lay in the fact that they could connect individual believers to a new society via a moral concept of nature, thus uniting the cultural with the natural level.[108] This was possible by using the abnormal behavior of the ascetics, which challenged not only the relation between man to nature but also the relation between man to society. In other words, the weird and insane behavior of such persons was marked as special and defined as spiritual to enable society to use them in order to apply a new type of theodicy, essential for its transformation.

Unlike Jewish ascetic rituals, Christian theodicy in Egypt required the demonstration of a triumph over the wilderness. The new societies depended on the Desert Fathers for their redefinition because more than in any other place in the Roman Empire, the desert was the most significant natural force behind Egyptian society. This is also why the sine qua non term for asceticism—wilderness (Greek: *erēmos*)—was in Egypt the desert. The required totem needed to control the desert. Socializing nature in Egypt needed to be achieved in and via the desert.[109] And hagiography was composed to model and sanctify the anchorite who moves into the desert as a local totem. The same process of "totemization" developed in Syria, but in a different manner.

Syria: The Ascetic Totem and the Community

In the concluding chapter of her book about Syrian asceticism in the work of John of Ephesus, Susan Ashbrook Harvey writes of the different collections about asceticism by John of Ephesus, Cyril of Scythopolis, and John Moschus: "each presents a different view of the relationship between asceticism and society and between the temporal and spiritual worlds in this same situation . . . a situation of a religious crisis in the midst of their worldly difficulties."[110] The impetus to examine different kinds of relations between asceticism and society came, in fact, from Ashbrook Harvey's book. In his *Lives of the Eastern Saints*, John of Ephesus shows the ascetic not as a self-denier, withdrawn from society, but on the contrary, as a vital figure for the functioning and the management of the religious community. We shall enlarge the scope of the analysis beyond the locality of Syria-Palestine and focus on the way in which society could establish a link with and rely on nature through asceticism. This is the reason why this comparative analysis of different forms of asceticism began and will end with Judaism. As we shall see, there are a number of common points in Mesopotamian Judaism and Syrian Christianity in constructing the holy man as a dynamic totem. In both cases, much like in the Egyptian case, control over nature fills a social function. However, while in Egyptian and Palestinian forms of asceticism this control stayed in the hands of the anchorites in the desert, in Syria it moved from the desert to the city.[111] We shall continue in the line of thought laid out by Ashbrook Harvey, but will begin the examination of the social function of Syriac asceticism with the "Letters to Virgins" and Theodoret of Cyrrhus.[112]

The "Letters to Virgins" reveals the uncontrollable situation of wandering prophets and apostles in the Syrian countryside in the beginning of the fourth century.[113] This text makes it clear that these were celibate women and men who moved around either in groups or individually. The "Letters" also reveal the social need in fourth-century Syria for ecstatic figures to perform miracles for society, imitating the example of the acts of Jesus in the Gospels. The *Acts of Thomas* have often been discussed in this context as an example of the particularity of the Syrian case. The *Acts* represent the ambivalent position of Thomas as magus or miracle worker.[114] Just as in the "Letters to Virgins," the text deals with an ambiguity in the behavior of the figure who is the subject of the text.[115] And in both cases, the text provides evidence, as well as a method of settling this ambiguity. Asceticism is defined both as the method and the means that developed in the fourth and fifth centuries to enable the separation of the true from the false ecstatic figure, the holy man from the magus or false prophet, as is stated in "Letters to Virgins." This is very similar to the ambiguity of the holy fool.

Theodoret of Cyrrhus wrote his *History of the Monks of Syria* (*Historia Religiosa*) between 386 and 393.[116] This is a collection of stories dedicated to different ascetics who had acquired a reputation in the cities and villages of Syria through their exemplary behavior as ascetics and their power over nature.[117] Loyal to the picture painted by the "Letters to Virgins," the activities of Theodoret's ascetics are situated in close proximity to society.[118] Although some ascetics do go out to the wilderness, their ascetic way of life (Greek: *askētikē politeia*) directs them to perform their acts of self-torment within close view of society.[119] Some attract followers and found communities of monasteries, others pass their life alone. But in either case their behavior—in a similar way to their Egyptian contemporaries—is aimed first at controlling and subduing their own nature, and with it at using this control in order to protect society by amending the behavior of its members.[120] We see here again that the main social function of asceticism is the equation between social and natural balances. In order to achieve it the ascetic needs to be socially present.[121] This is why these ascetics, although they wander, are located at the outskirts of cities and villages, or even within them.[122]

To amend society, these saints are attributed with absolute control over nature. In this way, they not only fight calamities but also bring them about. They can call upon rains, stop hail, dry up rivers, or cause winds to blow.[123] They can move mountains or call wild animals. In these ways they can fight their opponents (either human or demonic), but also the vices of the society they need to amend. One important fact must be noted: the author portrays them as such, not necessarily because Syrian ascetics followed this model exclusively, but because he expresses the way in which Syrian societies constructed their stories about their living totems within the framework of applying a new theodicy. A cardinal element in this theodicy is the conceptualization of epidemics and other calamities as punishment from God that requires repentance from men.[124]

Another point is the diffusion of the Syrian ascetic saints in such a way that Christian communities all over Syria seem to have developed their individual miracle workers. Theodoret of Cyrrhus used these stories in order to construct a single framework. Society defined and created the holy ascetics in the image of biblical prophets because it needed a new and tangible medium to generate a social and cultural transformation. This is clear from the types of miracles that the Syrian ascetic performs. The control of nature allows the ascetic to Christianize society and to restore social justice to it. Mar Jacob of Nisibis, for example, dries up a river and changes the hair of women to "hair of trees" in order to make them leave idolatry and teach them modesty.[125] He also protects the city from the Persians by manipulating his control of the animal kingdom (he calls upon mosquitoes to chase the Persian armies).[126] But he does so only after the city's inhabitants transform their Christian behavior and become worthy of such protection. The ascetic not only protects the community from the dangers that befall it, but even more so from the dangers that threaten from within. Theodicy serves here as a means of forming a new type of community in both cities and villages by applying repentance, modesty, and social justice on both the individual and the social levels.

In his *Lives of the Eastern Saints,* John of Ephesus uses the same *topos* of the ascetic, as the protector of the monophysite community. As Ashbrook Harvey demonstrates, the ascetic became institutionalized, a process that makes him both acceptable and accessible.[127] This is all the more important in the time of the crisis of the monophysite communities.[128] For the social crisis they were confronting, the monophysite literature of the sixth century used the same type of medium which was already institutionalized and had been functioning for over a century in Syria, but in a new and innovative manner. This is apparent, for example, in the diffusion of a unique type of an ascetic, typical of urban Syria: the "ascetic on a pillar," as Ashbrook Harvey has inspiringly named the stylite saints.

Asceticism on a Pillar: The Syrian Totem and Its Locus

The phenomenon of the holy man on a pillar (Greek: *stulitēs,* Syriac: *esṭonāyā, esṭonārā* or *desṭonā,* from "pillar"—*stulos* and *esṭonā,* respectively), has attracted the attention of modern research as a unique and unusual phenomenon of Syrian asceticism.[129] The first known Christian figure to have lived his life on top of a pillar was Simeon the Elder (c. 386–459). His life was narrated by three different authors. Theodoret of Cyrrhus visited Simeon during his lifetime and includes his report in his *History of the Monks of Syria.* The other two *Lives* were written by Antonius, who presents himself as Simeon's disciple and the author of the *Syriac Life,* who was Simeon's disciple.[130] The differences between the images of the stylite figure as constructed by these authors were treated at length by both Robert Doran and Susan Ashbrook Harvey.[131] Theodoret of Cyrrhus describes the "philosophy" that Simeon practices—meaning his way of life as an ascetic—as both an apprentice at a school of ascetic philosophy near the village of Teleda and a solitary ascetic.[132] Simeon received all kind of requests for what people "could not get out of nature [*phusis*]."[133] His mastery over nature brought him adherents for whom he performed miracles, but his reputation spread beyond his neighborhood and brought him visitors from afar. In this way he also managed to convert people who came from outside the Roman Empire: Persians, Armenians, Iberians, and Ishmaelites.[134] He ordered the construction of the column to separate himself from the large crowds of people who came to him.[135]

In contrast, the *Syriac Life*, written by Simeon's disciple, attributes his mounting on a pillar to a divine call, and presents it as a covenant (Syriac: *qyāmā*) between Simeon and God.[136] Although this could indeed be understood as part of the biblical image of the prophet that the author constructs for Simeon, as Doran argues, the author links it to Simeon's ascetic practices. In contrast to the description of Theodoret of Cyrrhus, in the the*Syriac Life* Simeon performs them in public.[137] In a similar way to other ascetics, Simeon performs miracles from his enclosure in the village of Telneshe, and even prior to the construction of his pillar. His miracles comprise the healing of diseases, conversion, protection from natural calamities, and also what can be termed "social miracles," that is, miracles that are aimed at establishing social justice for society.[138] In all these cases, he uses his power over nature to set up a new balance in society. In this, Simeon is very much in line with other ascetics. His power over nature enables him to save a region from rats.[139] When he receives a delegation from Lebanon about an attack of wild beasts, he identifies the reason as idolatry, and makes everyone repent (immediately hereafter the wild beasts die).[140] He dries up a river in order to examine the faith of a village's inhabitants, and brings rain in time of drought following the inhabitants' repentance.[141] He controls rivers, winds, and mountains.[142] A century later, John of Ephesus reveals the way in which this social power of the Syrian ascetics was diffused and institutionalized, and made the ascetics acceptable and accessible.[143] For example, the ascetics on the pillar of Zʿura as well as Abraham and Maro from Kalesh were made local totems for their nearby communities in the same way as the particular asceticism of Mare the Solitary, who walked around in the city with his eyes on the ground.[144] Nevertheless, what the stylites all have in common, and what differentiates them from other types of ascetics, is their catatonic localization. They seem to acquire their force from connecting their unmoving to a localization: the pillar.[145] In the "Life of the Brothers Abraham and Maro," John of Ephesus informs the readers that Abraham did not build the column which he mounted himself: "There was a high stone column [Syriac:

esṭonā] to which men used to come in order to stand upon it in that monastery; and after he [Abraham] had broken himself for a space of ten years by great labours, he himself ascended the column."[146]

The fact that the column was already there has tempted scholars to connect the stylite saints to local Syrian pagan cults where pillars ("phalluses," Greek: *phaloi*) were used. Lucian is our main literary source for pagan devotees who climbed the pillar (Greek: *phallobates*) and stayed there in a nest for a number of days without sleeping.[147] Such devotees then attracted others, who paid them in order to deliver their prayers. Modern scholarship has largely rejected a possible continuity between this pagan cult and the stylite saints. All the same, the possibility of the existence of a symbolism of pillars in Syria as a place of connection to the divine cannot be overruled.[148] To this we need to add one aspect which seems to have been marginalized in modern scholarship, and that is the catatonic nature of stylitism, which much more than any other form of asceticism acts through an immovable localization.[149]

Although stylites could get down from their column, they do so very rarely.[150] Most of the stylites stick to their pillar as an extreme form of asceticism. Moreover, the pillar in itself symbolizes the link to the divine in the eyes of their community. More than other forms of asceticism, stylitism connects the divine to the community via an abnormal self-control of human movement which in its behavior sanctifies a location.[151] In this, stylite ascetics correspond much more than wanderer ascetics to the way in which Syrian communities appropriate their saints. It goes without saying that a column normally stays in one place. But the catatonic staying in one place of the stylites precedes the pillar. As the author of the *Syriac Life* describes it, throughout his life Simeon's asceticism is expressed in training himself to stand still in one place, a practice which he begins right after his first vision.[152] Moreover, even before he mounts the pillar, he bounds himself within a circle of stones.[153] His supernatural power comes to him precisely from keeping his position still in one place as a symbol of his covenant with God. But for the people surrounding him, it is he who bestows power on the locus. This enables the saint to link heaven and earth through one locus. As with other ascetics, this locus is his body, but unlike other types of ascetic, it is also his location.[154] When Abraham of Kalesh dies after [28/]38 years of living on top of a column, his brother Maro replaces him to keep the functioning of the column as a means of miracle working.[155]

It should also to be noted that, since the stylites are not in tangible reach, some of their miracles are performed by liquids or powders. Mar Z'ura, for example, blesses water that is given to him and is later used for healing.[156] Both Maro and Simeon give powder or dust (Syriac: *ḥnānā*) to believers, who are ordered to sprinkle it as a miraculous powder.[157] This enables displacement of the stylites' power without moving their body from its location. Simeon can thus perform miracles without himself being present, which is what makes his power displaceable.[158] It is exactly what enables his cult to remain local and to be diffused without being detached from his community of origin. The meaning of the Syriac word for this miraculous powder (Syriac: *ḥnānā*) literally means clemency, mercy, or pardon (from the Syriac root *ḥ-n-n*, "to be merciful, to give clemency, to pardon"). It symbolizes very clearly the role of the stylites and the ascetics themselves in making the forces of the cosmos tangible for believers in the psychological dimension of the religious experience, by defining the dust of pardon as a divine reply to the believers' repentance.[159]

Even more than the Egyptian cases of asceticism, their contemporaneous Syrian narrations deal with what Brown has identified as "the rise and the function of the holy man."[160] The literature written about them places the Syrian ascetics in cities and the villages. They are always present, whether in body or spirit. As Brown has shown, their presence provides a community with protection. However, this protection is not the objective of their sanctification, but the means to generate a transformation of the individual and society by implementing a new theodicy to connect the two. Both the miracle and its story prove to be essential, because they set and give evidence of this transformation. This is precisely what magic lacks. Although magic is all about introducing a transformation of nature, it stays completely within the natural dimension. It is not aimed at transforming the individual or society. In the same way, even if it concerns and changes the social, it does not transform society as a whole. This is not its objective.

Asceticism is essential here in order to differentiate between these two types of intervention in nature. Asceticism can turn the practice (magic) into theodicy (miracle) because it gives a moral reasoning to the control of nature, thanks to its own definition as a control over nature in the framework of this theodicy.[161] It is constructed in this way so that its application will enable the development of the idea of a balance in nature as dependent on human actions toward God. Asceticism is therefore what enables people to relate culture to nature and nature to culture. A change of nature means a change of culture, just as a change of culture (sins, injustice) means a change of nature (calamities). This is the reason why throughout this chapter we have used the term "totem" to designate the ascetic figure. Here we observe how abnormal behaviors of social withdrawal, seclusion, and catatonia could become totemic through their sanctification and their definition as "ascetic." The fact that this is done through the psychological dimension is clear from the personal transformation of individuals via ascetics. The ascetics embody the link between society and nature through the connection between their abnormality and power to control nature. They also embody the link between the individual and society via nature. This is manifested clearly in the image of Symeon the Stylite, whose localization reveals his magical allure, but whose pillar enables society to use him in order to implement a new theodicy.

The power of the stylite saints that is connected to their localization in one spot, a round spot, invokes a comparison with one of the most famous miracle workers of ancient Judaism, Ḥoni Ham'agel, which leads us back to rabbinic Judaism.

The Palestinian Talmud: Between Public Asceticism and Miracle Workers

Ḥoni Ham'agel—Ḥoni "the circle maker"—is a historical figure who lived in the first century B.C. at the time of the Hasmonean civil war. His title, *"Ham'agel,"* is derived either from his profession of casting (round) roof tiles or his practice as a miracle worker: drawing circles. Our earliest evidence comes from Josephus, who ascribes to him the capacity to call upon rain in time of drought.[162] *Mishnah Ta'anit* gives him a major part in its third chapter:

> For any calamity upon the public they blow the ram's horn (Hebrew: *shofar*) except for excessive rain. Once it happened that they said to Ḥoni Ham'agel: Pray that rain may fall. He replied: Go out and bring the Passover ovens[163] inside, so that they will not be destroyed. He prayed, but no rain fell. What did he do? He drew a circle and stood within it, and said before him: Master of the universe, thy sons turned to me because before

> you I am like a "son of the house" [*ben baith*]. I swear by thy great name that I will not move from here until you have mercy upon your sons. Rains began to trickle. And he said: Not for this did I ask, but for rains to fill the cisterns, pits and caves. The rains began to come down violently. He said: Not for this did I ask, but for rains of benevolence, blessing and grace. The rains came down in orderly fashion until the Israelites had to go up from Jerusalem to the Temple Mount because of the rains. They came and said to him: Just as you prayed for them to come down, now pray that they will go away. He said to them: Go and see if the Strayers' Stone[164] has been washed away. Shim'on ben Shaṭaḥ sent for him: Had you not been Ḥoni, I would have decreed an excommunication ban against you. But what could I do to you when you indulge yourself before *the place* [God], and act as you wish, like a son indulging himself before his father? And of thee it is written [Prov. 23:25]: May thy father and thy mother rejoice, and may her who bore thee, be glad.[165]

The story refers directly to the subject of the tractate: public measures in times of drought. But in contrast to the elaborated ritual that the tractate defines, this story gives evidence of an alternative way to deal with drought. Alongside public repentance through collective asceticism, the story reveals a much simpler practice: turning to persons who have the power to bind nature (i.e., God) to their will. Ḥoni binds God by drawing a circle and swearing in God's name, a clearly magical practice.[166] He controls the intensity of the rain according to his will. The Mishnah depicts him as a true magician. The insertion of this story into the Mishnah raises two questions: First, why does the Mishnah include a story that goes against its main objective—to set out an ascetic public ritual—and in fact contradicts the theodicy that the tractate wishes to set out (to bring amendment through collective repentance)?[167] Second, why does the Mishnah give it such a central place? (The story about Ḥoni occupies one tenth of the whole tractate.)

The two questions are connected. This story receives such a central place precisely because it negates the theodicy that the tractate defines. Thus, the editor of the Mishnah decided to include it in order to oppose the norm of turning to magicians. To put it differently, the story about Ḥoni enables the Mishnah to show us exactly what not to do. This is clear already from the beginning. The Mishnah brings the story about Ḥoni in reference to the following regulation: "For any public calamity they blow the ram's horn [Hebrew: *shofar*], except for excessive rain."

Ḥoni acts precisely when the public claims that there is too much rain, and in contrast to this regulation. The regulation seems to be promulgated against this sort of case of people praying or turning to ecstatic figures like Ḥoni for rains.

In fact the Mishnah portrays Ḥoni as a magician who controls both rain and God, by using and swearing in God's name. This is a complete contrast to the tractate's rationale, which demands repentance by fasting and praying to God for forgiveness. Moreover, while the tractate defines an elaborated ritual of public praying and asceticism, the story about Ḥoni concerns an individual praying on behalf of the public. Ḥoni himself is depicted as an arrogant and dangerous figure, who does not question his own power to bind God, but, on the contrary, brags about it. The explanation of the insertion of such a long story in the middle of the definition of a new pubic ritual is made clear from the reaction of Shim'on ben Shaṭaḥ, the head of the halakhic authority. He would have excommunicated Ḥoni, but he cannot overpower him. Moreover, he does not ascribe Ḥoni's power to Ḥoni himself, but to God's (literally "the place," Hebrew: *haMakom*) love. Ḥoni acts, he explains, as a beloved son indulging himself before his father. In this, the Mishnah ascribes the power over nature of figures of the like of Ḥoni not to them, but to God. Although the story clearly shows that Ḥoni is perceived by the public as a magician, it negates this perception and replaces it with a hidden and mysterious love of God toward his favorite son, who can ask for and get whatever he desires. This clarifies what is *not* allowed in time of trouble: the public should not turn to ecstatic figures, magicians, and so on. On the other hand, it explains that the existence of such figures does not contradict the theodicy about nature and society. In this way, the Mishnah appropriates the existence of magicians within the theodicy it wants to set up. The Mishnah thus extends this theodicy, in determining that God bestows supernatural power on certain people whom he loves.

However, this extension sets up an ambiguity in the heart of the theodicy about the cosmic and moral balance. This ambiguity is dealt with by the Palestinian and the Babylonian sages of the Amoraic period, which immediately followed the compilation of the Mishnah. Note that the Mishnah was compiled before any story known to us about Christian ascetics was in circulation, and thus should not be considered as a response to the rise of the Christian holy man. The question of whether the cosmic order or God's order of nature is determined by the moral conduct of the community, or by God's beloved ones, preoccupied the amoraim. Their discussions in the two Talmuds over this chapter directly concern the tension that the Mishnah sets up between the two practices of regulation of the relationship between man and nature. The two Talmuds propose two different ways to understand this tension.

The Palestinian Talmud sets out a general rule that reflects the way in which *Mishnah Ta'anit* is understood: rains arrive on behalf of a certain human being, a certain grass weed, or a certain field.[168] It continues to develop the idea of what brings and what stops rains in the following passage: rain comes down thanks to the earth, through grace (Hebrew: *ḥesed*) or through suffering (Hebrew: *issurin*).[169] Rain stops because of four types of sin (Hebrew: *'avon*): idolatry, incest, murder, and refusal to give alms after alms have been declared. After setting out this reasoning, the Palestinian Talmud relates a series of stories that refer to the relationship between man and nature.[170] This starts with two stories about Rabbi Ḥaninah and the people of Tzippori.[171] In the first, Rabbi Ḥaninah fails to stop a plague in the city. He then teaches the people of the city that sinners are the reason for public sufferings.[172] In the second case, the *ta'anit* that he decrees in Tzippori does not succeed in bringing rain, to the public's great dissatisfaction. Rabbi Ḥaninah then invites Rabbi Yehoshu'a ben Levi to Tzippori to fast with them, in the hope that rain will come (since the *ta'anit* that the second declared previously in the south succeeded). However, the presence of Rabbi Yehoshu'a ben Levi in Tzippori does not help, and rain does not come. Rabbi Ḥaninah hence teaches the following conclusion to the people of Tzippori: the success of public asceticism depends not on the leading rabbi of the community, but on the public. But the story does not end there. When there is still no rain even after the public has learned their lesson, Rabbi Ḥaninah turns his eyes to the sky and expresses his wonder and sadness. Rain then finally falls as a reply. When he realizes his own powers, he immediately vows never to use his will again for such a purpose, in order not to intervene in God's ways of reward and punishment (i.e., theodicy).[173] The conclusion of the editor is that the public is judged by its majority and not by its leaders.[174]

In all of its stories in tractate *Ta'anit* , the Palestinian Talmud stays within the theodicy set out by *Mishnah Ta'anit*. It attributes imbalance in nature to God's punishment for human sins. The entire discussion is on the question of whether the imbalance is a collective or individual responsibility. In both cases, public ascetic rituals, as defined by *Mishnah Ta'anit*, are required to amend the imbalance. However, the Palestinian Talmud does recognize the power of certain individuals, God's beloved ones, to bypass the nature-to-society mechanism. In this, the Palestinian Talmud turns the figure who can intervene in the nature-to-society mechanism from the arrogant Ḥoni of the Mishnah to pious rabbis who are God's beloved. Nevertheless, by defining this method as intervention in God's ways, the Palestinian Talmud subscribes to the Mishnah's reluctance to turn to individuals like Ḥoni who can work miracles, and affirms the theodicy that necessitates public asceticism as a means of collective repentance. We will now see that the Babylonian Talmud refers to the same situations, but develops a totally different theodicy.

The Babylonian Talmud: From Asceticism to Nonascetic Totems

Tractate *Ta'anit* in the Babylonian Talmud uses the tension that *Mishnah Ta'anit* introduces between the two ways of controlling nature: public ascetic ritual on the one hand, and the ecstatic figure on the other, in order to develop an original theodicy for the benefit of the rabbis, the leaders of the Jewish communities in Mesopotamia. To this end, the Babylonian Talmud constructs the figure of the pious miracle worker in what could easily be described as a hagiographic cycle. This "cycle" is part of the third chapter of the tractate, which is a commentary and discussion on *Mishnah Ta'anit*'s third chapter.[175] It comprises thirty stories about miracle workers, among whom Ḥoni is just one example. In this way, the Babylonian Talmud establishes a context for the story of Ḥoni, but in fact turns the Mishnah's agenda on its head.

The thirty stories of the cycle concern the supernatural power of twenty-eight Jewish figures, twenty-five men and three women, two of whom are wives of miracle workers and have supernatural powers of their own. Twenty of the twenty-eight figures are identified as rabbis, and most of them are prominent figures. Some of them are famous rabbis from Palestine, others from Mesopotamia. The appropriation of supernatural power by the rabbinic authority is very clear: even Ḥoni is given the title "rabbi." If in both the Mishnah and the Palestinian Talmud Ḥoni appears as an ecstatic figure, a magician, the Babylonian Talmud names him a rabbi, a pious man (Hebrew: *ṣadik*), and places him in the rabbinic school. The Talmud elaborates on the story in the Mishnah, but introduces three major changes: First, Ḥoni's arrogance is completely attenuated. He does not brag about his capacities, but attributes them to God. Second, by comparing him with Habakkuk in guarding the people of Israel ("I will stand at my watch and station myself on the ramparts," Habakkuk 2:1), the Babylonian Talmud eliminates any connotation of magic from the Mishnah. Moreover, it equates Ḥoni's power with Elijah's in explaining that the drought is attributed to Elijah's will (1 Kings 17:1–18:41).[176] Third, the Babylonian Talmud emphasizes the love that Ḥoni receives from God, which is the reason why his will exceeds Elijah's.

The second story about Ḥoni concerns his miraculous sleep of seventy years in a cave, followed by his death.[177] Ḥoni's uncontrollable power makes his wishful thinking come true, but in a most horrific and ironic way that in fact deprives him of any control over his supernatural forces. The story places Ḥoni in the rabbinical school, where after seventy years of sleep in a cave he is not recognized as a great rabbi. This offends him so much that he finally dies of a broken heart (Aramaic: *ḥalaš daʿateih baʿei raḥamei umeit*).[178] But the story of Ḥoni does not end there. The Babylonian Talmud adds two anecdotes about his two grandchildren, who were also attributed with the power of calling up rain. Both Abba Ḥilkiyah and Ḥanan haNeḥba (Ḥanan "the hider," i.e., who hides himself) are called by the community in times of drought to bring about rain. And in contrast to Ḥoni, both react very modestly. They hide from the public, and attribute their power over the rain not themselves, but to God.[179] In contrast to Ḥoni, the power of his grandchildren is specifically attributed in these anecdotes to their modest and pious character. This, in fact, is the main statement that the Babylonian Talmud is making in its cycle of miracle workers: it establishes a close link between miracles and piety. An ignorant public can, in fact, attribute the descendants of Ḥoni with the hereditary qualities of a family of magicians, but the Babylonian Talmud portrays them as pious, in order to account for their supernatural powers. It needs to do this because neither of them were rabbis. Piety (Hebrew: *ṣadikut*) enables the Babylonian Talmud to construct a new theodicy around the figure of the miracle worker. A priori, the Mesopotamian rabbis develop a type of totem that is very similar to the early Christian ascetics, whose high degree of piety enables society to control nature. However, a closer examination will reveal a unique type of theodicy from which asceticism, both on the public and the individual levels, has been totally removed.

The hagiographic cycle in the Babylonian Talmud describes rabbis who prevent shaky walls from falling down, others who bring rain in time of drought, or who turn dust to magic powder.[180] There are rabbis who make trees grow fruits, turn sand into fine flour, or fill barns with wheat. Others turn people to rich and poor, and can change the form of another human being. There is a rabbi whose angry words can kill his own children, and pious men and women who stop plague and fire, or fill an empty oven with bread. Just like their contemporary Christian saints, these figures perform miracles for both the public and individuals. The fact that we are dealing here with miracles is specified by the use of the Hebrew term *nes*. The phrase "knowledgeable/educated in miracles" (Hebrew: *melumad/et benisim*) is used occasionally throughout the cycle to indicate the reputation that a certain man or woman has acquired as a miracle worker. However, no specific method is noted for the miracle to happen. Some miracles are brought about deliberately by the rabbi or the pious person, but most of them occur without the miracle worker's knowledge, thanks to his or her piety. Sometimes this is attributed to the presence of the prophet Elijah, or to God who makes the miracle on behalf of the pious person. But most of the time the miracle just happens with no mention of a deliberate hand. This is significant because here lies the essence of the theodicy that the Babylonian Talmud means to establish: miracles happen as a reward for piety and righteousness. Such, for instance, is the following story about the plague that hits the city of Sura. Only one neighborhood is spared because an anonymous man who lived there handed out his hoe for the burial of others, without thinking about the danger he risked in time of plague.[181] His piety thus not only protected himself but also his surroundings.[182] While the people of Sura attributed the miracle to Rav, it was revealed to them that Rav's level of righteousness is too great for such a petty thing.

If the Palestinian Talmud concludes that miracles depend on the behavior of the community, and not on that of individuals, the Babylonian Talmud teaches the opposite lesson: the level of the piety of individuals determines the level of protection for their society. At the basis of this lesson we find the same premise that piety and righteousness restore the balance in nature for the community because calamities are punishment for its unrighteousness. However, the Babylonian Talmud constructs this premise entirely on the individual level, and not on the public. What we see here is a new theodicy of reward and punishment, which is indeed social, but is based on the behavior of individuals, mainly rabbis. It is calculated according to acts of piety that rabbis consciously perform for their communities.[183] The Babylonian Talmud even draws here a scale of piety for the social deeds that people do for their communities. These deeds comprise almsgiving, distribution of food and money to the poor, ransoming of captives, regulation of marketing, teaching the Torah to small children, protecting the modesty of others, protecting the community from foreigners, and any kind of deeds that are done for the benefit of the public.

If we go back to the idea of the ascetic or the saint as a totem, we see that the Babylonian Talmud structures a new kind of totem, whose piety (i.e., social behavior) also acts on the level of nature. The piety of individual rabbis guarantees the balance of nature for the community. The fact that the objective here is to create a new theodicy, different from both that of *Mishnah Ta'anit* and that of tractate *Ta'anit* in the Palestinian Talmud, is clearly manifested in the aphorisms that the Babylonian Talmud quotes all through this hagiographic cycle. These sayings aim at explaining the theodicy that lies at the basis of the different hagiographic anecdotes, and thus mark the Babylonian Talmud's innovation in constructing a new type of totem for the community. This is the case, for instance, with the saying that it is not "the place" that bestows honor on individuals, but individuals on "the place," meaning that it is the pious who bestows their rights on their surroundings.[184] This is the opposite view to the one expressed in the Palestinian Talmud.[185] The editors of the Babylonian Talmud are totally conscious in their aim of constructing a new model of theodicy, when they emphasize the differences between the rabbis in Mesopotamia and Palestine in the way they react in time of drought: whereas the rabbis in Mesopotamia make a public statement that they will assemble to ask for rain, the rabbis in Palestine do this in secret, so that they will not be credited for the rain when it comes.[186] Thus the Babylonian Talmud affirms that in both cases rain comes thanks to the rabbis, and eliminates any need for the public ritual of collective asceticism. Moreover, it also raises a doubt about the practice of individual asceticism as a public means, when it quotes Rabbi Yose's statement that individuals are not allowed to torment themselves with fasting and other measures of self-denial, so that they will not be a burden on the public, which may not have mercy on them.[187] This is in complete contradiction to the Palestinian Talmud's attitude that rain is also brought by means of suffering (Hebrew: *issurin*).[188]

Indeed, the Babylonian Talmud completely abolishes the need for any kind of asceticism as a means of repentance. It cites the same story as in the Palestinian Talmud about the two rabbis who decree a *ta'anit* in time of drought, where one succeeded and the other did not.[189] However, the conclusion of the Babylonian Talmud is totally different from that of the Palestinian Talmud. The Palestinian Talmud concluded that rain comes or does not come because of the public, and not because of the rabbi. In the Babylonian Talmud, the story ends with the rabbi (here Rabbi Ḥama bar Ḥanina) ordering the sky to produce clouds. Only when this fails, and he declares that the sky is stubborn, do the rains come. In fact, in the Babylonian Talmud the power of the rabbi over nature can be so great that rains come just so that he will not be troubled with ascetic practices.[190]

The rabbis were involved in magic, and the very fact that the phrase "learned in miracles" (Hebrew: *melumad benisim/n*) is used of some of them reflects the capacity to either be knowledgeable (*melumad*) or to study these skills. We cannot differentiate between the concepts of magic and miracle working by their public versus individual character. Many miracles that the Babylonian Talmud describes are also performed on behalf of individuals. The main difference between magic and miracle, we see here, lies in the fact that the definition of supernatural phenomena as miracles is aimed at setting up and maintaining a theodicy. Although it is also defined as a way of controlling nature, the use of magic is not part of a moral conceptualization of nature. A theodicy makes nature affect and be affected by the social, with a direct relationship to human behavior. This is precisely why miracle is an intervention in nature that restores the just balance, meaning the moral balance between nature and society.[191]

Totemism, Theodicy, and Abnormality

Our analysis of the hagiographic cycle in tractate *Ta'anit* in the Babylonian Talmud revealed the way in which collective asceticism, formed and defined in second-century Palestine as a public ritual of repentance, was recontextualized in Mesopotamian Judaism in view of other social uses of asceticism.[192] A priori, the Babylonian Talmud introduces a completely new model by eliminating any need for public or private, collective or individual, asceticism. However, at the core of the discussion we find a close link between the rabbis' piety in relation to the community, and their capacity to save it by controlling nature. Piety thus equals the control of nature. We may also conclude that the same is true the other way around: controlling nature equals piety. Any supernatural intervention by the rabbis on behalf of the public is taken as a form of piety in itself, because piety in its social sense—defining and protecting the individual as part of the community—is here the main objective. This equation creates theodicy, while the miracle is simply a means of justifying and legitimizing this objective by employing nature.

According to the same reasoning, asceticism also appears to be a social means. It is not asceticism that provides the person with the capacity to perform miracles. It is the social need to control nature that finds a medium in the abnormal behavior of self-denial, and constructs it as a religious phenomenon: "asceticism." In both cases, the objective is to generate a psychological effect on the individual as part of a society which is linked to nature. The individual is thus connected to nature—affects it and is affected by it—through society. Whether this is attained through collective ritual of repentance, an individual ascetic figure, one's own asceticism, or piety toward the community, it provides the society with means of defining itself and its culture vis-à-vis nature, and making the individual a part of both society and nature. This is the reason why we have used the term "totem." It is the only model that can clarify that the relationship between man and nature and the relationship between man and the social are inseparable.

Lévi-Strauss has refuted the idea of the totem as the incarnation of both the relationship between man and nature and the cultural relationship between man and the group in a given society.[193] He has shown that the function of the totem is not to separate between groups, but to express the way in which the group portrays itself vis-à-vis nature. All the cases that were analyzed in this chapter show that the link between the relationship of man and culture and the relationship of man and nature is directed toward the creation of a theodicy through the totem's functioning on both the social and the psychological levels.

Asceticism proves here to be a powerful social tool precisely because it is performed on both the psychological and natural or biological levels. It is no wonder that it acquired such an important place in the period under examination. It offered a very *natural* method to generate a new theodicy by harmonizing society and its new culture with nature, and at the same time the individual with the collective. The ascetic itself proves to be here no more than a social function. The question about the motives, intentions, or consciousness of people in following the ascetic way is secondary for this purpose. The main question is what needs made them important. In comparison to Jewish communities that looked for protection and stabilization vis-à-vis nature and God, Christian communities needed a process of psychological transformation, cultural and social creation to attain the same objective. With this end, they found their totems in individual ascetics, whose abnormal/"pathological" behavior they defined in hagiographic narratives. The fact that ascetic behavior was abnormal both socially and biologically made such figures perfect totems of transformation.

To Conclude

Asceticism, which appears a priori as an individual phenomenon, the personal experience of an individual connecting to God, is made, by the hagiographic construction of a new moral framework connecting the cultural within nature, a public means of repentance in order to restore control, order, and balance in nature. But in fact, its objective is to transform society through nature. The miracle enables the functioning of asceticism as totemism. It acts on both private and public levels, and in this way connects man to society via nature. This means that the relationship of man and nature forms a single whole with the relationship of man and culture. For this purpose we have used the term "totem" here although these ascetic totems are human beings.

In order to change the cultural—asceticism shows us—humans transform their relationship to nature. People who act in "unnatural" and unsocial ways, such as the ascetics, could be used in order to generate a social movement. Their abnormal behavior is thus defined, not pathologically, but metaphysically as a control over nature. The need to find persons who control God's nature as a social means of transformation defined such abnormal behavior as a control over one's own body and nature. Such figures are chosen by society precisely because of their abnormality. They become symbols of breaking and changing social and cultural norms, and are thus used in order to generate a change. Early

Christian labeling of torments of the body as "asceticism" defined abnormal behavior within a moral framework, and enabled believers to relate to and control nature by moral conduct. Their contemporaneous rabbinic communities, which had no desire for change, simply attributed the control of nature to their pious rabbis excluding any inclination toward the abnormal.

EPILOGUE

Psychology, Religion, and Social Change

> When you stand before it, you see yourself, but not as you would in an ordinary mirror. You don't see your outward appearance; what you see is your real innermost nature. If you want to go through, you have to—in a manner of speaking—go into yourself.
>
> —Michael Ende, *The Neverending Story*

This book started with the assertion that we can never know whether true holy fools really existed in Byzantine Christianity, that is, whether real sane people simulated insanity as a spiritual practice. What is important, however, is that Byzantine society created this phenomenon of "faked insanity" as a cultural construction in order to open a zone of ambiguity in religious experience. From this perspective, holy fools exist once society defines them as such, while leaving the ontology of their abnormality intentionally unclear. The main question is to what end?

The previous chapters explored the scholarship, mainly of the twentieth century, which dealt with such phenomena. It is vital to go back to the beginning of this scholarship in order to understand the importance of the study of religion as a nexus between sociology, anthropology, and psychology, a study for which history serves as the main instrument of analysis. As far as the study of religion is concerned, we saw that the holy fool was not unique, but merely a particular sort of cultural phenomena of abnormal behavior, such as acts of self-denial and desire to die, created and formed as sanctified phenomena. These, of course, are not the only people who were sanctified. Many more "normal" types of saint existed in the same societies. However, as the previous chapters have shown, the abnormal behavior of certain figures was particularly functional, and was sanctified for good reason. The aim of their sanctification was to give a new meaning to religious experience, and through it to create and transform society. The ambiguity of the religious experience that such figures symbolized was the motor through which mental, political, social, and cultural changes could be generated. We saw this in the figure of martyrs, whose voluntary death was invented as a testimony for the inversion of accepted and rejected norms in both the political and mental fields. We also saw it in the figure of ascetics, whose abnormal behavior was invented within the framework of the relationship between nature and culture, in order to construct new theodicies for new societies, which would give them the affirmation they needed within the world of nature to transform themselves. We also saw it in sanctified insanity which came to be a symbol of a much larger ambiguity, needed to produce a change of mentality and perception of reality. By translating it into the practical social field, such figures incarnated in themselves the ambiguity of religious experience, rendering it functional and utilizable for society.

Religious Virtuosity

Ever since the works of Émile Durkheim, religion has become a unique prism for understanding the rationale for and the organization of the social environment. A fundamental touchstone was Max Weber's *The Sociology of Religion*, in which religion came to have a key role in explaining the elasticity of the social organization. In this study Weber coined the term "religious virtuosi" in order to explain the function of charismatic figures as means for changing the social order. Figures of religious virtuosity, such as ascetic monks and holy men and women, became one of the means of understanding how the dynamics of the social organization worked. By presenting an alternative to the social establishment, the charismatic leadership of these virtuosi challenged the established authority. The fact that their success was dependent on their ability to incarnate a larger social desire for change was exactly what made them leaders, that is, functional to their society. Religion, therefore, was understood as a vital aspect of the social organization, not only because it provided the psychological means for connecting the individual to society and its values, but also because it left an undefined space as a means of change. We have named it here "the ambiguous space of religious experience."

Weber paved the way not only for understanding the social functionality of religion, but also for understanding it within the framework of the power relations at play within a given society. Throughout the past century, society has been perceived and analyzed as a playground of power relations. Most of the studies that have focused on the social role of such religious phenomena and "religious virtuosi"—whether sanctified or not, whether or not we call them saints—understood them as a means for stabilizing, dynamizing, and symbolizing changes in the power relations that constitute the social structure. This is the case, for instance, with Ioan M. Lewis's *Ecstatic Religion,* where religion enables ecstatic experiences whose role is to act as a valve within the social organization. This is also the case in studies that look at holy figures as new patrons in a changing environment, as well as in studies that concentrate on sanctity as means of changing the social structure between center and periphery (adopting Victor Turner's modeling of "liminality").[1] Whether scholars see such religious figures and such religious phenomena as a means of change, stability, protection, or conflict management, they analyze them through the prism of social order and power relations. This, of course, makes a great deal of sense.

Nevertheless, by focusing mainly on the dynamics of social organization through the prism of power relations, these studies left out a particularly important aspect of the social organization, which is the role of interdependence within society and its importance to both the individual and the collective. This is the way in which society functions as a living organism through infinite relations of *interdependence,* to borrow a concept from group psychology (Kurt Lewin, Siegfried Foulkes).[2] The dynamics of social organization could not be merely the product of the ways in which power relations operate. As the analysis of religious phenomena in the previous chapters has shown, it also depends on psychological relations and the ways in which they situate the individual as part of the social, cultural, and cosmic fabric, as well as the conditions that change this fabric. The present study tried to bridge the incommensurability of psychology and history by using what seems the common perspective of analysis of historical societies and group psychology. This is particularly important to the analysis of the mechanism by which religious societies operate.

The present study has identified a zone of ambiguity around the definition of normality and abnormality, sanity and insanity, which worked within the religious experience of the evolving Byzantine society.[3] This zone of ambiguity plays a decisive role in the psychological dimension that forms the social. It makes it forever open and forever elastic, thanks to the ambiguity of the definition of abnormality and insanity as deviancy. The great theories in social psychology of the twentieth century by and large failed to explain this aspect of social evolution. They failed because most of them translated their psychological analysis from the individual level into the collective level. It was for group psychology, group analysis, and family psychology to rise to the challenge.

From the Holy Fool to the "Identified Patient"—A Case of Group Analysis

The previous chapters have shown the dynamics of social organization to be dependent on group psychology as much as on power relations. Of course, group psychology is also related to political organization and power distribution, as modern studies about the development of psychiatry have revealed.[4] Nevertheless, it has more functions than just the political aspect of social life.

The figure of the holy fool, as Chapter 2 has shown, presents not only as a symptom of the problems in Byzantine society but also as their means of change. In this, the holy fool acts as a mirror in the objective of transforming the social. The abnormality of the martyr is constructed in order to reflect a new type of mentality and a new perception of reality onto society, reversing the earlier norms of conduct, while the abnormality of the ascetic is constructed in order to connect the individual through nature to a new society. The very meaning of abnormality is here reversed by society. By looking up to these figures as "abnormal," not in the negative but the positive sense of the term, their society sanctifies them in order to justify and affirm the changes in the group that can be read in them. Unlike all other types of abnormality, the abnormality of sanctified insanity is concealed, unclear, and ambiguous, and thus leaves the decision between holiness and insanity to the beholder. The holy fool was constructed in this way in order to make it possible to read the symptoms of both individual and collective wrongs in Byzantine society.

The idea of personifying the symptoms of group behavior is familiar from family and group psychology, which has called this sort of figure "the identified patient."[5] The idea of the *identified patient* (the IP) is that an individual is unconsciously chosen in a family group as an emblematic figure to carry and personify the psychological problems within the family group.[6] Whether this individual becomes an identified patient through a "double bind" or in other different ways, it is clear that in group analysis individual abnormality is read as a collective symptom, mainly of the malfunctioning of this individual's group of origin (mostly the family).[7] Therapeutic strategies consist of providing individuals with a new setting through which they can be freed from their "role" as the identified patient. In individual-based therapy, this is done through the relationship between the patient and the therapist. In group therapy, this is done through a therapeutic group that enables individuals to experience themselves in a different human setting, as members of a different group.[8] Moreover, in the second case, the function of an identified patient in the therapeutic group can produce a collective change of this other group.[9] But, in either case, the therapeutic process pulls the individuals out of their group of origin. Of course, treating the group of origin itself is not always possible. It is more possible in family group therapy.[10]

Within the framework of a new therapeutic group, the integration and the dynamics between individuals and the group become a strategy of the therapist.[11] To put it differently, the identified patient is made here an object of therapy of the group, and vice versa[12]—so that the group becomes an object of therapy of the identified patient. The individual psychological difficulties appear here as an instrument of objectification of both the individual and the collective. In group psychological theories, this objectification is what enables therapeutic strategies of group psychology. These strategies are conditioned by the objectification of the collective or the group. However, the process of objectification through the identified patient, that is, through the abnormal member of the group, exists, regardless of their use. In other words, identifying abnormality within the social field objectifies the individual as well as the group. In group psychology strategies this objectification is used as means of psychological healing.[13]

In "The Group as an Object in the Cultural Field," Lawrence Jacobson articulated the need for using the group as a medium of therapy by constituting it as an object in the cultural field. He used the term "cultural" because he identified the psychotherapy group as a small temporary society with a therapeutic purpose. In his words, individuals can use the group as means of *play* in order to produce a change in the ways in which they relate to others.[14] Jacobson refers here to the psychotherapeutic group, but his insight can be used when we try to understand the social role of sanctified abnormality as a medium of *play*, that is, as a therapeutic instrument in historical context. The functioning of the group, the *interdependence* between its members, depends on communication.[15] And here ambiguity holds a special importance.

Donald Levine has argued for the important role of ambiguity in language and discourse as a means of rendering both culture and society dynamic.[16] He has shown the post-Cartesian scientific discourse to be centered on rendering language unambiguous, which to his mind is not only useless but completely wrong. Nonetheless, he does not refer to the role of the individual in group dynamics. In fact, he does not refer to the psychological dimension at all. But, ambiguity is extremely important to group psychology precisely because it affects the relationship between the individual and the group, and changes the group's behavior in relation to the individual and to itself. In other words, we have to focus here not on any behavioral ambiguity but on how an individual behavioral ambiguity is interpreted and affects the group. This is exactly what I have aimed to do in the previous chapters. To put it differently, the role of ambiguity seems here to enable what we could term a "social reflexive treatment."

Yvonne Agazarian developed Systems-Centered Therapy by applying Claude Shannon and Warren Weaver's mathematical theory of communication and Alan Howard and Robert Scott's theory of stress to her group psychology.[17] Ambiguity, noise, and chaos are perceived as failures and impediments to communication within groups that result in malfunctioning.[18] This is, of course, very logical in theories that attribute a major role to communication within the group (e.g., Foulkes). But, what we see in the Byzantine "Theater of Cruelty" of the sanctified abnormal behavior is exactly the reverse phenomenon: a social failure of one individual (the insane person, the fool, the martyr, the ascetic) is adopted as a symbol of ambiguity for the entire group. This, in turn, does not create any rupture in communication, but is used to transform the language of normal or accepted communication into a different kind of communication. In other words, the group chooses its identified patient as a mirror whose function is to produce a change. This is the main feature of sanctified abnormality, no matter what type. It plays on the undefined zone between sanity and insanity. To us it seems not only a cruel abuse of the insane person but also far from the experience of groups that we know and refer to. However, in societies that use religion as means of change this is a common aspect, which has social, cultural, and political roles to play. If we like to push this further, we should ask whether any common feature can be detected between such religious societies and modern group psychology.

A priori it would seem that group psychology is aimed in a totally different direction. A change that heals the identified patient, will also restore the identified patient's group of origin back to its normal behavior. Here we detect a major difference between modern group psychology and the functioning of a religious society. While the first aims to fix what went wrong in the social matrix, the religious environment that sanctifies insanity employs this wrong as means of transforming the social matrix, as means of collective change. If we look at the situation from a functionalistic point of view this is indeed a major difference, since psychology's objective is to correct the unhealthy environmental conditions of the psychological development of either the individual or the group. In contrast, in the cases analyzed in this book, abnormal behavior on the individual level is not "corrected," but serves as means of collective change. The ambiguous "noise" enables the group to develop and introduce a new mentality, a new interpretation of its world and to transform itself, its perception of reality, and its reality. By projecting new values and new perception of reality onto such "noise," society makes "noise" meaningful, and the perception of reality changes by using ambiguity about insanity as a mirror. Here the image of the mirror as a symbol of the ambiguity between the sane and the insane is telling and will help us to understand the psychological value of sanctifying such "identified patients."

The Mirror Effect and the Ambiguity Effect

In a foundational article from 1967, Donald Winnicott develops the idea of the mirror in the mother-baby relationship, where the baby needs its mother's eye contact as the mirror in which it can first perceive itself.[19] This mirroring is the first and most fundamental stage in psychological development. If something goes wrong and the parent cannot see the baby with the perception that the baby needs, the baby's perception of its *self* will develop abnormally. This represents a break from Freudian analysis, and forms the basis for any relational psychological perspective. Though object-relational, Winnicott's idea was explained and interpreted as interpersonal by Thomas Ogden. The mother-infant unit develops into interpersonal relationship in which the infant's perception of the mother as object (first internal and then external object) forms the basis of the infant's subjectivity.[20] If something goes wrong in this process, the infant's subjectivity will develop abnormally.[21]

This reading of Winnicott's model as interpersonal can also demonstrate the first stage of the creation of an identified patient, whose unhealthy psychological development in babyhood reflects the distorted image of its *self* that this baby received from its parent. In this way, we can elaborate, the infant is also a mirror in itself: as it grows, it reflects and projects back onto the parent the perception of its self and the image of the parent-infant relationship that it received.[22] Thus the mother will see herself as a mother in the eyes of her baby once the baby develops a reflection of its own. This is the infinite nature of the functioning of an interpersonal mirroring: being relational and interpersonal, it is forever dyadic. As much as the baby depends on the mother for its perception of its self, the mother, Jessica Benjamin shows, also depends on its reflection and recognition in order to perceive herself as a mother. Parents know, of course, that they are the parents of their baby. But since parenting is a relational association, they are in need of the approval of the object which they are parenting. In other words, the mirror that the baby gets in its parent's eye contact is answered by a second mirror, which reflects back not only the baby's selfhood but also the affirmation of its being related to the parent. This is why the baby's capacity to recognize the parent is so primal to the parent. Parents do not look for any kind of recognition from the baby except for the recognition of them*selves*.[23] This is also why the parent gives so much importance to the baby's first naming of the parent, the first uttering of "mom" and "dad." These are the stages when the mirror is reflected back, and parents can perceive themselves as parents. This relationship is fundamental to the psychological development of the baby, and it is also fundamental to the parent. Depressive parents, or parents who have problems in seeing themselves as parents, will undoubtedly get a different look back, as a token that something went wrong in this double-mirroring connection: miscommunication or malfunctioning. This is because in this case the parent has unconsciously prevented the healthy mirroring of parenthood.[24]

In his article from 1960, "The Theory of the Parent-Infant Relationship," Winnicott compares the parent-infant relationship to the therapist-patient relationship. The therapeutic encounter acts in a similar way, by producing a mirror which projects to the patient the new self-reflection that is needed in order to change self-perception. The point where the therapist needs to confront the projection of the patient through countertransference is crucial here.[25] This is the moment when a change in the self-perception of the patient is possible through the therapist's perception of the patient. In contrast to Freud, who gave a limited role to countertransference, Winnicott constructs it as the touchstone for any relational psychological perspective.[26] What Winnicott shows us here is that this dyadic relationship (parent-infant or therapist-patient) is what enables evolution, process, development, and change in the psychological dimension as a product of the social and relational dimension. In his treatment of schizophrenics, Harold Searles names this dynamic between patient and therapist "ambivalently symbiotic relatedness."[27] He goes even up to the point of defining the therapeutic process as a mutual two-way process. For Searles, the patient has "therapeutic strivings" that must be fulfilled in order for the therapeutic process to work. In other words, it is for the patient to change the therapist in order to be changed in return.[28] We find the same function of the therapeutic mirror in Foulkes's theory of group analysis. In order to change the way in which persons perceive themselves, he says, there is a need for "mirror reactions," which act within the "foundation matrix" of the group.[29] In theories of group analysis, any dyadic relationship is understood as part of a larger nexus of multidimensional relationships acting within the group. Here too, development and change—any change—in the psychological dimension are products of the social and relational dimension.[30] This is also how the ambiguity of abnormality functions in a religious environment.

The religious societies we have examined in the previous chapters did not care in particular about abnormal persons; nevertheless, they used them as instruments for their evolution. In fact, the study of the previous chapters suggests that this *is* the main function, the raison d'être even, of the religious environment: rendering abnormality or insanity socially functional. We have emphasized that abnormality is sanctified for different objectives, all of which concern the creation, affirmation, and transformation of the religious environment. The main objective of sanctified abnormality is to use the abnormal behavior of an individual as society's *identified patient* for the purpose of a collective transformation. In this, we perceived ambiguity to have a primal role because it enables the employment of individual insane state for a collective need. Looking at it in a relational perspective, this ambiguity creates a new type of relationship between the insane individual and the group. The abnormal person—any abnormal person—can indeed be a saint. This means that this ambiguity prevents any establishment of power relationship between the two sides. The beholders can never know whether the figure of abnormality is really insane and they themselves are sane, or whether they are "the patients" in a spiritual endeavor of a religious virtuoso in the role of a "therapist," who conveys a new code of truth to their society. This is why any evolution—and indeed real change—becomes possible. It is this ambiguous dyadic relationship that facilitates a mental change.

In the moving dedication of *Play and Reality*, Winnicott expresses his gratitude "to my patients who have paid to teach me." What he writes is, of course, also true of Freud's patients. However, Winnicott's acknowledgment that his patients have changed him is a recognition not only of the mechanism of transference and countertransference, but also of the ability of the patient to contribute to and change the therapist. To Harold Searles and Philip Bromberg, this is a necessary phase of the symbiotic process of therapy. This is not to say that we could equate the Byzantine holy man with the modern patient. However, we can observe that the idea of sanctified insanity works precisely on this dyadic relationship. The ambiguity that prevents us from knowing whether the person is insane ("patient") or a saint ("therapist") is what allows the communication between the two sides—the insane and their society—to be open to interpretation and to produce a change. To put it differently, the zone of ambiguity between insanity and holiness enables Winnicott's mirroring concept to function in both ways: communicating with such a person, one can consider him as a patient or a therapist. The consequence is that in such a society the beholders can never know for sure whether they themselves are normal or abnormal. In fact, this interpersonal relationship is all about seeing the patient as both.

Winnicott's ability to absorb and hold back the countertransference that he received from his patients is what enabled them to perceive themselves differently through the mirror of their therapist's eyes.[31] This reflects also the difference between group psychological theories and the way in which a religious environment functions. The first see the individual symptoms as reflecting a disturbance in the group that can be "cured" or "healed." In contrast, cases of sanctified abnormality are not alienated or cured, but are used as means of evolution of the group in a sort of a "Theater of Cruelty." In other words, psychology as it has evolved from medicine perceives the mental disturbance as a "noise," a sickness that needs to be cured. It is constructed with the objective of eliminating this "noise" by restoring the situation to "normality," stability. In contrast, sanctified abnormality precludes the notion of a stable and well-defined "normality," and aims to normalize the abnormal. This does not mean to change the abnormal to the normal, but the other way around. The zone of ambiguity between normality and abnormality is what enables society to transform itself. Alienating and curing are not the only ways of treating the abnormal person: there is also the option of using abnormality by legitimizing abnormal behavior in the framework of sanctification, and in this way to disturb, up-set, and transform normality.

We see here exactly what religion has that psychology does not. Psychology aims to cure patients and to make them "normal." But the study of religion shows us that a human environment requires an open definition of what is defined as sanity and insanity. This psychological aspect is what enables this environment to develop. Sanctifying abnormality provides the means of challenging the dichotomy between group and individual, life and death, nature and culture in order to produce a collective change.

The present study has shown the vitality that the ambiguity between sanity and insanity—indeed religion—provides for society by making it a living organism through the psychological dimension of the social fabric. Any social group is a living organism that cannot stop evolving.

In the period of great changes that transformed the world of antiquity, Christian societies found a way to use abnormal behavior as a mirror in order to project the required conditions for their evolution. The sanctification of abnormal behavior served them as means of change by playing on the ambiguity that they created between madness and holiness. In fact, we can argue that this is their particular and important feature, even their definition as "religious societies."

In this study we have followed the analysis of sanctification of different forms of social behavior, which are considered abnormal to us today and were considered as such also in their time. We have revealed the functionality of such figures, and made them relevant to our own lives. Our conclusion should not incite us to use insanity, to make it functional in a sort of a "Theater of Cruelty," or to sanctify it in a similar ways to the societies under examination. Our conclusion should lead us all the same to appropriate insanity, and look at it, with it and in it, with no fear. It is not our only means of change. It is, nevertheless, our only mirror.

Abbreviations

AASS *Acta Sanctorum*, 71 vols. Paris: Société des Bollandistes, 1863–1940.

BHG Halkin, *Bibliotheca hagiographica graeca troisième edition*. Brussels: Société des Bollandistes, 1957.

BT Babylonian Talmud, *Responsa Project: version 17+*. Ramat Gan: Bar Ilan University, 2009 (Vilnius: Romm, 1880–1886).

CCSL *Corpus Christianorum, Series Latina*.

CJ *Corpus Juris Civilis II: Codex Justinianus*, ed. Paul Krüger. Berlin: Weidmann, 1997 (1954).

CPJ *Corpus Papyrorum Judaicarum*, eds. Victor A. Tcherikover, Alexander Fuks. 3 vols. Cambridge, MA: Harvard University Press, 1957–1964.

CSEL *Corpus Scriptorum Ecclesiasticorum Latinorum*.

CSCO *Corpus Scriptorum Christianorum Orientalium*.

DSM *Diagnostic and Statistical Manual of Mental Disorders—DSM-5-TM* (fifth ed.). Washington, DC: American Psychiatric Publishing, 2013.

SC Sources Chrétiennes.

PG *Patrologiae cursus completus. Series Graeca*, ed. J. P. Migne, 161 vols. in 199 pts. Paris: 1857–1866.

PO *Patrologiae Orientalis*, eds. Graffin and Nau, Paris: 1904– .

PT Palestinian Talmud, ed. Yaacov Sussmann, *Talmud Yerushalmi: According to Ms. Or. 4720 (Scal. 3) of the Leiden University Library with Restorations and Corrections*. Jerusalem: The Academy of the Hebrew Language, 2001.

Notes

Prologue: Insanity and Religion

1. I am using both terms—"insanity" and "madness"—throughout this book as synonyms of the single French term *folie.* I use insanity when the context refers to an opposition to sanity, and madness otherwise.
2. See Foucault, *Les anormaux: Cours au Collège de France. 1974–1975.*

1. The Paradox That Inhabits Ambiguity

Epigraph: Laing, *The Divided Self,* p. 27.

1. Grosdidier de Matons, "Les Thèmes d'édification dans la Vie d'André Salos," pp. 279–292. Krueger, *Symeon the Holy Fool,* p. 63, n. 14. Ivanov, *Holy Fools in Byzantium and Beyond,* pp. 31–38.
2. Cf. Hosea 9:7: "The days of punishment are coming; the days of reckoning are at hand. Let Israel know this; because your sins are so many and your hostility so great, the prophet is considered a fool, the inspired person a maniac" (Hebrew: *evil hanavi' meshug'a ish haru'ḥ*). See the Babylonian Talmud: "Rabbi Yoḥanan said: From the day of the destruction of the Temple, prophecy was taken from the prophets and was given to the fools (*šoṭim*) and to the infants (*tinokot*)" (BT, *Bava Batra* 12b), which concerns the prophetic quality of the rabbis themselves. This passage starts with a quote from Rabbi Avdimi of Haifa who said that "from the day of the destruction of the Temple prophecy was taken from the prophets and was given to the sages" (loc. cit.).

3. Cf. 1 Cor. 1:25: "because the foolishness (*to mōron*) of God is wiser than men; and the weakness (*to asthenes*) of God is stronger than men."
4. See Jesus's own simulation of ecstasy in Mark 3:21.
5. Note that Paul contrasts folly (Greek: *mōria*) with wisdom (*sophia*), as well as with being sensible (*phronimos*), but not with reason (*noos*).
6. *The Sayings of the Desert Fathers*, trans. Wortley, pp. 60–63, 4211 (viii.31, vol. 1, p. 420). On the same question of "how to become a *mōros* in this world?" see PG 31:1272c.
7. *The Sayings of the Desert Fathers*, viii.32 (vol. 1, pp. 420–424, cf. PO 8:178–179).
8. This is, for instance, the case of the monk who puts stones in two different baskets, the monk who mixes salty water with drinking water, or the monk who buries gold coins: loc. cit. Ibid., viii.13 (vol. 1, p. 408). John Moschus, *Spiritual Meadow*, ch. 111 (pp. 162–163).
9. Cf. the abnormal behavior of Abba Ḥilkiyah, the son of Ḥoni's daughter, in BT *Ta'anit* 23a–b. Unlike a Christian *salos*, he explains his strange behavior to the beholders in the end of the story. See a parallel story in PT *Ta'anit* 1:4 (64b–c, Sussmann, p. 708) about an anonymous holy man (*ḥasid*). For an analysis, see Kalmin, "Holy Men, Rabbis, and Demonic Sages in Late Antiquity," pp. 222–234.
10. Palladius, *Lausiac History*, ch. 34 (pp. 162–166); also trans. Meyer, pp. 96–98 (with my alterations). See also *The Athenian Corpus of Saint Pachomius*, p. 97 (=*De monacha "Sala"*). Cf. *Saint Daniel of Sketis*, pp. 140–147 (story 5: "The Woman Who Pretended to Be a Drunkard").
11. De Certeau, "Le Silence de l'Absolu."
12. Lifshitz, "Beyond Positivism and Genre." Papaconstantinou, Debié, and Kennedy, eds., *Writing "True Stories."* Rapp, "The Origins of Hagiography and the Literature of Early Monasticism."
13. Leontius of Neapolis, *Life of Symeon salos*. Krueger, *Symeon the Holy Fool*. Déroche, *Études sur Léontios de Néapolis*. Mango, "A Byzantine Hagiographer at Work."
14. Ivanov, *Holy Fools in Byzantium and Beyond*, ch. 3.
15. Krueger, *Symeon the Holy Fool*. Déroche, *Études sur Léontios de Néapolis*. Mango, "A Byzantine Hagiographer at Work."
16. Evagrius Scholasticus, *Ecclesiastical History*, i.21 (p. 200).
17. Ibid. iv.34 (vol. 2, pp. 168-172), trans. Whitby, p. 238 (with my alterations).
18. *Life of Andrew the Fool*, vol. 1., pp. 27–71. Mango, "The Life of Saint Andrew the Fool Reconsidered." Rydén, "The Date of the Life of Andreas Salos."
19. The story about the nun came down to us in three versions: (1) the Tabennesiot nun in Palladius, *Lausiac History*, ch. 34 (pp. 162–166) and *The Athenian Corpus of Saint Pachomius*, p. 97; (2) the drunkard nun in a convent in Hermopolis in *Saint Daniel of Sketis*, pp. 140–147; and (3) Onesima in *Select Narratives of Holy Women from the Syro-Antiochene or Sinai Palimpsest*, pp. 81–93 (=*Life of Onesima*, fs. 85b–91b). Leontius of Neapolis, *Life of Symeon salos*.

Rydén, *Life of Andrew the Fool.* For Paul of Corinth (*BHG* 2362), see the first lines of his *Life* in Cod. Paris. 1452, f.227v, from the tenth century, as well as a short notice in the Synaxarion of Constantinople which does not provide much: *AASS Nov. III,* 130 a. Ehrhadr I, 570 (39). *Synaxarium Ecclesiae Constantinopolitanae,* p. 200, 495. Ivanov, *Holy Fools in Byzantium and Beyond,* pp. 142–147. *Saint Daniel of Sketis,* pp. 120–129 (Mark the Fool). John of Ephesus, *Lives of the Eastern Saints,* PO 82/17:64–65, 89/18:562–574, 92/19:183. PG 88:721a–d (=John of Climacus, *The Ladder of Divine Ascent,* step 4: "On Obedience"). *Life and Works of Saint Gregentios Archbishop of Taphar,* pp. 220–223, 238–240, 278, 324–328. Déroche, "Les variantes italiques de la folie en Christ."

20. Bell, *Holy Anorexia.* Kroll and Backrach, *The Mystic Mind.* Bushell, "Psychophysiological and Comparative Analysis of Ascetico-Meditational Discipline."
21. Gay, "Psychoanalysis in History."
22. Sacks, *Migraine,* ch. 3. Yarom, *Body, Blood, and Sexuality.*
23. William James had already expressed his opposition toward such an attitude in his *The Varieties of Religious Experience: A Study in Human Nature,* lecture I: "Religious and Neurology."
24. Two of the most characteristic examples in psychohistory are Erikson, *Young Man Luther: A Study in Psychoanalysis and History* and Scholem, *Sabbatai Ṣevi: The Mystical Messiah.* See also Freud's 1923 analysis in "A Seventeenth-Century Demonological Neurosis."
25. Porter, *A Social History of Madness,* p. 88, in reference to Freud's and others' interpretations of Haitzmann' pact with the devil (Freud, "A Seventeenth-Century Demonological Neurosis"): "All these psychiatric techniques of isolating figures like Haitzmann, putting them on the couch and diagnosing their problems can indeed become positively perverse. For doing so withdraws attention from the social, cultural, institutional, and linguistic environments which gave all their actions meaning."
26. For a social approach in psychohistory, see McKinley Runyan, "Reconceptualizing the Relationships between History and Psychology." For a theoretical discussion, see Hill and Kral, eds. *About Psychology: Essays at the Crossroads of History, Theory, and Philosophy.* For a general discussion of the problematic "instrumentalization" of both individual psychology and social psychology in the study of history, see Scott, "The Incommensurability of Psychoanalysis and History."
27. For a different approach, see Gianfrancesco, "Monachisme ancien et psychopathologie," which unravels the early Christian monastic notion of psychopathology and its treatment.
28. This line of investigation has been taken up by numerous scholars, beginning with John Saward, José Grosdidier de Matons, and Alexander Syrkin, and continuing more recently with Sergey Ivanov, Guy Stroumsa, and Andrew Thomas: Saward, *Perfect Fools;* Grosdidier de Matons, "Les Thèmes

d'édification dans la Vie d'André Salos" ; Syrkin, "On the Behavior of the 'Fools for Christ's Sake' "; Ivanov, *Holy Fools in Byzantium and Beyond*; Stroumsa, "Madness and Divinization in Early Christian Monasticism"; Thomas, *The Holy Fools*. Cf. Shoham-Steiner, "The Humble Sage and the Wandering Madman."

29. See Sinyavsky, *Ivan the Fool: Russian Folk Belief*. By putting the emphasis on the perceptions of the real and unreal worlds in Russian popular culture, Sinyavsky has unraveled a system of mentality in which "idiotism," or authentic folly (here rather than simulated holy madness), not only has precise meaning but also fills a defined cultural function.
30. I translate here the Syrian *šāṭyā* as an insane/madman in order to distinguish it from *saklā*, a fool/idiot, though the immediate Syrian term for madman is *šnāyā*. The *Peshiṭṭa* 1 Cor. 3:18 and 1 Cor. 4:10 uses *šnāyā* and *šāṭyṭyā*, respectively. See Sokoloff, *A Syriac Lexicon*, p. 1548, for the *Peshiṭṭa* using *šāṭyā* for the Hebrew bible's term of madman (*mešuga*ʿ). In transliterating the Syriac I used the Syriac Romanization of the Library of Congress: http://www.loc.gov/catdir/cpso/romanization/syriac.pdf (retrieved on March 20, 2014).
31. *The Book of Steps*, xvi.7 (ed. Kmosko, pp. 401–405), trans. Kitchen, Parmentier. See Thomas, *The Holy Fools*, p. 81. Ivanov, *Holy Fools in Byzantium and Beyond*, pp. 27–29.
32. *The Book of Steps*, xvi.8–9.
33. This is why I chose to translate Syriac *šāṭyā* as madman and not as fool (Greek: *mōros*). For *xeniteia*, see Guillaumont, "Le dépaysement comme forme d'ascèse, dans le monachisme ancien," especially p. 47 and n. 1 on the *peregrinatio* described in a poem of pseudo Ephrem. Déroche, *Études sur Léontios de Néapolis*, pp. 172–173 and n. 51.
34. This is different from the types of *xentieia* that Guillaumont analyzes in "Le dépaysement comme forme d'ascèse, dans le monachisme ancien." John of Ephesus, *Lives of the Eastern Saints*, PO 89/18:562–574. See Basil of Caesarea's answer on "How to become a *mōros* for this world?" PG 31:1272c (=Basil of Caesarea, *Regulae fusius tractate*, 274), p. 77, n. 13. The sixth-century correspondence between Barsanuphius and John underlines this; Barsanuphius and John of Gaza, *Letters*, no.185 (pp. 590–592).
35. Alternatively, as Gilbert Dagron explains in "L'homme sans honneur ou le saint scandaleux," the madman is someone who is devoid of honor (either from society or from within himself). See Thomas, *The Holy Fools*, p. 11, n. 12, and Ivanov, *Holy Fools in Byzantium and Beyond*, pp. 174–182.
36. Dagron, "L'homme sans honneur ou le saint scandaleux."
37. PG 88:721a–d. See Grosdidier de Matons, "Les Thèmes d'édification dans la Vie d'André Salos," p. 289, n. 39. Déroche, *Études sur Léontios de Néapolis*, pp. 171–172, n. 48.
38. *Saint Daniel of Sketis*, pp. 120–125. Note that Daniel refers to Mark as a vessel (Greek: *skeuos*), p. 122.

39. Logan, *The Medieval Historian and the Quest for Certitude.* I owe the following observations to a stimulating discussion with Susan Reynolds.
40. Leontius of Neapolis, *Life of Symeon salos,* p. 90 (p. 156).
41. Lévi-Strauss, "Le Sourcier et sa Magie."
42. Felman, *Writing and Madness,* ch. 7.
43. Wilson, "The Ambiguity of Henry James."
44. See Rimmon, *The Concept of Ambiguity—the Example of James,* ch. 5, who analyzes how the ambiguity is constructed on the literary level.
45. Felman, *Writing and Madness,* p. 159.
46. Ibid., p. 229.
47. Rimmon, *The Concept of Ambiguity—the Example of James,* ch. 5.
48. Rimmon analyzes how the ambiguity is produced on the literary level. Ibid.
49. *The Canons of the Council in Trullo,* can. 60 (p. 140). For the evidence see Agathias, *The Histories,* v.5.2 (p. 169), where people simulate demon possession.
50. Note that in Palladius's story about the *salē* (Palladius, *Lausiac History,* ch. 34, pp. 162–166), feigned folly and demon possession are synonyms. See Agathias, *The Histories,* v.5.2 (p. 169), and the following note.
51. This ambiguity is repeatedly stated in the *Life of Andrew the Fool* (see below). See the following characteristic examples: John of Ephesus, *Lives of the Eastern Saints,* PO 82/17:224–228; Theodoret of Cyrrhus, *A History of the Monks in Syria,* ix.9, xiii.13 (vol. 1, pp. 422–424, 492–498); Leontius of Rome, *Life of Gregory of Agrigento,* ch. 71 (64) (ed. Berger, pp. 228–229). Cf. *The Athenian Corpus of Saint Pachomius,* p. 97, and see the previous note.
52. *The Sayings of the Desert Fathers,* viii.32 (vol. 1, pp. 420–424). John of Ephesus, *Lives of the Eastern Saints,* PO 92/19:270–273, PO 82/17:64–65. Whitby, "Maro the Dendrite: An Anti-Social Holy Man?" Cf. in medieval Judaism: Shoham-Steiner, "The Humble Sage and the Wandering Madman."
53. Kekaumenos, *Stratigikon,* p. 196. Grosdidier de Matons, "Les Thèmes d'édification dans la Vie d'André Salos," pp. 300–201. Rallēs and Potlēs, *Suntagma tōn theiōn kai tōn hierōn kanonōn,* vol. 2, pp. 441–442. See other sources cited by Déroche, *Études sur Léontios de Néapolis,* pp. 204ff. Ivanov, *Holy Fools in Byzantium and Beyond,* chs. 6–7.
54. This incertitude has mostly been avoided by the modern scholarship that has addressed the phenomenon of the holy fool. Grosdidier de Matons indeed noted the danger in the *salos's* "ambiguous symbiosis" in "Les Thèmes d'édifications dans la Vie d'André Salos," p. 300. See Déroche, *Études sur Léontios de Néapolis,* pp. 186ff and n. 77, who argues that the ambiguity of the Byzantine holy fool was resolved by the canon of "the Council *in Trullo.*" See Ignatios the Deacon, *Life of Gregory the Decapolites,* ch. 39 (ed. Makris, pp. 102–104), where the devil appears in the form of a *salos* to distract the saint.

55. Agathias, *The Histories*, v.5.2 (p. 169). John of Ephesus, *Lives of the Eastern Saints*, 82/17:167–170. Kekaumenos, *Stratigikon*, p. 196. Grosdidier de Matons, "Les Thèmes d'édification dans la Vie d'André Salos," pp. 300–201. Rallēs and Potlēs, *Suntagma tōn theiōn kai tōn hierōn kanonōn*, vol. 2, pp. 441–442.
56. Dagron, "L'homme sans honneur ou le saint scandaleux," pp. 934–936.
57. Kekaumenos, *Stratigikon*, p. 196. See also Rallēs and Potlēs, *Suntagma tōn theiōn kai tōn hierōn kanonōn*, vol. 2, pp. 441–442. Grosdidier de Matons, "Les Thèmes d'édification dans la Vie d'André Salos," pp. 300–201. Agathias, *The Histories*, v.5.2 (p. 169), about "those who pretended to have mania and demon possession" (following Déroche, p. 161, n. 19).
58. This was a genuine problem in Byzantine society; see the previous note.
59. Scott, "The Incommensurability of Psychoanalysis and History," pp. 65–68.
60. De Certeau, *The Writing of History*, p. 96, quoted by Scott, "The Incommensurability of Psychoanalysis and History," p. 78.
61. To use once more Scott's phrasing ("The Incommensurability of Psychoanalysis and History," p. 81) in reference to Lyndal Roper, *Witch Craze* (New Haven, CT: Yale University Press, 2004).

2. Meanings of Insanity

Epigraph: "La littérature est le discours théorique des procès historiques. Elle crée le non-lieu où les opérations effectives d'une société accèdent à une formalisation. Bien loin d'envisager la littérature comme l'«expression» d'un référentiel, il faudrait y reconnaître l'analogue de ce que les mathématiques ont longtemps été pour les sciences exactes: un discours «logique» de l'histoire, la «fiction» qui la rend pensable." De Certeau, "Le 'roman' psychanalytique: histoire et littérature," p. 108 (my translation).

1. In chronological order: Grosdidier de Matons, "Les Thèmes d'édification dans la Vie d'André Salos" (1970) ; Saward, *Perfect Fools* (1980) ; de Certeau, "Le Silence de l'Absolu " (1979) ; Syrkin, "On the Behavior of the 'Fools for Christ's Sake" (1982); Dagron, "L'homme sans honneur ou le saint scandaleux" (1990); Dols, *Majnūn: The Madman in Medieval Islamic Society*, ch.13 (1992); Ivanov, *Holy Fools in Byzantium and Beyond* (1994, 2006); Déroche, *Études sur Léontios de Néapolis* (1995); Krueger, *Symeon the Holy Fool* (1996); Stroumsa, "Madness and Divinization in Early Christian Monasticism" (2002); Thomas, *The Holy Fools* (2009).
2. Weber, *The Sociology of Religion*.
3. Stroumsa, "Madness and Divinization in Early Christian Monasticism," p. 80.
4. Thomas, *The Holy Fools*.
5. Van Gennep, *Les rites de passage*. V. Turner, "Liminality and Communitas."
6. An excellent example is Bilu's *The Saints' Impresarios*, a study of the rise of

saints' cults in the Israeli periphery in the 1970s and 1980s. In this study, Bilu focuses not on social and political aspects, but rather on the psychological and anthropological aspects of the reinstallation of Jewish Moroccan saints' cults in today's Israeli society.

7. *The Canons of the Council in Trullo*, can. 60 (p. 140).
8. From this perspective the *Life of Symeon salos* by a seventh-century bishop, Leontius of Neapolis, can be understood as an appropriation of the legend about a person who acquired a reputation as an antiestablishment saint. Leontius simply "monasticizes" Symeon, and appropriates him by incorporating him into the religious establishment. Note that in Evagrius Scholasticus, *Ecclesiastical History* (PG 106b:2761), Symeon is not a monk, while Leontius dedicates a large part of his narrative to the monastic life of Symeon prior to his becoming a holy fool.
9. Lewis, *Ecstatic Religion.*
10. Cf. a specific example of this in Ernesto de Martino's *The Land of Remorse*, a study of the tarantella phenomenon in Southern Italy in the 1960s. Here de Martino shows how the bite of the spider works in a symbolic dimension, engaging the bitten person with his or her surroundings on both the social and psychological levels through a well-defined ritual. This ritual resolves and soothes the social and psychological tensions that the tarantella's bite expresses.
11. The literary phenomenon of the narrative of the sanctification of figures who are liminal to society can also serve as an essential means for changing the cultural and social structure. Kleinberg, *Brother Ginepro's Pork Leg*. Thomas, *The Holy Fools.*
12. Ivanov, *Holy Fools in Byzantium and Beyond.*
13. Ibid., p. 147.
14. Déroche, on the other hand, proposes a different approach. While he affirms the ontological existence of such persons, he shows that once they are acknowledged by society, their mode of sanctity is "frozen." *Études sur Léontios de Néapolis*, pp. 198ff.
15. Syrkin, "On the Behavior of the 'Fools for Christ's Sake,'" and Sinyavsky, *Ivan the Fool: Russian Folk Belief.* Cf. the figure of the "Stinking" *Lizaveta (Smerdyashchaya)* in Dostoevsky's *Brother Karamazov*. The same also goes for the cinematic figure of the idiot woman Durochka in Andrei Tarkovsky's *Andrei Rublev* (1966).
16. Their insanity is the insanity of which *The Book of Steps* speaks (xvi.7, ed. Kmosko, pp. 401–405), see above Chapter 1, p. 20. Thomas, *The Holy Fools*, p. 81. Ivanov, *Holy Fools in Byzantium and Beyond*, pp. 27–29.
17. Davis, "Crossed Texts, Crossed Sex."
18. Patlagean, "L'histoire de la femme déguisée en moine et l'évolution de la sainteté féminine à Byzance." See Bynum's critique of Turner's theory of liminality in "Women's Stories, Women's Symbols," in which she challenges the use of this concept in relation to women. See also Bynum's *Holy*

Feast and Holy Fast, pp. 283–287, about men calling themselves women in order to implement what she names "a symbolic inversion," while medieval women felt their being a woman as the manifestation of the humanity of God. In a similar way the woman dressed as a monk is symbolic to manly monastic environment, and in fact subversively reveals the failure to perceive woman as liminal (see following note).

19. The fact that any monk could be a woman in disguise guarantees a continuous combat against temptation of seduction even within a completely monastic male environment.
20. *The Sayings of the Desert Fathers*, viii.4, 13, 32 (vol. 1, pp. 402, 408, 420–424).
21. Cf. John Moschus, *Spiritual Meadow*, ch. 111 (pp. 162–163).
22. John of Ephesus, *Lives of the Eastern Saints*, PO 92/19:164–179.
23. Ibid., pp. 168–169.
24. Ibid., p. 179.
25. Ashbrook Harvey, *Ascetism and Society in Crisis: John of Ephesus and the Lives of the Eastern Saints*, pp. 91–93.
26. Cf. *La Légende Syriaque de Saint Alexis l'Homme de Dieu.*
27. Radin, *The Trickster: A Study in American Indian Mythology.*
28. As noted by Beidelman, "The Moral Imagination of the Kaguru," pp. 174–176.
29. Hynes, "Mapping the Characteristics of Mythic Tricksters," p. 34.
30. Leontius of Neapolis, *Life of Symeon salos*. Krueger, *Symeon the Holy Fool*. Déroche, *Études sur Léontios de Néapolis*. Mango, "A Byzantine Hagiographer at Work: Leontius of Neapolis."
31. The edition prepared by Lennart Rydén forms the basis for Festugière's edition from 1974. See previous note.
32. Leontius of Neapolis, *Life of Symeon salos*, pp. 55–71 (pp. 121–137).
33. Ibid., pp. 71–79 (pp. 137–145).
34. Ibid., pp. 73-76 (pp. 139–142).
35. Ibid., pp. 73–74 (pp. 139–140).
36. Ibid., pp. 76–77 (pp. 142–143).
37. Ibid., p. 77ff (p. 143ff).
38. Ibid., p. 82, 92 (p. 148, 158).
39. Krueger, *Symeon the Holy Fool.*
40. Leontius of Neapolis, *Life of Symeon salos*, p. 56 (p. 122).
41. Rapp, "Storytelling as Spiritual Communication in Early Greek Hagiography."
42. Déroche, *Études sur Léontios de Néapolis*, p. 198.
43. Leontius of Neapolis specifically states that Symeon was "as without a body" (Greek: *hōsper asōmatos*); *Life of Symeon salos*, p. 82 (p. 148).
44. Ibid., p. 80, 84, 88, 91–92 (p. 146, 150, 154, 157–158).
45. Ibid., p. 88 (p. 154).
46. Ibid., p. 97 (p. 163).
47. Déroche, *Études sur Léontios de Néapolis*, pp. 189–192.

48. Leontius of Neapolis, *Life of Symeon salos*, p. 84 (p. 150).
49. Ibid., pp. 83–84 (pp. 149–150).
50. Ibid., p. 96 (p. 162).
51. Ibid., p. 92 (p. 158).
52. Ibid., pp. 81–82, 90, 95–96 (pp. 147–148, 156, 161–162).
53. Ibid., pp. 81–821 (pp. 147–148).
54. Ibid., pp. 85–86 (pp. 151–152).
55. Loc. cit.
56. Ibid., pp. 87–88 (pp. 153–154). Note that another meaning of *pharmakos* is "scapegoat" (Liddell and Scott, *The Online Liddell-Scott-Jones Greek-English Lexicon*).
57. Ibid., p. 90 (p. 156).
58. Loc. cit.
59. Ibid., pp. 88, 96 (p. 154, 162).
60. Ibid., pp. 89–90 (pp. 155–156).
61. Ibid., p. 99 (p. 165).
62. Ibid., p. 103 (p. 169).
63. Ibid., pp. 89–90 (pp. 155–156).
64. Ibid., p. 103 (p. 169).
65. Cf. Bynum, *Holy Feast and Holy Fast*, especially chs. 9–10. But here, as Bynum clearly reveals, the meaning of *woman*, of *feminine*, was employed differently by men and women. To women the female body was a means to become God, "God who feeds and saves" (ibid., p. 275). We are using here terminology taken from relational psychology, i.e., "relational object," which will be dealt with at length later in this chapter in the section titled "The Psychic Logic."
66. De Certeau, "Le Silence de l'Absolu."
67. Palladius, *Lausiac History*, ch. 34 (pp. 162–166); see also Chapter 1.
68. Kleinberg, *Brother Ginepro's Pork Leg*, pp. 146–149.
69. *Select Narratives of Holy Women from the Syro-Antiochene or Sinai Palimpsest*, pp. 81–93 (=*Life of Onesima*, fs. 85b–91b).
70. Déroche, *Études sur Léontios de Néapolis*, p. 198.
71. De Certeau, "Le Silence de l'Absolu." Cf. Déroche, *Études sur Léontios de Néapolis*, p. 188.
72. Just as Kekaumenos describes happening with the encounter of madmen in his society. *Stratigikon*, p. 196.
73. The distinction between active and passive holy fools is Déroche's (*Études sur Léontios de Néapolis*, pp. 170, 177–181), who raises the question of a parallel geographic distinction: the Egyptian *saloi* incline to be passive while the Syrian incline to be active. Déroche links this to the difference in the meaning of *apatheia* in the two religious cultures.
74. For this verb—*skandalein*—see Dagron, "L'homme sans honneur ou le saint scandaleux," as well as *The Sayings of the Desert Fathers*, viii.32 (vol. 1, pp. 420–424), v.30 (vol. 1, pp. 266–268).

75. Leontius of Neapolis, *Life of John of Cyprus*, ch. 38 (pp. 387–391).
76. Ibid., pp. 389–390.
77. Ibid., p. 390.
78. The bishop John, who is the hero of this oeuvre, is aware of Vitalius's spiritual character.
79. Rapp, "Storytelling as Spiritual Communication in Early Greek Hagiography." Krueger, *Writing and Holiness*. Leontius of Neapolis, *Life of Symeon salos*, p. 56 (p. 122).
80. Theodoret of Cyrrhus, *A History of the Monks in Syria*, xxvi.12–14 (vol. 2. p. 186) in his description of Symeon Stylite.
81. Kekaumenos, *Stratigikon*, p. 196.
82. Agathias, *The Histories*, v.5.2 (p. 169). John of Ephesus, *Lives of the Eastern Saints*, 82/17:167–170. Kekaumenos, *Stratigikon*, p. 196. Grosdidier de Matons, "Les Thèmes d'édification dans la Vie d'André Salos," pp. 300–201. Rallēs and Potlēs, *Suntagma tōn theiōn kai tōn hierōn kanonōn*, vol. 2, pp. 441–442.
83. Agathias, *The Histories*, v.5.2 (p. 169), about "those who pretended to have mania and demon possession" (following Déroche, p. 161, n. 19). This ambiguity is exemplified in the use of the Greek term *salos*. This term, whose origin is obscure, was first attributed to genuine madmen, imbeciles as well as to fools (synonym of Greek *mōros*): Grosdidier de Matons, "Les Thèmes d'édification dans la Vie d'André Salos," pp. 279–292; Krueger, *Symeon the Holy Fool*, p. 63, n. 14; Ivanov, *Holy Fools in Byzantium and Beyond*, pp. 31–38. *Salos* as synonym of *mōros*: *The Sayings of the Desert Fathers*, viii.32 (pp. 420–424). See ibid., xv.13 (vol. 2, p. 296), regarding *ktēsasthai salotēta*, "acquiring the character of a *salos*." Other sources use the term as the object of simulation ("making him-/herself *salos/salē*"). In later sources, however, the same term came to designate both the *authentic* and the *fake* madman: Ivanov, *Holy Fools in Byzantium and Beyond*, p. 141; Leontius of Rome, *Life of Gregory of Agrigento*, ch 49 (ed. Berger, pp. 204–205); *Life of Gregory the Decapolite*, 15 (ed. Dvornik, pp. 59–60).
84. Kekaumenos, *Stratigikon*, p. 196. Grosdidier de Matons, "Les Thèmes d'édification dans la Vie d'André Salos," pp. 300–201. Rallēs and Potlēs, *Suntagma tōn theiōn kai tōn hierōn kanonōn*, vol. 2, pp. 441–442. *The Canons of the Council in Trullo*, can. 60 (p. 140).
85. Jung, "On the Psychology of the Trickster-Figure."
86. On the role of literature in representing this part of the human psyche of the reader, see the illuminating article by Le Guin, "The Child and the Shadow."
87. Jung, "On the Psychology of the Trickster-Figure," § 488.
88. Hynes compares the trickster's embodiment of Jung's shadow with the embodiment of Freud's id and the id-super ego struggle: in Hynes and Doty, eds., *Mythical Trickster Figures*, p. 209 (=Hynes, "Inconclusive Conclusions"). He follows here both Edward Piper and Bruno Bettelheim. In the words of

Daniel Burston, *The Wing of Madness*, p. 3, "mainstream psychoanalysis has yet to recognize the power and significance of the trickster motif." This is because psychoanalysis, in contrast to analytical psychology, does not use archetypes in its structuring of the human psyche.

89. Bakhtin, "Response to a Question from the *Novy Mir* Editorial Staff," pp. 5–7.
90. Bakhtin, "From Notes Made in 1970–71," pp. 144–145. These notes predate his main works on the dialogue.
91. De Certeau, "Le Silence de l'Absolu." Krueger, *Symeon the Holy Fool.*
92. See Rapp's studies on the spiritual function of writing the tales about saints in "The Origins of Hagiography and the Literature of Early Monasticism" and "Storytelling as Spiritual Communication in Early Greek Hagiography."
93. Bakhtin, "Author and Hero in Aesthetic Activity," p. 110.
94. Palladius, *Lausiac History*, ch. 34 (pp. 162–166). *The Athenian Corpus of Saint Pachomius*, p. 97. Ivanov, *Holy Fools in Byzantium and Beyond*, pp. 51–62.
95. Paul of Corinth (*BHG* 2362). We have only the first lines of his *Life* in Cod. Paris. 1452, f.227v, from the tenth century. Otherwise, a short notice in the Synaxarion of Constantinople which does not provide much: *AASS Nov. III*, 130 a. Ehrhadr I, 570 (39). *Synaxarium Ecclesiae Constantinopolitanae*, p. 200, 495. Ivanov, *Holy Fools in Byzantium and Beyond*, pp. 142–147.
96. *Saint Daniel of Sketis*, pp. 120–129 (Mark the Fool), pp. 140–147 (the woman who pretended to be drunkard). John of Ephesus, *Lives of the Eastern Saints*, PO 82/17:64–65, 89/18:562–574, 92/19:183. PG 88:721a–d (=John of Climacus, *The Ladder of Divine Ascent*, step 4: 'On Obedience,' following A. Thomas). *Life and Works of Saint Gregentios Archbishop of Taphar*, pp. 220–223, 238–240, 278, 324–328.
97. Déroche, "Les variantes italiques de la folie en Christ."
98. Morson and Emerson, *Mikhail Bakhtin: Creation of a Prosaics*, p. 192.
99. Bakhtin, "The Problem of the Text in Linguistics, Philology, and the Human Sciences," a compilation of Bakhtin's thoughts in his notebooks.
100. Bakhtin, "Author and Hero in Aesthetic Activity," pp. 30–31.
101. Ibid., p. 51. "Only the other's action is capable of being artistically understood and formed by me, whereas from within myself my own action does not yield in principle to artistic forming and consummation. What we mean here is, of course, action in a purely plastic-pictorial sense." Ibid., p. 45.
102. Ibid., p. 52ff.
103. Todorov, *Mikhaïl Bakhtine: Le principe dialogique*, pp. 145–146.
104. Cf. Winnicott, "Ego Distortion in Terms of True and False Self." Priel, "Bakhtin and Winnicott." According to Wachtel, *Relational Theory and the Practice of Psychotherapy*, pp. 42–49, in relational psychology the psychic development of the baby in relation to the mother continues on in the "ongoing relationships, interactions, and circumstances of the person's

life." Wachtel proposes to replace the "one-person" versus "two-persons" theories by considering the person in "context" in contrast to an acontextual perspective. Ibid., pp. 67–74. And cf. Benjamin, *The Bonds of Love*, ch. 1: "The First Bond," who builds her theory of intersubjectivity on the premise of a psychological individual need to be in a dynamic relationship of mutual recognition with the *other*.

105. Priel, "Bakhtin and Winnicott."
106. Note that the difference between the analyses of Bakhtin and Winnicott comes not so much because of different theoretical perspectives, but because the two thinkers (who were born within a half year of each other and died within four years) have developed them with different objectives: Winnicott aimed to explain psychological problems in adulthood, while Bakhtin was interested in understanding the aesthetic role of literature.
107. For different attitudes about "relation structure" model versus "drive structure" model, see Bromberg, "Shadow and Substance"; Mitchell, *Relational Concepts in Psychoanalysis*; Wachtel, *Relational Theory and the Practice of Psychotherapy*, ch. 5.
108. Although as Bromberg explains, Winnicott, like other parental figures of the relational perspective, does not carry parental authority. *The Shadow of the Tsunami and the Growth of the Relational Mind*, p. 68.
109. Winnicott, "Primitive Emotional development"; "Mirror-role of Mother and Family in Child Development"; and *The Maturational Processes and the Facilitating Environment*.
110. Winnicott, "Ego Distortion in Terms of True and False Self." Eleven years later Kohut published his own model in *The Analysis of the Self*. Note that in his relational model of the development of the psyche in infancy, Kohut depends on Freud's model of ego-id-super ego, while Winnicott avoids it altogether.
111. Note that although I referred to Kohut above, I intentionally do not enter here into theories about the self. See Sedikides and Brewer, *Individual Self, Relational Self, Collective Self*.
112. Philo, *Opera* 6, p. 127 (=*In Flaccum*, vi.36–39), trans. F. H. Colson, pp. 322–325.
113. See Porter, *A Social History of Madness*, and *Madness: A Brief History*.
114. Porter, *A Social History of Madness*. Fromm-Reichmann, *The Philosophy of Insanity by a Late Inmate of the Glasgow Royal Asylum for Lunatics at Gartnavel*. Reicher, *Madness*. See three examples of cinematic works: Roberto Rossellini, *The Miracle* (second part of *L'amore*, 1948); John Casavettes, *A Woman Under the Influence* (1974); and François Truffaut, *L'histoire d'Adèle* (1975).
115. See the figure of Maro in John of Ephesus, *Lives of the Eastern Saints*, who simulates insanity in order to be a *xenos*, but unsuccessfully; PO 82/17:64–65.
116. This can also be explained by an enlargement of Thomas Ogden's idea of the way in which "projective identification" functions. Ogden takes here

Melanie Klein's concept of "projective identification" and adapts it to Winnicott's model. Ogden, *The Matrix of the Mind*, pp. 34–37. Ogden then uses it to explain what happens in a relation when there is no empathy in object-relatedness because of a psychological disorder. Ibid., pp. 227–232.

117. Laing, *The Divided Self*. De Certeau, "Le Silence de l'Absolu."
118. *Select Narratives of Holy Women from the Syro-Antiochene or Sinai Palimpsest*, pp. 86–87 (=*Life of Onesima*, fs. 88a–b).
119. As Rapp and Krueger have shown, both its writing and its reading are a spiritual experience. See Rapp, "The Origins of Hagiography and the Literature of Early Monasticism" and "Storytelling as Spiritual Communication in Early Greek Hagiography"; and Krueger, *Writing and Holiness*.
120. This is in contrast, for example, to the phenomenon of the possession at Loudun and its achievements at the public level. De Certeau, *La Possession de Loudun*.
121. Todorov, *The Fantastic: A Structural Approach to a Literary Genre*, p. 43. Todorov gives two examples: Henry James's *The Turn of the Screw* and Prosper Mérimée's *La Vénus d'Ille*. For the first, see Chapter 1 where I have used Felman, *Writing and Madness* (ch. 7).
122. Todorov, *The Fantastic*.
123. Ibid., p. 46.
124. Ibid., p. 44.
125. See Miller, "Is There a Harlot in This Text? Hagiography and the Grotesque," which reveals the conscious strategy of the hagiographer, here dealing with sexuality.
126. Freud, "A Disturbance of Memory on the Acropolis," pp. 244–245; emphasis added. For a full analysis, see the commentary of Henri Vermorel and Madeleine Vermorel in Freud and Rolland, *Correspondence 1923–1936*, pp. 400–419, 463ff.
127. Freud, "The 'Uncanny' (1919)." H. Vermorel and M. Vermorel make this connection in Sigmund Freud and Romain Rolland, *Correspondence 1923–1936*, pp. 560–566.
128. Masschelein, *The Unconcept: The Freudian Uncanny in Late-Twentieth-Century Theory*.
129. Shklovsky, "Art as Device," otherwise translated as "Art as Technique." L. Crawford, "Viktor Shklovskij: différenace in defamiliarization."
130. As Benjamin Sher explains in his introduction to Shklovsky's *Theory of Prose* (p. xix): "Shklovsky's process is not a transition from the 'familiar' to the 'unknown' (hence, not 'defamiliarization'), but proceeds from the cognitively known (the language of science), the rules and formulas that arise from a search for an economy of mental effort, to the familiarity known, to real knowledge that expands and 'complicates' our perceptual process in the rich use of metaphors, similes and a host of other figures of speech."
131. See Brecht, "Alienation Effects in Chinese Acting" (1935), analyzed by Carney, *Brecht and Critical Theory*, pp. 14–22 ("*Verfremdungseffekt and Unheimlich*").

Though translated as "alienation" by Willett, the German *Verfremdungseffekt* corresponds perfectly to Shklovsky's Russian *priem ostrannenniya*, "the device of making strange." See Tian, *The Poetics of Difference and Displace*, p. 43. Carney, op. cit., p. 15, who emphasizes that Brecht's *Verfremdungseffekt* is clearly not alienation (German *Entfremdung*). For this, see Bloch, "Entfremdung, Verfremdung: Alienation, Estrangement."

132. Rapp, "The Origins of Hagiography and the Literature of Early Monasticism," and "Storytelling as Spiritual Communication in Early Greek Hagiography."
133. The question of Andrew's existence is here irrelevant. *Life of Andrew the Fool*, vol. 1, p. 32ff. Also "The Date of the Life of Andreas Salos" and "The Life of St. Basil the Younger and the Date of the Life of St. Andreas Salos" in ibid. Mango, "The Life of St. Andrew the Fool Reconsidered," dates it to the beginning of the eighth century in contrast to the accepted dating of Rydén to the second half of the tenth century.
134. *Life of Andrew the Fool*, vol. 2, pp. 12–14.
135. Ibid., pp. 14–18.
136. Ibid., pp. 18–20.
137. Ibid., pp. 20–26.
138. Ibid., p. 28.
139. Ibid., p. 40.
140. Ibid., pp. 140, 186, 188, 256.
141. Ibid., pp. 36, 44.
142. Ibid., pp. 62, 92–102, 256.
143. Ibid., p. 96.
144. Ibid., pp. 170–184, 198, 256. Cf. Ignatios the Deacon, *Life of Gregory the Decapolites*, ch. 39 (ed. Makris, pp. 102–104).
145. *Life of Andrew the Fool*, vol. 2, pp. 38, 140.
146. This happens, for example, when he performs his miracle of catching thieves, after which people start to believe in him. Ibid., pp. 106–112. The people of the city have three interpretations for Andrew's behavior and powers: some refuse to believe it, some marvel, and others think Andrew speaks from the devil. Ibid., p. 198. Cf. Leontius of Neapolis, *Life of Symeon salos*, pp. 85-86 (pp. 151-152).
147. *Life and Works of Saint Gregentios Archbishop of Taphar*, pp. 220–223, 238–240, 278, 324–328. And the contrary in Ignatios the Deacon, *Life of Gregory the Decapolites*, ch. 39 (ed. Makris, pp. 102–104), where the *salos* represents the enemy of the saint.
148. *Life of Andrew the Fool*, vol. 2, pp. 20–26, 44–58, 134–136.
149. Greek: *ide, pōs eimi meta alētheias exēchos*. Ibid., p. 46.
150. Ibid., p. 48.
151. Ibid., pp. 52–58.
152. Ibid., pp. 56–58.
153. Ibid., p. 60.

154. Ibid. pp. 164–168.
155. Ibid., p. 166.
156. This is very similar to Bakhtin's analysis of Rabelais in his *Rabelais and His World*.
157. *Life of Andrew the Fool*, vol. 2, p. 38, 140, 198. Cf. Leontius, *Life of Symeon salos*, p. 88 (p. 154). For the holy fool as a Gnostic, see Stroumsa, "Madness and Divinization in Early Christian Monasticism." See Epiphanios's discussion with the philosophers about *gnōsis* in ibid., vol. 2, pp. 68–70.
158. *Life of Andrew the Fool*, vol. 2, p. 194.
159. Artaud, *Le théâtre et son double*, p. 139 (=id. "Le théâtre de la cruauté" from 1932).
160. "Le théâtre contemporain est en décadence parce qu'il a perdu le sentiment d'un côté du sérieux et de l'autre du rire. Parce qu'il a rompu avec la gravité, avec l'efficacité immédiate et pernicieuse—et pour tout dire avec le Danger. Parce qu'il a perdu d'autre part le sens de l'humour vrai et du pouvoir de dissociation physique et anarchique du rire. Parce qu'il a rompu avec l'esprit d'anarchie profonde qui est à la base de toute poésie." Artaud, *Le théâtre et son double*, p. 61 (="La mise en scène et la métaphysique" from 1932) ; my translation.
161. "Or tirer les conséquences poétiques extrêmes des moyens de réalisation c'est en faire la métaphysique, et je crois que nul ne s'élèvera contra cette manière de considérer la question." Ibid., p. 66.
162. Through this process Artaud equates theater with alchemy. Ibid., p. 73 (=id. "Le théâtre alchimique").
163. Gorelick, "Life in Excess," pp. 5–7.
164. See, for example, Andrew's ambiguous prophecy in *The Life of Andrew the Fool*, vol. 2, pp. 140-142.
165. Ibid., vol. 2, pp. 106–110.
166. Ibid., vol. 2, pp. 116–118.
167. See Foulkes's definition: "*The Matrix* is the hypothetical web of communication and relationship in a given group. It is the common shared ground which ultimately determines the meaning and significance of all events and upon which all communication and interpretations, verbal and nonverbal, rest." *Therapeutic Group Analysis*, p. 292. We shall return to Foulkes and his theory of group analysis below.
168. *The Life of Andrew the Fool*, vol. 2, pp. 198–200.
169. Ibid., vol. 2, pp. 200–234, 258–284.
170. Ibid., vol. 2, p. 212. Cf. the clairvoyance of Petros or Moryne the holy fool in the *Life and Works of Saint Gregentios Archbishop of Taphar*, pp. 220–222.
171. *The Life of Andrew the Fool*, vol. 2, 286–288.
172. Ibid., vol. 2, p. 424.
173. Virmaux, *Le théatre et son double: Antonin Artaud*, pp. 34–36.
174. See Artaud's third letter about "Le théâtre de la cruauté" from 1932 in *Le théâtre et son double*, pp. 156–157. And ibid., p. 186 (=id. "Le théâtre de la

cruauté [Second Manifeste]"). For the plague as theatre due to staging life in crisis, see ibid., pp. 19–45 (=id., "Le théâtre et la peste" from 1933).

175. "C'est par la peau qu'on fera rentrer la métaphysique dans les esprits." Ibid., p. 151.
176. Ibid., p. 187.
177. Ibid., pp. 99–101 (=id. "Sur le théâtre balinais" from 1931). Ibid., p. 126 (=Id. "En finir avec les chefs-d'œuvre" from 1935–1936).
178. Gorelick, "Life in Excess," p. 12.
179. "Le théâtre ne pourra redevenir lui-même, c'est-à-dire constituer un moyen d'illusion vraie, qu'en fournissant au spectateur des précipites véridiques de rêves, ou son gout du crime, ses obsessions érotiques, sa sauvagerie, ses chimères, son sens utopique de la vie et des choses, son cannibalisme même, se débondent, sur un plan non pas suppose et illusoire, mais intérieur. En d'autres termes, le théâtre doit poursuivre, par tous les moyens, une remise en cause non seulement de tous les aspects du monde objectif et descriptif externe, mais du monde interne, c'est-à-dire de l'homme, considéré métaphysiquement." Artraud, *Le théâtre et son double*, pp. 139–140 (="Le théâtre de la cruauté"); my translation.
180. Bromberg, "Shadow and Substance." See Bromberg, *The Shadow of the Tsunami and the Growth of Relational Mind*, p. 68: "The name [i.e., 'relational psychoanalysis'] was selected for two reasons: It clearly and concisely represented the core viewpoint that united us, namely that the human mind, its normal development, its pathology, and the process of its therapeutic growth are relationally configured; at the same time, the term was not so conceptually specific that it would convey adherence to one given set of ideas." For another view about this, see Wachtel, *Relational Theory and the Practice of Psychotherapy*, ch. 5.
181. Mitchell, *Relational Concepts in Psychoanalysis*, ch. 1.
182. Ibid., p. 3.
183. Bromberg, "Shadow and Substance," p. 166.
184. Mitchel, *Relational Concepts in Psychoanalysis*, p. 41. To be differentiated from Foulkes's idea of the "foundation matrix" as relational and communicational web within a group. Foulkes, *Therapeutic Group Analysis*, p. 292.
185. The concept of the *self* is here relational configured. Bromberg, "Shadow and Substance," p. 157. Here he follows Aron ("The Patient's Experience of the Analyst's Subjectivity") and Hoffman ("Discussion: Toward a Social-Constructivist View of the Psychoanalytic Situation"). I avoid the psychoanalytical discourse about the definition of the "self." The basic reference is, of course, to Kohut, *The Analysis of the Self.* Note that this discussion is very different from Freud's concept of the self, and also from Jung's concept of the self as a gathering of contradictory subjectivities. Young-Eisendrath, "The Self in Analysis."
186. Bromberg, *The Shadow of the Tsunami and the Growth of the Relational Mind*, p. 18.

187. Bromberg deals here with post-trauma psychological dissociation, and emphasizes the importance of the *enactment* of the patient's dissociation. Ibid., ch. 5.
188. Here (ibid., pp. 107–110) Bromberg draws on Winnicott's dyadic mirror to which we will return below.
189. Cf. Jung, "Psychology of the Transference" (§ 353–401), where he points to the relational psychic zone between the patient and therapist.
190. Bromberg, *The Shadow of the Tsunami and the Growth of the Relational Mind*, p. 56.
191. Ibid., p. 70.
192. Ibid., chs. 3–4.
193. Ibid., p. 72.
194. Ibid., p. 87.
195. Ibid., pp. 121, 140, 162.
196. Amati Sas, "Situations sociales traumatiques et processus de la cure" and "L'interprétation dans le trans-subjectif."
197. Bleger equates his *self* to the ego. *Symbiosis and Ambiguity*, pp. 163–164, 172–173.
198. Bleger explains this as a defense mechanism related to states of ambiguity. Ibid., pp. 35–46.
199. Ibid., pp. 188–191.
200. "Dans l'ambiguïté (à la différence de l'ambivalence), les termes opposés, antinomiques ou contradictoires sont interchangeables; car ils ne sont pas encore précises, ni contrastés, ni hiérarchisés . . . en conséquence, la présence de l'ambiguïté donne aux phénomènes psychiques un caractère oscillatoire de malléabilité, d'élasticité et d'adaptabilité protéiforme qui permet l'adaptation à la culture, aux habitudes et la réalité contextuelle, et au climat affectif des rapports inter- et trans-subjectifs." Amati Sas, "Situations sociales traumatiques et processus de la cure," pp. 927–928 ; my translation.
201. This is precisely the danger that Kekaumenos warns against when confronting an insane person. *Stratigikon*, p. 196.
202. Here following Mitchell, *Relational Concepts in Psychoanalysis*, p. 33.
203. Bromberg, *The Shadow of the Tsunami and the Growth of the Relational Mind*, p. 162.
204. To Bleger this is a product of an unhealthy subjective symbiosis. Although today largely rejected; nevertheless, cf. Laing and Esterson, *Sanity, Madness, and the Family* (1964), where the authors explain schizophrenia as "a social praxis," i.e., a product of an unhealthy interfamily symbiosis.
205. Cf. Searles, "Concerning Therapeutic Symbiosis" and "The Patient as Therapist to His Analyst." I owe this reference to Ruth Sarig.
206. This is exactly the subject of Bateson, Jackson, Haley, and Weakland, "Toward a Theory of Schizophrenia." See Cox and Paley, "Families as Systems," and cf. Laing and Esterson, *Sanity, Madness, and the Family*.

207. In contrast, see the therapy of the family as a whole in the detailed case description of Napier and Whitaker, *The Family Crucible*. We shall get to group psychology and group analysis in the Epilogue.
208. Napier and Whitaker, *The Family Crucible*, who show precisely how the behavior of the "Identified Patient" (i.e., IP, see below) within the family is a product of their entire group's interdependence (for the importance of interdependence in group analysis, see the Epilogue). The IP here is not schizophrenic.

3. Abnormality and Social Change: Insanity and Martyrdom

Epigraph: Lewin, *Resolving Social Conflicts*, p. 165.

1. Baars, "Why Volition Is a Foundation Problem for Psychology." Draguns and Tanaka-Matsumi, "Assessment of Psychopathology across and within Cultures." I am thankful to Inbar Graiver for her contribution to this discussion.
2. McNally, *What Is Mental Illness?* p. 18ff. Scheff, *Being Mentally Ill.*
3. Wakefield, "The Concept of Mental Disorder," p. 374.
4. McHugh, "Striving for Coherence."
5. McNally, *What Is Mental Illness?*
6. Cf. Dols's third model of insanity, "the intelligibility model," in his *Majnūn: The Madman in Medieval Islamic Society*, chs. 14–15.
7. Wakefield, "Evolutionary versus Prototype Analyses of the Concept of Disorder."
8. I have referred here to only three recent theories about mental illness as representative examples of the different approaches. For Thomas Szasz's opposition to the term "mental illness" in his *The Myth of Mental Illness*, see below. His views were severely criticized for ignoring evidence that psychiatric illness has a biological basis. For a recent example, see Shorter, "Still Tilting at Windmills."
9. A few examples include: Dols, "Insanity in Byzantine and Islamic Medicine"; Horden, "Responses to Possession and Insanity in the Earlier Byzantine World"; Giafrancesco, "Monachisme ancien et psychopathologie" ; Ahonen, *Mental Disorders in Ancient Philosophy*; and Draguns and Tanaka-Matsumi, "Assessment of Psychopathology across and within Cultures."
10. See McNally, *What Is Mental Illness?* ch. 5: "Does Society Create (Some) Mental Disorders?" and especially the example of schizophrenia in contrast to posttraumatic stress disorder (pp. 143–156).
11. Foucault, *Histoire de la folie à l'âge classique*, published first as *Folie et Déraison: Histoire de la folie à l'âge classique* (Paris: Plon, 1961). Translated into English by Richard Howard from the abbreviated French edition (1963) as *Madness and Civilization: A History of Insanity in the Age of Reason* (London: Tavistock, 1967), and in its integrality only in 2006 as *History of Madness*, trans. Jonathan Murphy and Jean Khalfa (London: Routledge, 2006). For critical

reviews, see Still and Velody, eds., *Rewritings the History of Madness;* and in France, Artières et al., eds., *Histoire de la folie à l'âge classique de Michel Foucault.*

12. Porter, "Foucault's Great Confinement," p. 119.
13. As stated above I am using both "insanity" and "madness" throughout this book as synonyms of the single French term *folie.* I use insanity when the context refers to as an opposition to sanity, and madness otherwise.
14. Some of the severe criticism that this theory has received is largely due to the relationship it established between "reason" and the confinement of unreason. Foucault describes this process as an inevitable means of producing a new concept of reason. Naturally such a theory is not easy to accept, all the more so since "the great confinement" outside France is a matter of debate. See MacDonald, "Insanity and the Realities of History in Early Modern England." Also Porter, *Mind-Forg'd Manacles,* and "Foucault's Great Confinement."
15. This is the main subject of the second part of Foucault's *Histoire de la folie à l'âge classique,* especially pp. 264–303, 355–374.
16. Gauchet and Swain, *La pratique de l'esprit humain: L'institution asilaire et la révolution démocratique,* first published by Gallimard in 1980. Translated into English by C. Porter in an abbreviated form as *Madness and Democracy: The Modern Psychiatric Universe* (Princeton, NJ: Princeton University Press, 1999).
17. Ibid., pp. 47–51.
18. Ibid., pp. 317ff.
19. "La démarche est au fond similaire: c'est là aussi en dernier ressort du schème de la Volonté qu'il s'agit de se libérer, du mythe de la Souveraineté personnelle, comme si l'individu, de par la puissance que lui confère l'extériorité consciente, pouvait à son gré disposer de lui-même." Ibid., pp, 352–353.
20. Ibid., pp. 369ff.
21. Ibid., pp. 67–78.
22. Ibid., pp. 407–412: "De l'inégalité comme principe de communication."
23. "De guérison, écrit Esquirol, il n'est 'qu'en donnant une secousse morale, qu'en plaçant l'aliéné dans un état opposé ou contraire à celui dans lequel il était avant de recourir à ce moyen.'" Ibid., p. 479.
24. In Gauchet's words in his preface to the 2007 edition. Ibid., p. ii.
25. This attempt was already made by Thomas Szasz in *The Myth of Mental Illness,* which threatened to pull the rug out from under psychiatric practice. Also see Szasz's *The Age of Madness,* and Shorter, "Still Tilting at Windmills."
26. Clément and Kakar, *La folle et le saint.*
27. Ibid., p. 17.
28. Ibid., p. 82.
29. Ibid., pp. 83–99. There is also a very significant difference here between the attitude to male and female mystics.

30. See Porter, *A Social History of Madness*, ch. 2: "Madness and Psychiatry Talking: A Historical Dialogue."
31. "The Lord might show us a witness from heaven." *The Martyrdom of Polycarp*, § 1 (p. 210).
32. In transliterating the Syriac I used the Syriac Romanization of the Library of Congress: http://www.loc.gov/catdir/cpso/romanization/syriac.pdf (retrieved on March 20, 2014).
33. I borrow here the term of Glen Bowersock, *Martyrdom and Rome*, p. 7, who paraphrased the "pathological yearning for martyrdom" of De Ste. Croix, "Why Were the Early Christians Persecuted?" See Weiner and Weiner, *The Martyr's Conviction*, p. 1.
34. Stein, "Evil as Love and as Liberation."
35. For martyrdom as collective memory, see Castelli, *Martyrdom and Memory*, who gives the example of the way in which the victims of September 11 are commemorated (pp. 198–199).
36. Cf. Riley-Smith, "Crusading as an Act of Love."
37. On the sacrificed self as a social necessity of the group, see Girard, *La violence et le sacré*. On the passage from animal sacrifice to the Christian concept of human sacrifice, see Stroumsa, *La fin du sacrifice*, ch. 3.
38. The scale of the Roman persecutions has been a matter of recent scholarship. Among the most provoking theses: Castelli, *Martyrdom and Memory*; De Ste. Croix, *Christian Persecution, Martyrdom, and Orthodoxy*; Luijendijk, *Greetings in the Lord*; Barnes, *Early Christian Hagiography and Roman History*; Moss, *Ancient Christian Martyrdom*, and *The Myth of Persecution*.
39. Van Hanten and Avemarie, *Martyrdom and Noble Death*.
40. This is the way in which the Roman authority's stand is portrayed in the Christian sources: Barnes, *Tertullian: A Historical and Literary Study*, ch. 11: "Persecutions." De Ste. Croix, *Christian Persecution, Martyrdom, and Orthodoxy*, ch. 3: "Why Were the Early Christians Persecuted?' shows this to be a Christian propaganda. Buell, *Why This New Race*, pp. 52–59.
41. Musurillo, *Acts of the Pagan Martyrs*. Harker, *Loyalty and Dissidence in Roman Egypt*.
42. Van Hanten and Avemarie, *Martyrdom and Noble Death*. Cohen, "Masada: Literary Tradition, Archaeological Remains, and the Credibility of Josephus." Cf. Bowersock, *Martyrdom and Rome*, ch. 1, where the subject is the particularity of the Christian case.
43. Musurillo, *The Acts of the Christian Martyrs*, p. 100 (=*The Martyrdom of the Saintly and Blessed Apostle Apollonius, also called Sakkeas*, § 38). Justin Martyr, *Apology I*, 5, *Apology II*, 10 (p. 138, 350). Tertullian, *To the Nations*, i.4.6, i.10.42 (p. 15, 28). For other ancient Greek examples, see Clement, *Stromata*, iv.48 (p. 138), iv.56 (p. 150).
44. See Clement, *Stromata*, iv.48 (p. 138). Moss, *Ancient Christian Martyrdom*, pp. 29–30, does discuss her.
45. Berthelot, "L'idéologie maccabéenne." See Honigman, *Tales of High Priests and Taxes*.

46. The political revolt was targeted in fact not against the Seleucid ruler, but against their representatives, the priestly division that controlled Jerusalem.
47. Musurillo, *Acts of the Pagan Martyrs*. Tcherikover and Fuks, *CPJ* vol. 2, p. 55, also named them "Acts of Alexandrian Martyrs" and followed in that Musurillo, Bauer and Rostovtzeff (*CPJ* vol. 2, p. 55).
48. Harker distinguishes between *Acta Alexandrinorum* and other *acta* related literature.
49. *CPJ* ii 159, p. 101. Harker, *Loyalty and Dissidence in Roman Egypt*, pp. 80, 90–91. The emperor has been identified as Commodus.
50. *CPJ* ii 159b, col. 5 (p. 103).
51. Schwartz, "Quelques réflexions à propos des Acta Alexandrinorum."
52. Although we do not know whether these texts were ever grouped or circulated together.
53. Philo, *Embassy to Gaius*. Josephus, *Antiquities of the Jews*, xix.278ff.
54. *CPJ* ii 155, 156a–d. Harker, *Loyalty and Dissidence in Roman Egypt*, pp. 39–45.
55. *CPJ* ii 157–158.
56. *CPJ* ii 156.
57. An exception to that is the intervention of Serapis on behalf of the Alexandrians in Rome (*CPJ* ii 157), which could be understood as a local Alexandrian cultural symbol, rather than as an expression of religious dispute. *CPJ* ii 154; Harker, *Loyalty and Dissidence in Roman Egypt*, pp. 37–38.
58. Van Henten and Avemarie, *Martyrdom and Noble Death*, ch. 2.
59. The author of 2 Maccabees evokes the prototypes of the binding of Issac and the trial of Hananiah, Mishael, and Azariah (Dan. 3) and uses them in the exhortation speech of the mother. 2 Maccabees 4:20-23.
60. Kahana, "The Halakhic Midrashim," p. 57.
61. *Tosefta, Berakhot*, 4:18: the story of the people of Judah who, of all the tribes of Israel, jumped first into the Red Sea, thus putting their lives in God's hands. The same is mentioned also in BT, *Soṭah*, 36b. This, however, seems exceptional in contrast to the other references to *kiddush hašem* in the tannaitic literature; see Safrai, "Kiddush haShem in the Teaching of the Tannaim," pp. 29–32.
62. *Tosefta, Shabbat*, 15:17.
63. *Sifra Leviticus*, *"Emor"* parasha 8, ch. 9:4 (p. 104b). But see the complete contrast in *Sifra Leviticus*, *"Aḥrey mot"* parasha 9, ch. 13:14, on Leviticus 18:5: "'Keep my ordinances and commandments, which in doing them a man shall live' . . . 'shall live and not die': according to Rabbi Ishma'el this means that a man can transgress the commandment as if he is forced to idolatry as long as it is in private." *Sifra Leviticus*, *"Emor"* is considered an Akivan exposition. We may find here a tannaitic debate about giving one's life for God's commandments. On the date of these halakhic midrashim, see Kahana, "The Halakhic Midrashim," p. 78. While *Sifra Leviticus* on *"Emor"* chapter 9 is considered an Akivan exposition, *Sifra Leviticus*, *"Aḥrey mot"* chapter 13 belongs to a later period.

64. Most of the anecdotes place the execution of the two brothers in Laodicaea (Lydda) under Trajan. The Palestinian Talmud, on the other hand, puts them in the framework of sanctifying God's name by refusing to drink from painted glass vessels, thus connecting the term to their submission to the tannaitic halakhah. PT *Shevi'it*, 4:2 (35a, p. 189). PT *Sanhedrin* 3:3 (21b, p. 1281). The story about the two brothers is mentioned also in order to explain why they were not saved by a miracle, like the three whom God saved from Nebuchadnezzar's furnace in Daniel 3 (*Treatise Semaḥot*, 8:15. BT *Ta'anit* 18b). The message is clear: one should be conscious about dying for God and should not expect a miraculous intervention.
65. Trajan's name has many versions in the rabbinic anecdotes related to Papus and Lulianus: Traianus, Targinus, Turinus, Trakhianus, Marianus. Vered Noam points rather to a confusion here between Trajan and Lusius Quietus: *Megillat Ta'anit*, p. 296 and n. 9.
66. See Oppenheimer, "Heiligkeit und Hingabe des Lebens in der Folge des Bar-Kochba Aufstands."
67. PT *Berakhot* 9:5 (14b, pp. 74–75). PT *Soṭah* 5:5 (20c, pp. 929–930). BT *Berakhot* 61b. Boyarin, *Dying for God*, ch. 4. Safrai, "Kiddush haShem in the Teaching of the Tannaim," pp. 32–36.
68. *Midrash Genesis Rabbah* 65:27 (pp. 740–744). *Sifrei Deuteronomy* 207 (pp. 344–346).
69. BT *Berakhot* 61b. BT *'Avodah Zarah* 17b–18a.
70. Cf. J. Cohen, *Sanctifying the Name of God*, where the presentation of martyrdom in medieval Jewish chronicles from the Crusades is shown to play a psychological function in constructing and managing traumatic collective events. This is also the case as far as the Alexandrian, Jewish, and Christian texts which deal with the victims of Roman violence that they commemorate.
71. And in competition with the Christians. Boyarin, *Dying for God*.
72. Lifshitz, "The Martyr, the Tomb, and the Matron." Castelli, *Martyrdom and Memory*. Barnes, *Early Christian Hagiography and Roman History*. Moss, *The Myth of Persecution*.
73. Musurillo, *Acts of the Christian Martyrs*, Introduction. Also *The Martyrdom of Pionios*, Robert, ed. and trans.
74. See Barnes, *Tertullian: A Historical and Literary Study*, ch. 11: "Persecutions."
75. See also the resemblance to the conflict between Antigone and Kreon, depicted in a dialogue in the tragedy genre, and the resemblance to the drama set in 2 Maccabees 6–7.
76. "The Lord might show us a witness from heaven." *The Martyrdom of Polycarp*, § 1 (p. 210). Carpus and Papylus are called "witnesses of Christ" (Musurillo, *Acts of the Christian Martyrs*, p. 22). The same for Cyprian who "was chosen as a holy martyr by God" (ibid., p. 170). The same in regard to Fructuosus: "For it was necessary that the martyr Fructuosus should finally 'prove' [Latin: *comprobare*] in his own bodily suffering and resurrection that which he had

by God's mercy in our Lord and Savior, when he was alive and teaching in the world" (ibid., p. 182). The fact that the Christian martyrologies were constructed in the Roman juridical language was the subject of Brox, *Zeuge und Märtyrer*; for critics, see Moss, *Ancient Christian Martyrdom*, pp. 3–4, 169, n. 3. If we consider the fact that the torture of slaves was a common practice of Roman investigation for *maiestas* crimes, depictions of Christians as tortured slaves could well prove their loyalty to their master in heaven and to his innocence, as Chariton the martyr says: "once Caesar's slave (Greek: *doulos*), I am now a slave of Christ, winning freedom by his favor." Musurillo, *The Acts of the Christian Martyrs*, p. 56 (=*The Martyrdom of Saints Justin, Charion, Charito, Evelpistus, Hierax, Paeon, and Valerian: Recension C*, § 3).

77. The sanctification of God's name is seldom used in the Christian texts. In the Latin recension of *The Martyrdom of Carpus, Pamphilus, and Agathonicē* (§ 5) Carpus cries: "Lord Jesus Christ, you know that we suffer this for your name's sake" (Latin: "*Domine Iesu Christe, tu cognoscis quia propter nomen tuum haec patimur*"). Musurillo, *The Acts of the Christian Martyrs*, p. 34.
78. *The Martyrdom of Pionios*. For the authenticity of the Christian martyrs, see Tacitus, *Annales* xv.44. De Ste. Croix, *Christian Persecution, Martyrdom, and Orthodoxy*. Luijendijk, *Greetings in the Lord*. Barnes, *Early Christian Hagiography and Roman History*. Moss, *The Myth of Persecution*.
79. *The Martyrdom of Polycarp*. Musurillo, *Acts of the Christian Martyrs*: "The Letter of the Churches of Lyons and Vienne," "The Martyrdom of Saints Marian and James," "The Martyrdom of Saints Montanus and Lucius," "The Martyrdom of Saints Pepetua and Felicitas," and "The Letter of Phileas."
80. This is the case in the writings of Eusebius, who compiled collections of martyrologies, and also took special care in his *History of the Church* to include them: Eusebius of Caesarea, *On the Martyrs in Palestine* (Greek); *History of the Martyrs in Palestine* (Syriac); and *The Encomium of the Martyrs*. The last two are from the Ms. BL. Add. 12150, dated to 411 A.D. Musurillo, *The Acts of the Christian Martyrs*, Introduction. Eusebius of Caesarea, *Ecclesiastical History*, vol. 4: Pierre Périchon, loc. cit., index, pp. 252–254.
81. Buc, "Martyre et ritualité dans l'Antiquité tardive."
82. Weiner and Weiner, *The Martyr's Conviction*, pp. 76–77.
83. Any analysis of this subject is completely dependent on the following studies, organized here by their publication date: *Midrash Elleh Ezkherah*, ed. Reeg, *Die Geschichte von den Zehn Märtyren*; Shepkaru, "From After Death to Afterlife"; Boustan, *From Martyr to Mystic*; Welner, *The Ten Slain by the Kingdom in the Midrash and Piyyut*.
84. The piyyut *Elleh Ezkherah* is said to this day as part of the Ashkenazi liturgy of Yom Kippur before the reenactment (the whole congregation fall to their knees four times) of the high priest's service in the Temple, as well as on Tisha B'Av in the Sephardic liturgy.
85. See the table of versions in Welner, *The Ten Slain by the Kingdom in the Midrash and Piyyut*, p. 38.

86. *Midrash Elleh Ezkherah*, pp. 33–34. Boustan, *From Martyr to Mystic*, chs. 1, 2.
87. *Midrash Canticles*, 1:3 (pp. 8–24). *Heikhalot Rabbati*, ed. Schäfer, §§ 107–129, 198 (pp. 50–63, 86–87); see Boustan, *From Martyr to Mystic*, ch. 1, in particular table 1.1 (pp. 41–42). *Heikhalot Rabbati*, ed. Oron. *Midrash Elleh Ezkerah*. *Midrash Proverbs* 1:13, p. 18.
88. In the version of this story in *Heikhalot Rabbati*, on the other hand, the sages are not only saved, but Rabbi Ḥananyah ben Teradyon is miraculously replaced with the Roman emperor, a position which he then uses in order to revenge Rome by ordering a massacre of its elite. *Heikhalot Rabbati*, ed. Schäfer, § 120 (pp. 58–59).
89. Boustan, *From Martyr to Mystic*, p. 55.
90. Ibid., ch. 2.
91. Ibid., ch. 3. Boustan, "A Hebrew Hymn of Praise for a High-Priestly Rabbinic Martyr."
92. I leave aside the immediate parallelism between Rabbi Ishma'el and the executions of the nine other sages to the atonement of Jesus's crucifixion.
93. Boustan, *From Martyr to Mystic*, pp. 63ff.
94. God's vengeance on Rome as depicted in *Heikhalot Rabbati* (ed. Schäfer, § 120, pp. 58–59) reflects the Jewish need of moral comfort, rather than a political perspective envisaging the destruction of Rome. God's revenge on the execution of the ten sages is also a theme in *Midrash Psalms*, 9:13, pp. 88–89.
95. Dan. "*Aseret Harugei Malkhut*, Martyrology and Mysticism."
96. An exception to this rule is the story about the death of Rabbi Akiva as narrated in the Babylonian Talmud (*Berakhot* 61b), which will be discussed below.
97. Boustan, *From Martyr to Mystic*, p. 55.
98. Aristides, *Apology*, pp. 32–37. "The martyrdom of Polycarp" is considered to be the first to be written in the form of a martyrology. For its date, see *The Martyrdom of Polycarp*, pp. 199–200. Dehandschutter, *Polycarpiana*, pp. 50ff. Moss, *Ancient Christian Martyrdom*, pp. 58ff.
99. Justin Martyr, *Apology I*, 68 (p. 314, n. 2).
100. Justin Martyr, *Apology I*, 68.
101. Before the city prefect Urbicus (140–160 A.D.). In *Apology II*, 2.15 (p. 324), Justin Martyr uses the Greek term *alogeōs*—illogically—when he refers to the accusation of Christians who have not committed any crime (the execution of Ptolemy, Lucius, and a third Christian). This narration is considered by Musurillo as a martyrology in *The Acts of the Christian Martyrs*, pp. xvi–xvii, pp. 38–41.
102. Note that in *Apology II*, 12.4 (p. 356), Justin depicts a Roman juridical procedure when describing the measures taken against the Christians: "after putting so many as prosecutors [Greek: *epi sukophantiai*] against us, they interrogated under torture [Greek: *eis basanous heilkuan*] our slaves, adolescent servants, and women, and forced them to accuse us of their own

crimes. But none of this concerns us since we have God as witness—*martur.*" Compare this with the lack of a single specific meaning of *marturein* in the book of Revelation: Dehandschutter, *Polycarpiana,* pp. 181–187; and Bowersock, *Martyrdom and Rome,* pp. 14–17.

103. Justin Martyr, *Apology II,* 2.
104. See the evidence from Egypt: Luijendijk, *Greetings in the Lord;* Bisbee, *Pre-Decian Acts of Martyrs and Commentarii;* and de Ste. Croix, *Christian persecution, martyrdom, and Orthodoxy.*
105. Ignatius of Antioch, *Letters,* pp. 106–119 (=*Epistle to the Romans*). Yet, as Bowersock (*Martyrdom and Rome,* pp. 6–7) observed, this in no way is articulated as "martyrdom." Neither does he refer to himself as a "martyr."
106. Clement, *Stromata,* iv.81–88 (pp. 188–200).
107. Ibid., iv.81–88 against Basilidis, and iv.89–94 against Valentinian. See van den Hoek comments (ibid., p. 188, n. 2, p. 200, n. 2). Clement also writes directly against those who think that martyrs commit suicide in *Stromata,* iv.16 (pp. 82–84). Bowersock, *Martyrdom and Rome,* pp. 67–71.
108. Clement, *Stromata,* iv.39.1 (p. 122). See Moss, *Ancient Christian Martyrdom,* pp. 147–149.
109. Clement, *Stromata,* iv.14 (p. 78).
110. Ibid., iv.15–17, 56 (pp. 80-86, 150).
111. Ibid., iv.101–104 (pp. 224–228). Compare with Origen: the confession (Greek: *to homologēthēnai*) is the moment of unification with God, and a denial (Greek: *to arnēthēnai*) is a separation from him. PG 11:576c–d (=Origen, *Eis marturion,* ch. 10).
112. Clement, *Stromata,* iv.104, 163ff (p. 228, 328ff). Clement also presents other forms of accomplishment which concern life on earth, but express the same parallel Christian perfection in the knowledge and love of God, and can thus lead to unification with him without a denial of the body ibid., iv.147–155ff (pp. 300-318ff).
113. Tertullian, *Apology,* xli.1 (pp. 88–89) (and *Apology,* trans. Rendall, p. 187).
114. Ibid., xliv–xlv (pp. 92-94).
115. Ibid., l (p. 105ff).
116. Ibid., l.16, the last phrase of the *Apology* (p. 108).
117. Ibid., l.13 (p. 108).
118. But cf. Tertullian, *To Scapula,* ii (pp. 1127–1128).
119. Tertullian, *Apology,* l.
120. I owe Susan Weingarten this observation.
121. PG 11:563a–637 (=Origen, *Eis marturion*).
122. PG 11:584c–589b (=Origen, *Eis marturion*).
123. PG 11:617c–620a (=Origen, *Eis marturion*).
124. Clement, *Stromata,* iv.16.1 (p. 82). See Perkins, *The Suffering Self,* pp. 32-33 on the martyr as a warrior and an athlete.
125. Note that unlike Pericles's funeral oration the Christian writers must use an implicit language in their speeches (hence "principalities and powers"

instead of the Roman state), otherwise they risk high treason. This is the reason why, to my mind, they use an ambiguous and a symbolic language to articulate their political battle.

126. To state a few examples: Musurillo, *The Acts of the Christian Martyrs*, pp. 22, 80, 290.
127. See the resistance of El'azar in 2 Maccabees 6:29 to eat pork, which is considered an act of madness—*aponoia*—because it did not tally with the logics of a reasonable man.
128. PG 11:592a–596c (=Origen, *Eis marturion*).
129. *Midrash Lamentation Rabbah*, p. 84.
130. The exception to that is the rabbinic take on the trials of the seven sons of 2 Maccabees 7 in BT *Giṭṭin* 57b.
131. See Bowersock, *Martyrdom and Rome*, pp. 77–81, who shows how the idea of self-sacrifice of the Maccabees is adopted by Ignatius. Van Henten, "The Martyrs as Heroes of the Christian People" and idem, *The Maccabean Martyrs as Saviours of the Jewish People*.
132. For example, John Chrysostom's three homilies *In Sanctos Maccabaeos* (PG 50:617–628), and *De Eleazaro et de septem pueris* (PG 63:523–530). Christo, *Martyrdom according to John Chrysostom*, pp. 32, 41. Gregory of Nazianzus, *Orations*, 15 (*In Machabaeorum Laudem*): PG 35:912–933. Ziadé, *Les martyrs Maccabées*.
133. *Select Narratives of Holy Women from the Syro-Antiochene or Sinai Palimpsest*, vol. 1, pp. 118–144. See Van Esbroeck, "The Saint as a Symbol."
134. For a different interpretation on the relationship between 1 and 2 Maccabees, see Berthelot, "L'idéologie maccabéenne," and Honigman, *Tales of High Priests and Taxes*.
135. See T. Rajak, "Reflections on Jewish Resistance and the Discourse of Martyrdom in Josephus," for the way in which Josephus constructs the Maccabean model of martyrs, thus attesting to a "missing link" that may connect the Maccabean martyrs of 2 Maccabees 6–7 to early Christian martyrologies.
136. Here concurrent with the way in which Josephus represents their revolt (see previous note).
137. Woolfenden, *Daily Liturgical Prayer*, p. 26.
138. *The Didascalia Apostolorum in Syriac*, chs. 19–20 in vol. 407 (t. 179) pp. 185–202.
139. Ibid., ch. 19, pp. 186, 188. For the practice, see Musurillo, *The Acts of the Christian Martyrs*, p. 108 (=*The Martyrdom of Saints Perpetua and Felicitas*, § 3).
140. *The Didascalia Apostolorum in Syriac*, ch. 19, p. 188.
141. Ibid., ch. 19, p. 191.
142. The idea of the resurrection can already be discerned in 2 Maccabees 7:14.
143. *The Didascalia Apostolorum in Syriac*, ch. 20, pp. 201–202.
144. Cyprian, *Epistularium*, 6 (vol. IIIb, pp. 29–37), 10 (vol. IIIb, pp. 46–55), 15

(vol. IIIb, pp. 85–89), 58 (vol. IIIc, pp. 319–335), 60 (vol. IIIc, pp. 374–379), 77–79 (vol. IIIc, pp. 618–625).

145. Cf. El'azar ben Yair's exhortation prior to the suicide on Masada in Josephus, *Jewish War*, vii.320ff.

146. Cyprian, *Ad Fortunatum*, i–v (pp. 187–193).

147. See Boyarin, *Dying for God*, pp. 100ff. Note that the anti-Roman provocation of Rabbi Akiva who teaches the Torah publically is used here in order to attract the attention of Paphos ben Yehudah, who would not have otherwise known about Rabbi Akiva's transgression. Note that this story is not repeated in any of the cycles about "The Ten Slain by the Kingdom."

148. In a different story about Rabbi El'azar ben Pratha and Rabbi Ḥananyah ben Teradion, who are also caught for studying the Torah, the second is burned alive while the first publically renounces his activities and tries to convince the authorities that he is a master (*rabbi*) of weavers: *'Avodah Zarah* 17b. El'azer ben Pratha is saved by a miraculous intervention of Elijah, while Rabbi Ḥananyah ben Teradion is punished for studying in public the letters of God's name (i.e., practicing magic). Boyarin has shown the trickster feature of such figures in *Dying for God: Martyrdom and the Creation of Christianity and Judaism*, ch. 2. Both portray a sharp contrast to the figure of the Christian martyr.

149. In *The Myth of Persecution*, Moss argues that the myth of persecutions was aimed at inventing the notion of the persecuted church, and that historical victimization enabled the church to build its authority."

150. Dehandschutter draws attention to the earliest use of the Greek term in the context of Roman persecution in "The Martyrdom of Polycarp"; see "Martyr—Martyrium," pp. 35–36 (repr. p. 107).

151. Musurillo, *The Acts of the Christian Martyrs*, pp. 18, 20, 104, 160, 292. See the debate between Dehandschutter, "Martyr—Martyrium" and Ruysschaert, "Les 'martyrs' et les 'confesseurs' de la lettre des églises de Lyon et de Vienne." The first argues that the meaning of *marturion* as martyrology is already apparent in the Greek in "The Martyrdom of Polycarp." The second argues for a technical juridical sense of the term until the mid-third century. The terms *marturion* and *marturia* as used in "The Martyrdom of Polycarp" could all be understood as "testimony/ies." See also Barnes, *Tertullian*, ch. 12: "Martyrdom," in particular pp. 176–183.

152. For the Greek *marturologion* (the martyr's life story, i.e., martyrology), see *The Canons of the Council in Trullo*, can. 63 (p. 144) from 691/2, which anesthetizes false martyrologies.

153. *"Martyrizauerunt autem testes dei Carpus episcopos Pomfilius et Agathanice apud provinciam Asiam"* ends the Latin recension of *The Martyrdom of Carpus, Pamfilus, and Agathonicē*, § 7 (Musurillo, *The Acts of the Christian Martyrs*, p. 36), and is missing from the Greek recension.

154. See ibid., p. 106 (=*The Martyrdom of Saints Perpetua and Felicitas*, § 1), where

Latin *in martyrum* and *in testimonium* are used in the same sentence, the first for "martyrdom" and the second for "testimony."

155. See Musurillo, *The Acts of the Christian Martyrs*, p. 292 (*The Martyrdom of Agapē, Irenē, and Chionē*, § 7), where the verb *marturein* is used to designate the act of execution—here burning alive. Cf. Bowersock, *Martyrdom and Rome*, pp. 69–71, who shows "martyr" to be constructed by Clement in order to refute the idea of suicide. And Moss, *Ancient Christian Martyrdom*, pp. 2–6.
156. Tertullian, *To the Martyrs*. In *De anima*, 55.4–5 (pp. 862–863) Tertullian writes about the special place where the souls of the Christian martyrs are taken upon their death. The term enters the official juridical language in the constitutions of the fourth century: *CJ* i.2.2 (from 381) and i.2.3 (from 386), where both *martyr* and *martyrium* appear in Latin in reference to Christians who were executed in the persecutions by the Pagan state. See also Hoppenbrouwers, *Recherches sur la terminologie du martyre de Tertullien à Lactance*.
157. See Barnes, *Early Christian Hagiography and Roman History*. Lifshitz, "The Martyr, the Tomb, and the Matron." Buc, "Martyre et ritualité dans l'Antiquité tardive." Moss, *Ancient Christian Martyrdom*.
158. Moss, *Ancient Christian Martyrdom*.
159. In her book *The Suffering Self*, Perkins shows how martyrologies created a representation of the Christian community as a community of sufferers. The desire to be tortured and executed was an empowering experience for Christians. In her words, the figure of the sufferer hero created a new subjectivity, a new "cultural subject," in its alternative image of the human body and the human self. For the martyrs, see especially chs. 1, 4.
160. In ibid, pp. 32–33, Perkins indeed refers to the martyr as a warrior and an athlete, and also states the importance of this figure's abnormality. For Christian repudiation of the normal social nexus, see Brown, *The Body and Society*, pp. 1–64.
161. Barnes, *Early Christian Hagiography and Roman History*, ch. 3: "The Great Persecution (303–313)."
162. See the attack on the cult of martyrs and their grave led by Julian the Apostate, as described in Gregory of Nazianzus, *Orations*, 4.24–27, 4.68.
163. Lactantius, *Divine Institutions*, v.1 (pp. 435–436), addressed to Constantine himself.
164. Ibid., v.1.23–28, v.4.3–4.
165. Ibid., v.8.
166. Ibid., v. 13.6–14.
167. Ibid., v.14–15.
168. Ibid., v.5.22–23.
169. Eusebius of Caesarea, *On the Martyrs in Palestine* (Greek); *History of the Martyrs in Palestine* (Syriac); and *The Encomium of the Martyrs*. Basil the Great's homilies 5, 17, 18, 19, and 23 (PG, 31:238–260, 483–525, 590–599, =*In mar-*

tyrem Iulittam, In Barlaamum martyrem, In Gordium martyrem, In Quadraginta martyres, In Mamantem maryrem). Gregory of Nyssa's sermons on Saint Stephen, Praise of Theodore the Martyr, and sermons on the Forty Martyrs (PG 46:701–721; 735–772). John Chrysostom's extensive homilies as is indicated by Christo, *Martyrdom according to John Chrysostom*, appendix B (pp. 205–206), p. 26.

170. Christo, *Martyrdom according to John Chrysostom*. Straw, "Martyrdom and Christian Identity."
171. See, for example, in his homily *In S. Ignatium Martyrem*. Christo, *Martyrdom according to John Chrysostom*, pp. 102ff.
172. Christo, *Martyrdom according to John Chrysostom*, pp. 184ff.
173. In particular, Gregory of Nazianzus, *Orations*, 11 (pp. 336–340) and 15 (*In Machabaeorum Laudem*, PG 35:912–933). For the second, see Ziadé, *Les martyrs Maccabées*.
174. Gregory of Nazianzus, *Orations*, 35, which is probably not his own as the editor of the text explains (Moreschini, pp. 38–39). The author evokes the figure of the martyr in order to light the flame of Christian battle, this time against the Arian apostates.
175. Evagrius Ponticus's Disciples, *Chapters*, 15 (p. 118), see also chs. 45–47 (pp. 148–150).
176. Markus identifies the origin of this tradition already in the writings of Clement and Origen in *The End of Ancient Christian*, pp. 71–72.
177. Lactantius, *Divine Institutions*, vi.4, vi.24.
178. Jerome, *Letters*, xiv (to Heliodorus), especially §§ 4–5.
179. This is in line with the classic studies of Peter Brown on the beginning of the cult of martyrs' tombs in the West. Brown, *The Cult of the Saints: Its Rise and Function in Latin Christianity*.
180. Rajak, "Reflections on Jewish Resistance and the Discourse of Martyrdom in Josephus."
181. Josephus, *Jewish War*, vii.410–419.
182. Note his use of the term *aponoia:* "the madness of the Sicaii attacking like a disease in the cities of Cyrene." Ibid., vii.437.
183. Rajak, "Reflections on Jewish Resistance and the Discourse of Martyrdom in Josephus."
184. In *The Myth of Persecution*, Moss shows that they continue to fulfill this function to this day.
185. Musurillo, *The Acts of the Christian Martyrs*, pp. 22, 80, 290, 302.

4. Socializing Nature: The Ascetic Totem

Epigraph: Durkheim and Mauss, "De quelques formes de classification—Contribution à l'étude des représentations collectives," p. 87 (82).

1. Hadot, *Philosophy as a Way of Life*, chs. 3–4, 7.

2. See Miller, "Shifting Selves in Late Antiquity." Flood, *The Ascetic Self.*
3. See all the same Valantasis's attempts in defining asceticism in his conclusive article, "A Theory of the Social Function of Asceticism."
4. Glucklich, *Sacred Pain,* and Flood, *The Ascetic Self,* reveal the psychological effect of pain and asceticism respectively, and their importance to the religious experience. The first reveals how physiological pain becomes imbued with cultural significance that makes it a meaningful religious phenomenon. The second sees asceticism as a ritual of transformation of the self, through which the self internalizes the tradition about the body and reaches subjectivity by ritual of asceticism. Both focus on the subjective experience of the ascetic and the way in which it connects and is fed by the cultural setting.
5. But was brought back recently by Descola, *Beyond Nature and Culture.*
6. Lévi-Strauss, *Le Totémisme aujourd'hui,* ch. 1.
7. Descola, *Beyond Nature and Culture,* pp. 144ff.
8. Durkheim, *Les formes élémentaires de la vie religieuse.* Durkheim and Mauss, "De quelques formes de classification—Contribution à l'étude des représentations collectives" (translated into English as *Primitive Classification*).
9. Lévi-Strauss, *Le Totémisme aujourd'hui,* p. 84 (my translation).
10. Ibid., introduction.
11. Descola, "Societies of Nature and the Nature of Society," p. 110.
12. Already in Schama, *Landscape and Memory.*
13. Descola, *In the Society of Nature.* In the 1970s the Achuar still maintained a way of life largely unaffected by outsiders' contacts.
14. Ibid., p. 3.
15. Ibid., pp. 93–101.
16. This is not an argument that Descola makes, but my own deduction from his book, one which I do not think he will object to.
17. Ibid., ch. 5.
18. Ibid., ch. 6, e.g., pp. 260–262. Descola, *Beyond Nature and Culture,* ch. 6.
19. Descola, *In the Society of Nature,* pp. 47ff.
20. See Descola, "Human natures" and *Beyond Nature and Culture.*
21. Berger, *The Sacred Canopy,* ch. 3.
22. Ibid., ch. 1.
23. Ibid., p. 55.
24. Today, *ta'anit* normally refers to the act of fasting. But the biblical origin is "torment your souls" on the Day of Atonement (Leviticus 16:29–31). For this Hebrew root see below in this chapter.
25. This is already set out in the Bible, where the calamities that God inflicts on earth always arrive as punishment for a sinful collective (e.g., the Flood, the Tower of Babel, Sodom and Gomorrah, the destruction of Nineveh).
26. The sect at Qumran offers such an alternative already in the Second Temple period. For Second Temple prayer houses, see Levine *The Ancient Synagogue,* chs. 2–5.

27. Loc. cit., Feldman, "Diaspora Synagogues."
28. Leviticus 16:29–31, which connects the "torments of the *souls*" to the idea of purification from all sins and atonement. The Septuagint translates it using the verb *tapeinoō* (to reduce, to lower, to humble), here in the meaning of lowering oneself. See the second-century A.D. Jewish inscription from Rhenea about lowering of the soul (*psuchē*) on a fast day (*Sylloge inscriptionum graecarum,* iii, 1181). This method of repentance was practiced in daily life in the Second Temple period as an individual act; see Finn, *Asceticism in the Graeco-Roman World,* p. 44ff.
29. The book of Jonah could well have served as an example for collective fasting and repentance which prevented God's punishment for the people of Nineveh; the book is included to this day in the reading for Yom Kippur.
30. This is 17th MarHeshvan; *Mishnah Ta'anit,* 1:3.
31. Some, not all, of the torments concern the using of water.
32. *Mishnah Ta'anit,* 1:6
33. *Mishnah* (Kaufmann MS) *Ta'anit,* 3:4.
34. *Mishnah Ta'anit,* 1:7.
35. Including the seventh of the Eighteen Benedictions and the six additional ones.
36. Note that the two biblical senses of the verb *'a-n-h,* to answer and to torment, are used with the accusative "answer someone" (in contrast to the modern Hebrew where "to answer" takes the dative). Thus "God answers" is morphologically equivalent to "God torments man"/"man torments himself."
37. Note the place that the priests get in this ritual (especially *Mishnah Ta'anit,* ch. 4), while the rabbis are those who define, control, and govern the rituals (ibid., chs. 2–3).
38. This is one of the five models, the "juridical model" that Glucklich brings for the use of pain in *Sacred Pain,* pp 16–21.
39. PT *Ta'anit* 3:3 (66c, pp. 719–720). See below toward the end of the present chapter for the discussion on the Palestinian Talmud.
40. BT *Ta'anit* 16a.
41. As noted above (n. 25), this is already set out in the Hebrew Bible, where the calamities that God inflicts on earth always arrive as punishment for a sinful collective (the Flood, the Tower of Babylon, Sodom and Gomorrah, Nineveh).
42. Note also that this biblical word for sinful in a specific sense of unlawfulness (*anomia*) is very rare in the Talmud.
43. This is regardless of the question of whether this ritual also created social distinction and hierarchy. For an in-depth summary on the social theories about ascetic rituals, see Clark, *Reading Renunciation,* ch. 8, pp. 204ff.
44. Ibid.
45. Ibid., ch. 1. See also Vööbus, *History of Asceticism in the Syrian Orient,* vol. 1; and Caner, *Wandering, Begging Monks,* ch. 2.

46. Public Christian fasting is attested already in the first century A.D. Finn, *Asceticism in the Graeco-Roman World,* pp. 58–71.
47. Especially Tatian; see Vööbus, *History of Asceticism in the Syrian Orient,* vol.1, pp. 31–39. See also Vaage and Wimbush, *Asceticism and the New Testament.*
48. Virginity is not necessarily related to the idea of self-denial and social withdrawal. The Vestal Virgins are just one example to the contrary.
49. Clark, *Reading Renunciation,* pp. 212ff. Vööbus, *History of Asceticism in the Syrian Orient,* vol.1, p. 35. This is also related to the idea of man made in God's image; Gen 1.26. I owe this observation to Susan Weingarten.
50. As is shown by both Clark and Finn.
51. The descriptions are from the fourth–sixth centuries: Sozomen, *Ecclesiastical History* vi.33.2–4; Theodoret of Cyrrhus, *A History of the Monks in Syria,* i.2; Evagrius Scholasticus, *Ecclesiastical History* i.21 (pp. 198–200); Caner, *Wandering, Begging Monks,* pp. 50–53; and Vööbus's description from pseudo-Ephrem, *History of Asceticism in the Syrian Orient,* vol. 1, pp. 152–154.
52. Patlagean, "*Ancienne hagiographie* byzantine et histoire sociale," pp. 114–115. "They reject the nourishments of human beings" in the words of Evagrius Scholasticus, *Ecclesiastical History,* i.21 (p. 198).
53. Patlagean, "*Ancienne hagiographie* byzantine et histoire sociale," pp. 114–115. See Antony and Paul of Thebes wearing animal skin, though inside out, in Athanasius of Alexandria, *Life of Antony,* 47. Jerome, *Three Lives of Monks: Paul, Malchus, Hilarion,* pp. 154, 296 (=*Life of Paul of Thebes,* § 6. *Life of Hilarion,* § 32). Theodoret of Cyrrhus, *A History of the Monks in Syria,* i.2, xxvi.12–14. *A History of the Monks in Egypt,* vi.3 (p. 45). PG 87/3:3705a,c (=*The Life of Mary of Egypt,* §§ 10, 12). Leontius of Neapolis, *Life of Symeon salos,* pp. 67, 71 (pp. 133, 137).
54. Theodoret of Cyrrhus, *A History of the Monks in Syria* xxii.3-5, xxiv.6–7. Ševčenko, "The Hermit as Stanger in the Desert."
55. Theodoret of Cyrrhus, *A History of the Monks in Syria,* prol.5, vi.2, 10. See also the multiple descriptions of communicating, controlling, and blessing wild beasts (both real and mythological creatures) in John Moschus, *Spiritual Meadow,* ch. 58 (pp. 101–2); *A History of the Monks in Egypt,* vi, ix.8–10 (pp. 43-44, 73-74); and Jerome, *Three Lives of Monks: Paul, Malchus, Hilarion,* pp. 156, 178 (=*The Life of Paul of Thebes,* §§ 7ff, 16).
56. Theodoret of Cyrrhus, *A History of the Monks in Syria,* xxii.3–9, xxiv.6. The love towards God enables man "to pass beyond natural limits" (Greek: *ho peri ton theon erōs huperbēnai tous tēs phuseōs pareseuasen horous*). Theodoret of Cyrrhus, "On divine love," passim. and ch. 4 (pp. 262–264). *The Sayings of the Desert Fathers,* xviii.53 (vol. 3, pp. 134-136).
57. The first two things that the ascetic fights are the passions of the body and demons. The demons themselves represent forces which induce humans to evil through their corporality. Characteristic examples from *A History of the Monks in Egypt* include: when Father Hellē had a sudden desire for honey, he interpreted it as an attack of a passion of a body (xii.2, pp. 92–93);

and when Father Pityrion taught that gluttony is controlled by a demon, and in order to beat it one needs to subdue gluttony, not surrender to it (x.23, xv.2, pp. 85, 111). More examples of demons as a source of passions and troubles for humans include: Athanasius of Alexandria, *Life of Antony*, chs. 23, 26; and Jerome, *Three Lives of Monks*, p. 226ff (=*Life of Hilarion*, §§ 5–11). The means of the devil's battle here is the senses, while asceticism is the way for people to fight back. The body is perceived as a battlefield.

58. This idea is laid out in the first of the letters attributed to Antony the Great in *The Letters of St. Antony*, pp. 197–202. Palladius, *Lausiac History*, ch. 38 (pp. 192–202). See the incorruptibility of the soul in contrast to the body in the *Acts of Thomas* (in *Apocryphal Acts of the Apostles*, trans. Klijn, pp. 10–11). Sebastian Brock, "Early Syrian Asceticism," pp. 8–9. PG 11:188–189 (=Origen, *On the First Principles*, ii.3.2). See Athanasius of Alexandria, *Life of Antony*, ch. 74 (pp. 324–326).
59. Wild beasts are described as both innocent and dangerous to man. The ascetic is never attacked by wild animals. On the contrary, the ascetic makes contact with them, and vice versa, by acknowledging the ascetic's divine supernatural power over them. Ševčenko, "The Hermit as Stanger in the Desert." See Onesima reading the Gospels to wild animals nine hours a day in *Select Narratives of Holy Women from the Syro-Antiochene or Sinai Palimpsest*, p. 84 (=*Life of Onesima*, f. 86b–87a). For an in-depth analysis of mastery over the animal world as part of a moral perception of nature and man in Christian and Jewish Palestinian sources, see Diamond, "Lions, Snakes, and Asses."
60. PG 11:181–183 (=Origen, *On the First Principles*, ii.1.1–2).
61. Diamond has noted the similarity between Jewish and Christian texts in regard to mastery over the animal world as a restoration of the world of animals and humans to its "natural" form in "Lions, Snakes, and Asses," pp. 265–267. Antony, for example, wraps himself in an animal skin, but wears it inside out as a hair shirt, thus becoming one of the animals but also controlling his own nature with the hair shirt (Athanasius of Alexandria, *Life of Antony*, ch. 47). See his frowning on nakedness (ibid., ch. 60).
62. Here in line with Descola, *In the Society of Nature*.
63. Just like the Achuar in the study of Descola, *In the Society of Nature*.
64. The Old Testament is, of course, full of miracles, although to a much lesser degree compared to the New Testament and Christian hagiography. Miracles do occur in the Hebrew Bible, but they do not often determine the course of events. However, there are several biblical figures who perform miracles as part of their function: Moses, Elijah, and Elisha. This capacity is naturally bestowed on them from God, whose power they express. Interestingly, the first two figures also spent part of their life in the desert.
65. Titus Lucretius Carus, *De rerum natura*, vi.173ff, 495ff.
66. Ibid. vi.50–55 (trans. Rouse). See also the use of vows in times of trouble in ibid., v.1226–1232.

67. Ibid., ii.62ff, v.195ff.
68. Ibid., i.146–158.
69. In contrast to Plotinus, for example, see Dodds, *Pagan and Christian in an Age of Anxiety*, pt. 2, "Man and the Divine World."
70. Philostratus, *The Life of Apollonius of Tyana*, i.3.
71. Ibid., i.2.
72. Ibid., i.1–2, 32.
73. Ibid., i.1–2. Cf. *The Acts of Thomas*, below in this chapter.
74. Philostratus, *The Life of Apollonius of Tyana*, i.11.
75. Ibid., i.8–15. Cf. *The Acts of Thomas* in *Apocryphal Acts of the Apostles*, ch. 20.
76. He does it by convincing the wheat merchants to release their stocks, which he does without uttering a word, solely by writing. Philostratus, *The Life of Apollonius of Tyana*, i.14–15.
77. Ibid., i.32.
78. Greek: *para tēn phusin tēn heautōn*. Ibid., i. 38.
79. Ibid., i.8–9, 22, 38, iv.13ff, 24.
80. Ibid., iii.38, iv.2,10,13–16, vi.29–34, 41.
81. Ibid., iv.19–20, 30–31, 35–45.
82. Ibid., iv.45, v.24.
83. When he is in Athens, for example, he refuses to enter the amphitheater because it is an impure place, defiled by blood. Ibid., iv, 22.
84. Ibid., vi.29–34.
85. Greek: *hoi gumnoi*, "the Naked Wise" in Christopher Jones's translation. Apollonius's encounter with them comprises most of the sixth book. Ibid., vi.5–23.
86. Apollonius and Damis reach them after they had paid a visit to the sanctuary of Memnon, and before they continue to the Cataracts of the Nile.
87. Ibid., vi.16.
88. For example, their chief makes a tree speak to Apollonius. Ibid., vi.10.
89. Ibid., vi.10.6.
90. "They follow their head as *Hellanodikai* follow their presbyter." Ibid., vi.10.
91. Ibid., vi, 5.
92. Du Toit, *Theios Anthropos: Zur Verwendung von θεῖος ἄνθρωπος und sinnverwandten Ausdrücken in der Literatur der Kaiserzeit*, ch. 12. Fowden, "The Pagan Holy Man in Late Antique Society." Cf. Marinos of Neapolis, *The Life of Proclus*, and Iamblichus, *On the Pythagorean Life*.
93. Cf. Marinos of Neapolis, *The Life of Proclus*, especially §§ 7, 19–20. Iamblichus, *On the Pythagorean Life*, §§ 13, 24 (60, 106).
94. Judge, "Fourth-Century Monasticism in the Papyri," pp. 613–615.
95. Rapp, "The Origins of Hagiography and the Literature of Early Monasticism."
96. Rapp, "Storytelling as Spiritual Communication in Early Greek Hagiography."
97. John of Ephesus, *Lives of the Eastern Saints*, PO 82/17:238–242.

98. Theodoret of Cyrrhus, *A History of the Monks in Syria,* prol. 10 (pp. 140–142), i.13, xxvi.17.
99. Rapp, "'For next to God, you are my salvation.'"
100. Rapp, "The Origins of Hagiography and the Literature of Early Monasticism." In her book *The Saint's Saints,* Weingarten argues convincingly for the Jewish model of ascetic loner in Jerome's writings in rabbinic tales about Rabbi Shim'on bar Yoḥai. See in contrast, Bar-Asher Siegal, *Early Christian Monastic Literature and the Babylonian Talmud,* ch. 5.
101. *The Sayings of the Desert Fathers. The Greek Lives of Pachomius.* Pachomius and his disciples, *Works. A History of the Monks in Egypt.* See the "five thousand" monks in the city of Oxyrhynchus and the same number living in monasteries in the city's outskirts in *A History of the Monks in Egypt,* v.
102. *The Sayings of the Desert Fathers,* v.30, v.40 (vol. 1, pp. 266–268, 280–282). Rapp, "Storytelling as Spiritual Communication in Early Greek Hagiography." See Krueger, *Writing in Gold,* for writing hagiography as a spiritual rapprochement to the anchorites.
103. Athanasius of Alexandria, *Life of Antony,* 87 (p. 358). See *The Sayings of the Desert Fathers,* xviii: "On the clairvoyants" (vol. 3, pp. 38–137). *A History of the Monks in Egypt,* i.1–2, ii, vi.1 (pp. 9–10, 12, 43). Cf. Syria: Theodoret of Cyrrhus, *A History of the Monks in Syria,* vii.1–3. xiii.15.
104. Philostratus, *The Life of Apollonius of Tyana,* iv.2,10, 19–20, 30–31, 35–45, vi.41.
105. *A History of the Monks in Egypt,* vi, viii.22–37, xxii.3–6 (pp. 44, 55–61, 93–94). Cf. Syria: Theodoret of Cyrrhus, *A History of the Monks in Syria,* i.4–6.
106. *The Sayings of the Desert Fathers,* vi.27, xviii.53 (vol. 1, p. 334, vol. 3, pp. 134–6). John Moschus, *Spiritual Meadow,* chs. 173, 183 (pp. 227–228, 239–240). *A History of the Monks in Egypt,* ix.8–10. Jerome, *Three Lives of Monks,* pp. 274, 286 (=*Life of Hilarion by Jerome,* §§ 22, 29).
107. See Dunn, *The Emergence of Monasticism.* For fighting demons as means of psychological transformation, see the works of Cassian (*Conferences*) and Evagrius Ponticus (*Praktikos, On Thoughts*). I rely here on the PhD dissertation of Inbar Graiver on *Self-Transformation and Self-Formation in Early Christian Asceticism,* currently under preparation at the School of History, Tel Aviv University.
108. *The Sayings of the Desert Fathers,* v.30, 40, vi.1, ix. See father Apollo on pagan worship of nature forces in Egypt, and its replacement with a Christian theodicy. *A History of the Monks in Egypt,* viii.16, 22–37, x.28, xviii.1–3. Cf. Syria: Theodoret of Cyrrhus, *A History of the Monks in Syria,* i.4–6.
109. Compare this with the central role of *hoi gumnoi* in Apollonius of Tyana discussed above in this chapter.
110. Ashbrook Harvey, *Ascetism and Society in Crisis,* p. 135.
111. Ibid. Theodoret of Cyrrhus, *A History of the Monks in Syria,* iv.1.
112. Ashbrook Harvey, *Ascetism and Society in Crisis,* pp. 13–21, sets out this difference between Egypt and Syria and attributes it to the precarious situation of the Syrian desert between the Roman and the Persian Empires.

Brown also marked this difference in his article "The Rise and Function of the Holy Man in Late Antiquity."

113. PG 1:379–451 (=*Epistolae ad virgines*). These are letters of instruction, probably from the third century, addressed to wandering ascetics who spread the Christian faith in Syria and provided Christian believers with moral support. They indeed testify to wandering ascetics, but are not a call to social withdrawal. Quite the contrary, they provide strict instructions for conduct among these "apostolic wanderers," as Caner calls them in *Wandering, Begging Monks*, pp. 65–77.
114. *Apocryphal Acts of the Apostles*, pp. 173–333, especially pp. 187ff.
115. Brock, "Early Syrian Asceticism."
116. Theodoret of Cyrrhus, *A History of the Monks in Syria*, vol. 1, p. 30. Krueger, *Writing in Gold*, ch. 2.
117. Theodoret of Cyrrhus, *A History of the Monks in Syria*, prol. 5.
118. Ibid., ii.9, iii. 20, iv.1, xxv.1.
119. Ibid., prol. 10., iv.1, xxix.2.
120. Ibid. vii.1–3, viii.7. John of Ephesus, *Lives of the Eastern Saints*, PO 82/17:21–22, 26.
121. Theodoret of Cyrrhus uses the term *anachōrēsis* very rarely: when Symeon is expelled from Teleda (*A History of the Monks in Syria*, xxxvi.5.25, p. 170), for his own departure (ibid., xxix.5), and when he describes the exceptionality of Asclepius having lived a life both of a city dweller and an anchorite (ibid., xxv.1, Greek: *diaprepsas biōi, tōi te politikōi kai anachōrōtikōi*).
122. Ibid., ii.9, vi.6, viii.7, ix.1–4.
123. Ibid., i.11–14. ii.7–8, vi.6, viii.14, x.7, xiii.14, xxiv.7. John of Ephesus, *Lives of the Eastern Saints*, PO 82/17:12–14, 123, PO 92/19:252–253, 257. Cf. Jerome, *Three Lives of Monks*, pp. 274, 286 (=*Life of Hilarion*, §§ 22, 29).
124. See Ashbrook Harvey, *Ascetism and Society in Crisis*, p. 59ff, and especially John Ephesus's account of "the plague of madness" that struck Amida and its neighborhood in 560. Ibid., pp. 64–65, 171–173 (n. 44–50). John of Ephesus, *The Second Unedited Part of the Ecclesiastical History* (ed. Nau), pp. 488–489. Cf. John of Ephesus's description of emperor Justin's madness, which is perceived here as a divine punishment for his impiety (antimonophysite persecutions). John of Ephesus, *The Third Part of the Ecclesiastical History*, iii.2ff.
125. Theodoret of Cyrrhus, *A History of the Monks in Syria*, i.4–5. The same Jacob reverses a verdict of a judge by miraculously smashing a big jar into pieces (ibid., i.6).
126. Ibid., i.4–14, xxi.2, as noted by Brown, "The Rise and Function of the Holy Man in Late Antiquity."
127. Ashbrook Harvey, *Ascetism and Society in Crisis*, pp. 51–52.
128. See the "Life of Z'ura" in John Ephesus, *Lives of the Eastern Saints*, who after mounting a pillar gets down to be sent to the capital to defend the case of his monophysite community by punishing the emperor (PO 82:21ff).

129. See the elaborated discussion about the archaeological evidence in Schachner, "The Archaeology of the Stylite," including a map of its dispersion (p. 331). This study shows that the phenomenon did not stay in Syria, but appeared also in other regions in the early Christian Near East, although to a much lesser extent.
130. *The Syriac Life of Symeon the Stylite.* For the pagan archetype of the saint on a pillar in Syria, see Frankfurter "Stylites and Phallobates," discussed below.
131. Doran *The Lives of Simeon Stylites.* Ashbrook Harvey, "The Sense of a Stylite."
132. Theodoret of Cyrrhus, *A History of the Monks in Syria,* xxvi.4–11, and prol. on asceticism as a philosophy.
133. Ibid., xxvi.11.
134. Ibid., xxvi.13, 18.
135. Ibid., xxvi.12.
136. *The Syriac Life of Symeon the Stylite,* p. 308. Doran, *The Lives of Simeon Stylites,* p. 33.
137. *The Syriac Life of Symeon the Stylite,* pp. 302ff.
138. Such, for instance, is the disease that he inflicts on the consul of Antioch, who oppresses the poor of the city, a disease which leads to the consul's death. Ibid., pp. 311–313. Cf. Philostratus, *The Life of Apollonius of Tyana,* i.14–15.
139. *The Syriac Life of Symeon the Stylite,* pp. 318–319.
140. Ibid., pp. 319–322.
141. Ibid., pp. 323–324, 339–342.
142. Ibid., pp. 335–336, especially p. 355 where Simeon stops a mountain from crawling toward the village in Lycia.
143. Harvey Ashbrook, *Ascetism and Society in Crisis,* pp. 43–52.
144. John of Ephesus, *Lives of the Eastern Saints,* PO 82/17:18–35, 56–84, PO 89/18:663.
145. Schachner, "The Archaeology of the Stylite."
146. John of Ephesus, *Lives of the Eastern Saints,* PO 82/17:56–57.
147. In the second century Lucian documented this sort of use of mounting a pillar (*phallobates*) in the cult of the goddess Atargatis at Hierapolis, in his *On the Syrian Goddess,* §§ 16, 28–29 (Lightfoot, pp. 256, 266–268). For a full discussion see ibid., pp. 417–427. Frankfurter, "Stylites and Phallobates."
148. Frankfurter "Stylites and Phallobates."
149. Theodoret of Cyrrhus, *A History of the Monks in Syria,* xxi.4–6, 13: where father Jacob "passes over nature" (Greek: *huper phusin agōnas*) in order to fight with nature to triumph over it. He stays catatonic under the burning sun and dropping snow, not even moving for his natural needs. People from the city who approach him, dig him out of the snow.
150. Mar Z'ura gets down from his pillar in order to defend his community's case in Constantinople. John of Ephesus, *Lives of the Eastern Saints,* PO 82/17:21.

151. Doran explained the stylite as a biblical prophet who is placed in the heavenly temple between earth and heaven, symbolizing "the flight of the soul towards heaven." Doran, *The Lives of Simeon Stylites,* pp. 34–35, quoting Theodoret of Cyrrhus, *A History of the Monks in Syria,* xxvi.12.
152. *The Syriac Life of Symeon the Stylite,* pp. 301–302, 275. Cf. Father Jacob in Theodoret of Cyrrhus, *A History of the Monks in Syria,* xxi.4–6, 13, who is catatonic without mounting on a pillar.
153. Or to a single stone. *The Syriac Life of Symeon the Stylite,* pp. 301–302, Theodoret of Cyrrhus, *A History of the Monks in Syria,* xxvi.10. Cf. the practices of catatonia in the convent in Amida in John of Ephesus, *Lives of the Eastern Saints,* PO 89/18:612–618.
154. In much a similar way to what Brown, *The Cult of the Saints,* has shown about the saint's tomb as a conduit of holiness between heaven and earth.
155. John of Ephesus, *Lives of the Eastern Saints,* PO 82/17:59–60. The same for Z'ura who replaces his master Habib after his death on the pillar. Ibid., PO 89/18:663.
156. Ibid., PO 82:20.
157. Ibid., PO 82:70. *The Syriac Life of Symeon the Stylite,* pp. 295, 336. Sokoloff, *A Syriac Lexicon,* p. 472: "dust of a place where people were martyrized, which is diluted with oil and water and is applied for extreme unction" (following Feige, *Dies Geschichte des Mar ʿAbhdiso und seines Jüngers Mar Qardagh,* 2 vols., Kiel, 1889, 51:6). See also *Select Narratives of Holy Women from the Syro-Antiochene or Sinai Palimpsest,* p. 92 (=*Life of Onesimah,* f. 91a), where the dust of the paths of Saint Onesima is used by the sisters as ointment, "as *ḥnanā.*" Cf. BT *Sanhedrin* 68a.
158. *The Syriac Life of Symeon the Stylite,* pp. 334, 353–354.
159. See below in the last part of this chapter for the use of the same root in the Mishnah and the Palestinian and Babylonian Talmuds in the names attributed to the miracle workers: *Ḥanina, Ḥaninah, Ḥanan,* and even *Ḥoni.*
160. As he himself stated. Brown, "The Rise and Function of the Holy Man in Late Antiquity," p. 82.
161. In this, asceticism combines Glucklich's four models of pain in *Sacred Pain*: the juridical, the athletic, the magical, and the purifying. For a theoretical discussion, see Hill and Kral, *About Psychology.* A general discussion of the problematic "instrumentalization" of both ego-psychology and social psychology in the study of history is found in Scott, "The Incommensurability of Psychoanalysis and History."
162. Josephus, *Antiquities of the Jews,* xiv.4, where the two camps in the Hasmonean civil war fight over his powers. Cf. Theodoret of Cyrrhus, *A History of the Monks in Syria,* xxvi.15
163. Large ovens that were constructed especially for the Passover Sacrifice (*korban pesah*) in Jerusalem (*Tosefta,* ed. Lieberman, *Pesahim* 5:11; BT *Sanhedrin* 11a).

164. Hebrew: *Even haṬoim*, a high public rock in Jerusalem, used in the Second Temple period to declare lost and found (BT *Bava Metzi'a* 28a)
165. *Mishnah Taʿanit*, 3:8 (3:7–12 in MS Kaufmann A 50).
166. Bohak, *Ancient Jewish Magic*, pp. 45, 53, 128–129.
167. Ḥoni first tries the usual way and prays to God for rain. Only when this fails, does he turn to his magic practices.
168. PT *Taʿanit* 3:2 (66c, p. 719).
169. Ibid., 3:3 (66c, pp. 719–720).
170. Ibid., 3:3–3:9 (66c–67a, pp. 719–724).
171. Note that his name literally means "forgiveness" or "clemency" and derives from the same root of Ḥoni's name: *ḥ-n-n*. For an equivalence to the Syriac *ḥnānā*, see the discussion above.
172. Ibid., 3:4 (66c, p. 720) evoking the biblical case of Zimri ben Salu's sin which caused the death of twenty-four thousand people in a plague.
173. This anecdote was analyzed at length by Zalkhah, "The Prayer, the Miracle and the Miracle-Worker."
174. Cited from Rabbi Zeʿurah in the name of Rabbi Ḥaninah. The editor brings biblical cases to support this argument, which in fact opposes the biblical story about Zimri ben Salu' and Rabbi Ḥaninah's first conclusion that disasters come because of individual sinners. In the continuation of this passage, the editor evokes two cases of public fasting. The first was declared by Rabbi Eliʿezer and did not succeed, and the second by Rabbi Akiva and did succeed. The Talmud brings two explanations to account for this difference between the two sages. According to the first explanation, God loved Rabbi Eliʿezer so much that he wanted to continue hearing his prayers, and hence did not answer them. But according to the second explanation, the rain did not come so that Rabbi Eliʿezer would not be discredited for intervening with God's ways of reward and punishment (i.e., theodicy).
175. BT *Taʿanit* 19a–26a.
176. Cf. John of Ephesus, *Lives of the Eastern Saints*, PO 82/17:21.
177. BT *Taʿanit* 23a. For more on this, see a forthcoming article by Youval Rotman, "The Wormhole: Contracting Space-Contracting Time in Jewish, Christian and Muslim Sources."
178. The Bavli's conclusion: if you do not study along with others, you will die (Aramaic: *ḥavruta o mituta*). This conclusion needs to be taken as the Bavli's main emphasis in its interpretation of the tractate: the social importance of the rabbi as a miracle worker.
179. BT *Taʿanit* 23a–b. Abba Ḥilkiyah attributes the miracle to his wife's prayers. The story about Abba Ḥilkiyah is also narrated in the Palestinian Talmud (64b–c, p. 708), but is related to an anonymous miracle worker from the village of Eimi. See Kalmin, "Holy Men, Rabbis, and Demonic Sages in Late Antiquity," pp. 222–234.
180. BT *Taʿanit* 19b–25a.

181. BT *Ta'anit* 21b.
182. The same is also narrated about a pious woman in the city of Drokart who in time of a big fire still handed her oven to her neighbors (loc. cit.).
183. See, for instance, the competition between Abaye, the head of the community of Pumbedita, who receives greetings from heaven only once a week, while Aba Umana, who is but a simple bloodletter, receives greetings everyday because of fine deeds that he undertakes anonymously, which raises his level of piety. BT *Ta'anit* 21b–22b.
184. BT *Ta'anit* 21b.
185. See in particular the lesson that Rabbi Ḥaninah and the people of Tzippori. PT *Ta'anit* 3:4 (66c, p. 720), discussed above.
186. BT *Ta'anit* 23b. No such reference exists in PT *Ta'anit.*
187. And thus will die. BT *Ta'anit* 22b. The Bavli quotes the *Tosefta, Ta'anit,* ch. 2, 12 (ed. Lieberman, p. 334).
188. PT *Ta'anit* 3:3 (66c, p. 719). This difference between the two Talmuds is parallel to the difference in the ways in which Palestinian and Babylonian amoraim treat the suffering of the righteous as a theodicy. Elman, "The Suffering of the Righteous in Palestinian and Babylonian Sources."
189. BT *Ta'anit* 25a. Cf. PT *Ta'anit* 3:3–3:9 (p. 719–724) above. See Zalkhah, "The Prayer, the Miracle and the Miracle-Worker," for an analysis of this comparison. Note that many of the rabbis mentioned in the cycle in BT *Ta'anit,* ch. 3, are from Palestine. The fact that the Babylonian Talmud constructs the legends about Palestinian rabbis also in a different manner from the Palestinian Talmud is significant. Although the first was compiled later than the second, we cannot be sure in most cases which of the two has preserved a more ancient version, and which one introduced changes. See Noam, "A Tale of a Captured Story," on the case where the more "authentic" version of a story is found in the Babylonian Talmud. However, for our purpose the importance lies not in the question of which version is older, but what is the main intention of the editors in bringing the different anecdotes they recount.
190. As with Rabbi Yehuda in BT *Ta'anit* 24b, in comparison with Rabbi Yehuda haNasi's repeated attempts that fail to bring rain. Only when he loses confidence in his powers does the rain come.
191. The supernatural force should not be used as magic for harming people. See the case of Rabbi Yose demin Yukrat, who is angry about his son "troubling his creator." The son used his power to get the fig tree to grow figs for his father's workers. His father declares his wish that his son would die for "troubling his creator" (for such a petty thing), and his son dies on the spot. BT *Ta'anit* 24a (cf. Mt 21:18–22, Mk 11:12–14).
192. This analysis was not meant to show the rabbinical attitude toward either miracle working or asceticism (*issurin*) with the objective of underlining the similarities and differences to equivalent concepts in Christianity. On Jewish ascetics, see "beloved torments," Rabbi Shim'on bar Yoḥai and his

model adopted by Jerome. Weingarten, *The Saint's Saints*; and Bar-Asher Siegal, *Early Christian Monastic Literature and the Babylonian Talmud*, ch. 5, who argues differently. And on suffering as expiation and the difference between the two Talmuds' attitudes, see Kraemer, *Responses to Suffering in Classical Rabbinic Literature*. Elman, "The Suffering of the Righteous in Palestinian and Babylonian Sources." BT *Berakhot* 5a. BT *Bava Metzia* 85a ff.

193. Lévi-Strauss, *Le Totémisme aujourd'hui*, ch. 2: "Le nominalisme australien," where he has shown that the two do not necessarily overlap.

Epilogue: Psychology, Religion, and Social Change

Epigraph: Ende, *The Neverending Story*.

1. Van Gennep, *Les rites de passage*. Thomassen, "The Uses and Meanings of Liminality." Szakolczai, "Liminality and Experience."
2. Lewin, *Resolving Social Conflicts*. Bennis and Shepard. "A Theory of Group Development." Dalal. *Taking the Group Seriously*, p. 53ff. Connors and Caple. "A Review of Group Systems Theory," pp. 99–100. Cox and Paley, "Families as Systems."
3. In *The Flight from Ambiguity*, Levine has shown the importance of the ambiguity of language to the dynamics of social and cultural evolution, and the opposing "frozen" model that modern cultures present in their "flight from ambiguity." See in particular his ch. 2 on the comparison between ambiguity in Amhara and American cultures (pp. 25ff).
4. Foucault, *Histoire de la folie à l'âge classique*. Swain, *Le sujet de la folie*. Gauchet and Swain, *La pratique de l'esprit humain*. Basaglia, *Psychiatry Inside Out*. Ettin, Cohen, and Fidler, "Group-as-a-Whole Theory Viewed in Its 20th-Century Context." Dalal, *Taking the Group Seriously*. Bennis and Shepard, "A Theory of Group Development." See also Bion's observation about the need of authority in group behavior in *Experiences in Groups and Other Papers*.
5. Gerson, *The Embedded Self*, pp. 150–156.
6. Coming from the psychological stream of group analysis, Pichon-Rivière, a Swiss-Argentinean psychiatrist, has named this phenomenon *portavoz*, the "carrying voice," the spokesman. Pichon-Rivière, *El proceso grupal: Del psicoanalisis a la psicologia social*.
7. Gibney, "The Double Bind Theory." Napier and Whitaker, *The Family Crucible*. Bateson, Jackson, Haley, and Weakland, "Toward a Theory of Schizophrenia."
8. Foulkes, *Therapeutic Group Analysis*. Foulkes and Anthony, *Group Psychotherapy*. Ettin, Cohen, and Fidler, "Group-as-a-Whole Theory Viewed in Its 20th-Century Context."
9. Ettin, "From Identified Patient to Identifiable Group."
10. Napier and Whitaker, *The Family Crucible*. Gerson, *The Embedded Self*. Cox

and Paley, "Families as Systems." See, nevertheless, the development of new group therapeutic method by Agazarian, *Systems-Centered Therapy for Groups*, focusing on "functional subgrouping" and "boundarying" within the operation of the group.

11. Foulkes, *Therapeutic Group Analysis*. Foulkes and Anthony, *Group Psychotherapy*.
12. Ettin, "From Identified Patient to Identifiable Group."
13. Loc. cit.
14. This idea was further developed by Ettin, "From Identified Patient to Identifiable Group."
15. Foulkes, *Therapeutic Group Analysis*. Foulkes and Anthony, *Group Psychotherapy*. Dalal, *Taking the Group Seriously*, ch. 2.
16. Levine, *The Flight from Ambiguity*.
17. Agazarian, *Systems-Centered Therapy for Groups*, pp. 5–7. Shannon and Weaver, *The Mathematical Theory of Communication*.
18. See previous note, as well as Bennis and Shepard, "A Theory of Group Development."
19. Winnicott, "Mirror-Role of Mother and Family in Child Development."
20. Ogden, *The Matrix of the Mind*, ch. 6: "Internal Object Relations," and ch. 7: "The Mother, the Infant, and the Matrix in the Work of Donald Winnicott."
21. Through an analysis of different case studies Ogden reveals how this abnormal development in infancy is reenacted in the framework of the patient-therapist relationship. Ibid., ch. 7.
22. This was defined by Jessica Benjamin "as the development of the capacity for mutual recognition, the development of intersubjective relatedness," which distinguishes between intersubjectivity and object-relational perspective. "Recognition and Destruction," pp. 46–47.
23. Benjamin defines this as "mutual recognition," a pivotal concept to explain the infant-mother relationship in terms of intersubjectivity. *The Bonds of Love*, ch. 1: "The First Bond."
24. Benjamin calls this "a negative circle of recognition." Ibid., p. 28.
25. Winnicott, "Hate in the Countertransference."
26. Jung, "Psychology of the Transference" (introduction to *The Collected Works*, vol. 16, § 353–401) emphasizes that the psychic process of the unconscious is relational and is realized in therapy between patient and therapist.
27. Searles, "Concerning Therapeutic Symbiosis." He has also used the terms "pathogenic symbiosis" and "therapeutic symbiosis" in "Countertransference and Theoretical Model." I am thankful to Ruth Sarig for this reference.
28. Searles, "The Patient as Therapist to His Analyst." Transference and countertransference are precisely the means that enable this dynamic. Searles compares this process to the act of parenting, where the infant requires the parent to become a parent, that is, to change in order to care for the infant and to take responsibility over it.

29. *"Mirror reactions* are characteristically brought out when a number of persons meet and interact. A person sees himself, or part of himself—often a repressed part of himself—reflected in the interactions of other group members. He sees them reacting in the way he does himself, or in contrast to his own behaviour. He also gets to know himself—and this is a fundamental process in ego development—by the effect he has upon others and the picture they form of him." Foulkes, *Therapeutic Group Analysis,* p. 110. Note that Searles too equates the way this "ambivalent symbiotic relatedness" functions as group relationship in "Concerning Therapeutic Symbiosis," p. 190.
30. In group analysis, too, the importance of transference and countertransference, and the way in which they are handled within the group are crucial. Agazarian and Peter, *The Visible and Invisible Group,* ch. 9.
31. Winnicott, "Hate in the Countertransference."

Bibliography

Primary Sources

Acta Sanctorum Martyrum Orientalium et Occidentalium, Acta S. Simeonis Stylitae, 2 vols. Ed. Stephanus Evodius Assemanus. Westmead, UK: Gregg International, 1970 (Rome, 1748).

Agathias. *The Histories.* Ed. Rudolph Keydell, *Agathiae Myrinaei Historiarum libri quinque.* Berlin: De Gruyter, 1967.

A History of the Monks in Egypt. Ed. and trans. André-Jean Festugière, *Historia monachorum in Aegypto.* Brussels: Société des Bollandistes, 1971. Trans. Norman Russell, *The Lives of the Desert Fathers: The Historia monachorum in Aegypto.* Kalamazoo, MI: Cistercian Publications, 1981.

Apocryphal Acts of the Apostles. Ed. and trans. William Wright. Amsterdam: Philo Press, 1968 (London, 1871). Trans. A. F. J. Klijn, *The Acts of Thomas.* Leiden: Brill, 2003 (1962).

The Arab Life of Theodosius the Cenobiarch. Ed. and trans. Michel van Esbroeck, "La vie arabe de saint Theodose le Cenobiarque." *Parole de l'Orient* 18 (1993): pp. 45–73. M. van Esbroeck, "La vie arabe de saint Theodose le Cenobiarque," *Parole de l'Orient* 18 (1993) pp. 45–73.

Aristides. *Apology.* Eds. and trans. Bernard Pouderon, Marie-Joseph Pierre, *Apologie.* Paris: Éd. du Cerf, "SC 470," 2003.

Athanasius of Alexandria. *Life of Antony.* Ed. and trans. G. J. M. Bartelink, *Vie d'Antoine.* Paris: Éd. du Cerf, "SC 400," 1994.

The Athenian Corpus of Saint Pachomius. Ed. François Halkin, trans. André-Jean Festugière, *Le Corpus athénien de Saint Pachome.* Geneva: Patrick Cramer, 1982.

Barsanuphius and John of Gaza. *Letters.* Eds. François Neyet and Paula de

Angelis-Noah, trans. L. Regnault, *Correspondence*, vol. 1/2. Paris: Éd. du Cerf, "SC 427," 1998.

The Book of Steps. Ed. Michael Kmosko, *Liber Graduum.* Patrologia Syriaca 1/3, ed. R. Graffin (Paris, 1926). Trans. Robert A. Kitchen and Maartien F. G. Parmentier, *The Book of Steps: The Syriac Liber Graduum.* Kalamazoo, MI: Cistercian Publication, 2004.

The Canons of the Council in Trullo. Eds. and trans. George Nedungatt and Michael Featherstone. In *The Council in Trullo Revisited,* pp. 41–186. Rome: Pontificio Istituto Orientale, 1995.

Cassian, John. *Conferences.* Eds. Michael Petschenig and Gottfried Kreuz. *Collationes.* Vienna: Verlag der Österreichischen Akademie der Wissenschaften, "CSEL 13," 2004.

Clement. *Stromata.* Ed. and trans. Alain Le Boulluec, *Les Stromates: stromate vii.* Ed. and trans. Patrick Descourtieux, *Les Stromates: stromate vi.* Ed. A. Van den Hoek, trans. Cl. Mondésert, *Les Stromates: stromate iv.* Paris: Éd. du Cerf, "SC 428, 446, 463," 1997–2001. For *Stromata* i–iii: Ed. Otto Stählin, *Clemens Alexandrinus: Stromata Buch I–VI.* Berlin: Akademie Verlag, 1960.

Cyprian. *Ad Fortunatum.* Ed. R. Weber. In *Sancti Cypriani Episcopi Opera,* pp. 180–216. Turnout: Brepols, "CCSL III," 1972.

———. *Epistularium.* Ed. G. F. Diercks. In *Sancti Cypriani Episcopi Opera.* 3 vols. Turnhout: Brepols, "CCSL IIIb–d," 1994–1999.

Cyril of Scythopolis. *Lives of the Monks of Palestine.* Ed. Eduard Schwartz, *Kyrillos von Skythopolis.* Leipzig: J. C. Hinrichs, 1939.

The Didascalia Apostolorum in Syriac. Ed. and trans. Arthur Vööbus. 4 vols. Louvain, Belg.: Secrétariat du CSCO, "CSCO 401–402/175–176, 407–408/179–180," 1979.

Eusebius of Caesarea. *Ecclesiastical History* Ed. and trans. Gustave Bardy, index by Pierre Périchon, *Histoire ecclésiastique,* 4 vols. Paris: Éd. du Cerf, "SC 31, 41, 55, 73," 1952–1967.

———. *The Encomium of the Martyrs.* Ed. and trans. B. H. Cowper. In W. Wright, "The Encomium of the Martyrs." *Journal of Sacred Literature* 5 (1864): 403–408, 6 (1864–65):129–133.

———. *History of the Martyrs in Palestine: Discovered in a Very Ancient Syriac Manuscript* (Syriac). Ed. and trans. William Cureton. London: Williams and Norgate, 1861.

———. *On the Martyrs in Palestine* (Greek) Ed. and trans. Gustave Bardy. Appendix In *Ecclesiastical History,* vol. 3, pp. 121–174.

Evagrius Ponticus. *On Thoughts.* Eds. and trans. Paul Géhin and Claire Guillaumont, *Sur les pensées.* Paris: Éd. du Cerf, "SC 438," 1998.

———. *Praktikos.* Eds. and trans. Antoine Guillaumont and Claire Guillaumont, *Traité pratique ou le moine.* Paris: Éd. du Cerf, "SC 170, 171," 1971.

Evagrius Ponticus's Disciples. *Chapters.* Ed. and trans. Paul Géhin, *Chapitres des disciples d'Évagre.* Paris: Éd. du Cerf, "SC 514," 2007.

Evagrius Scholasticus. *Ecclesiastical History.* Eds. J. Bides and L. Parmentier, trans. André-Jean Festugière, Bernard Grillet, and Guy Sabbah, *Histoire Ecclésiastique*, 2 vols. Paris: Éd. du Cerf, "SC 542, 566," 2011, 2014. Trans. Michael Whitby, *The Ecclesiastical History of Evagrius Scholasticus*. Liverpool: Liverpool University Press, 2000.

The Greek Lives of Pachomius. Ed. François Halkin, *Sancti Pachomii Vitae Graecae*. Brussels: Société des Bollandistes, 1932.

Gregory of Nazianzus. *Orations*. Ed. and trans. Jean Nernardi, *Discours 4–5: Contre Julien*. Paris: Éd. du Cerf, "SC 309," 1978. Ed. and trans. Marie-Agne Calvet-Sebasti, *Discours 6–12*. Paris: Éd. du Cerf, "SC 405," 1995. Ed. Claudio Moreschini, trans. Paul Gallay, *Discours 32–37*. Paris: Éd. du Cerf, "SC 318," 1985.

Heikhalot Rabbati. Ed. Peter Schäfer in collaboration with Margarete Schlüter and Hans Georg von Mutius, *Synopse zur Hekhalot-Literature*. Tübingen: Mohr Siebeck, 1981.

Heikhalot Rabbati: Aseret Harugei Malkhut. Ed. Oron, Michal. "Parallel Versions of the Story of *Aseret Harugei Malkhut* and of *Hekhalot Rabbati*." *Eshel Beer-Sheva: Studies in Jewish Thought* 2 (1980): 81–95.

Iamblichus. *On the Pythagorean Life*. Ed. L. Devbner, *De Vita Pythagorica liber*. Stuttgart: Teubner, 1975.

Ignatios the Deacon, *Life of Gregory the Decapolites*. Ed. Georgios Makris, *Ignatios Diakonos und die Vita des Hl.Gregorios Dekapolites*. Stuttgart: Teubner, 1997.

Ignatius of Antioch. *Letters*. Ed. and trans. Pierre Thomas Camelot. In *Ignace d'Antioche, Polycarpe de Smyrne: Lettres. Martyr de Polycarpe*. Paris: Éd. du Cerf, "SC 10bis," 1998.

Jerome. *Letters*. Ed. Isidorus Hilberg, *Epistulaum pars I: Epistulae I–LXX*. Vienna: Verlag der Österreichischen Akademie der Wissenschaften, "CSEL 54," 1996.

———. *Three Lives of Monks (Paul, Malchus, Hilarion)*. Ed. Edgardo M. Morales, trans. Pierre Leclerc, *Trois Vies de moines (Paul, Malchus, Hilarion)*. Paris: Éd. du Cerf, "SC 508," 2007.

John Moschus. *Spiritual Meadow*. Ed. and trans. M.-J. Rouët de Journal, *Le Pré Spirituel*. Paris: Éd. du Cerf, "SC 12," 1946.

John of Ephesus. *Lives of the Eastern Saints*. Ed. and trans. Ernest Walter Brooks, 3 vols. PO 82/17.1, 89/18.4, 92/19.2.

———. *The Second Unedited Part of the Ecclesiastical History*. Ed. and trans. F. Nau, "Analyse de la seconde partie inedited de l'*Histoire Ecclesiastique* de Jean d'Asie, patriarche jacobite de Constantinople (d. 585)." *Revue de l'Orient Chrétien* 2 (1897): 455–493.

———. *The Third Part of the Ecclesiastical History*. Ed. and trans. E. W. Brooks, *Ioannis Ephesini historiae ecclesiasticae pars tertia*. Louvain: Secrétariat du CSCO, "CSCO 105/54, 106/56," 1935–1936.

Josephus. *Antiquities of the Jews*. Ed. Benedikt Niese, *Flavii Iosephi Opera*. vols. 1–4. Berlin: Apud Weidmannos, 1955 (1888–1895).

———. *Jewish War*. Ed. Benedikt Niese, *Flavii Iosephi Opera*. vol. 6. Berlin: Apud Weidmannos, 1955 (1895).

Justin Martyr. *Apology I–II.* Ed. and trans. Charles Munier, *Apologie Pour les Chrétiens.* Paris: Éd. du Cerf, "SC 507," 2006.

Kekaumenos. *Strategikon.* Ed. Maria Dora Spadaro, *Raccomandazioni e consigli di un galantuomo.* Alessandria, It.: Ed. dell'Orso, 1998.

Lactantius. *Divine Institutions.* Eds. Eberhard Heck and Antonie Wlosok, *Divinarum Institutionum libri septem.* Berlin: De Gruyter, 2005–2011. Trans. Anthony Bowen and Peter Garnsey. Liverpool: Liverpool University Press, 2003.

La Légende Syriaque de Saint Alexis l'Homme de Dieu. Ed. Arthur Amiaud. Paris: Émile Bouillon, 1889.

Leontius of Neapolis. *Life of John of Cyprus.* Ed. and trans. André-Jean Festugière. In *Vie de Syméon le Fou et Vie de Jean de Chypre,* pp. 253–632. Paris: Libraire Orientalis Paul Geuthnes, 1974.

———. *Life of Symeon salos.* Ed. Lennart Rydén, trans. André-Jean Festugière. In *Vie de Syméon le Fou et Vie de Jean de Chypre,* ed. André-Jean Festugière, pp. 1–253. Paris: Libraire Orientalis Paul Geuthnes, 1974. All references are to pages in Festugière's publication including in parentheses the pages in Rydén's edition in his *Bemerkungen zum Leben des heiligen Narren Symeon von Leontius von Neapolis.* Uppsala: Almqvist & Wiksell, 1970.

Leontius of Rome. *Life of Gregory of Agrigento.* Ed. Albrecht Berger, *Das Leben des heiligen Gregorios von Agrigent.* Berlin: Akademie Verlag, 1995.

The Letters of St. Antony: Monasticism and the Making of a Saint. Ed. Samuel Rubenson, Minneapolis, MN: Fortress Press, 1995.

Life and Works of Saint Gregentios Archbishop of Taphar. Ed. and trans. Albrecht Berger. Berlin: De Gruyter, 2006.

Life of Andrew the Fool, ed. Lennart Rydén, vol. 1: *Introduction, Testimonies and Nachleben, Indices;* vol. 2: *Text, Translation and Notes, Appendices.* Uppsala: Almqvist & Wiksell International, 1995.

Lucian. *On the Syrian Goddess.* Ed. J. L. Lightfoot. Oxford: Oxford University Press, 2003.

Lucretius Carus Titus. *De rerum natura.* Ed. and trans. A. Ernout, *De la nature.* 2 vols. Paris: Les Belles Lettres, 1967–1968 (1964–1966). Eng. trans. W. H. D. Rouse. The Loeb Classical Library. Cambridge, MA: Harvard University Press, 1949.

Marinos of Neapolis. *The Life of Proclus.* In *The Extant Works or the Life of Proclus and the Commentary in the Dedomena of Euclis,* ed. and trans. Al. N. Oikonomides. Chicago: Ares Publishers, 1977.

The Martyrdom of Pionios. Ed. and trans. Louis Robert, comp. and pub. Glen Warren Bowersock and Christopher P. Jones, *Le martyre de Pionios, prêtre de Smyrne.* Washington DC: Dumbarton Oaks Research Library and Collection, 1994.

The Martyrdom of Polycarp. Ed. and trans. Pierre Thomas Camelot. In *Ignace d'Antioche, Polycarpe de Smyrne: Lettres. Martyre de Polycarpe,* pp. 197–239. Paris: Éd. du Cerf, "SC 10bis," 1998.

Megillat Ta'anit [in Hebrew]. Ed. Vered Noam, *Megillat Ta'anit: Versions, Interpretation, History, with a Critical Edition*. Jerusalem: Yad Ben-Zvi Press, 2003.

Midrash Canticles. Ed. Eliezer Halevi Grünhut, 2nd ed. Joseph Chaim Wertheimer, *Midrash Shir haShirim: Printed from a Geniza Manuscript*. Jerusalem: Ktav Yad vaSefer Institute, 1971.

Midrash Genesis Rabbah. Ed. Hanokh Albeck, *Midrash Bereshit Rabba*. 3 vols. Jerusalem: Sifre Waherman, 1965.

Midrash Lamentations Rabbah. Ed. Salomon Buber, *Midrash Eikhah Rabbah*. Vilnius: Romm, 1899.

Midrash Eleh Ezkherah. Ed. Gottfried Reeg, *Die Geschichte von den Zehn Märtyren*. Tübingen: Mohr Siebeck, 1985. Ed. Adolf Jellinek, *Bet ha-Midrasch: Sammlung kleiner Midraschim und vermischter Abhandlungen aus der ältern jüdischen Literature*, vol. 1, pt. 2, pp. 64–72, vol. 2, pt. 6, pp. 19–35. Jerusalem: Wahrmann Books, 1967.

Midrash Proverbs. Ed. Burton L. Visotzky, *Midrash Mishle: A Critical Edition Based on Vatican MS. Ebr. 44, with variant Readings from All Known Manuscripts and Early Editions, and with an Introduction, References and a Short Commentary*. New York: Jewish Theological Seminary of America, 1990.

Midrash Psalms. Ed. Salomon Buber, *Midrash Tehillim haMekhuneh Shoḥer Tov*. Vilnius: Romm, 1891.

Mishnah. Ed. Hanokh Albeck, 6 vols. Tel Aviv: Devir, 1957–1959. Ms. Kaufmann A 50. National Library of Israel. http://jnul.huji.ac.il.dl.tlamud. Consulted throughout 2011–2015.

Musurillo, Herbert, ed. and trans. *Acts of the Christian Martyrs*. Oxford: Clarendon Press, 2000 (1954).

———. *Acts of the Pagan Martyrs*. Oxford: Clarendon Press, 2000 (1972).

Pachomius and His Disciples. *Works*. Ed. and trans. L. Th. Lefort, *Œuvres de S. Pachôme et de ses disciples*. 2 vols. Louvain: L. Durbecq, "CSCO 159–160/23–24," 1956.

Palladius. *Lausiac History*. Ed. G. J. M. Bartelink, trans., Marino Barchiesi, *La Storia Lausiaca*. Milan: Arnoldo Mondadori, 1990. Ed. Cuthbert Butler. *The Lausiac History of Palladius*. Hildesheim: Georg Olms, 1967. Trans. Robert T. Meyer. *The Lausiac History*. New York: Newman, 1964.

Peshiṭta: The Old Testament in Syriac: According to the Peshiṭta Version. Ed. *The Peshiṭta Institute*. Leiden: Brill, 1966–.

Philo. *Embassy to Gaius*. Ed. and trans. E. Mary Smallwood, *Philonis Alexandrini Legatio ad Gaium*. Leiden: Brill, 1970.

———. *Opera*. Eds. Paul Wendland and Leopold Cohn, *Philonis Alexandirini Opera quae supersunt*, 7 vols. in 8 pts. Berlin: De Gruyter, 1962–1963 (Berlin: Reimer, 1896–1930). Eng. trans. F. H. Colson, *In Flaccus*. The Loeb Classical Library, *Philo*, vol. 9, pp. 295–403. Cambridge, MA: Harvard University Press, 1967.

Philostratus. *The Life of Apollonius of Tyana*. Ed. and trans. Christopher P. Jones, 3 vols. The Loeb Classical Library. Cambridge, MA: Harvard University Press, 2005–2006.

Rallēs, Georgios Alexandrou, and Michael Potlēs, eds. *Suntagma tōn theiōn kai tōn hierōn kanonōn*, 6 vols. Athens: Gregore, 1966 (1852–1859).

Saint Daniel of Sketis: A Group of Hagiographic Texts. Ed. Britt Dahlman. Lund: Wallin & Dalholm, 2007.

The Sayings of the Desert Fathers. Ed. and trans. Jean-Claude Guy, *Les Apophtegmes des Pères: Collection systématique*. Paris: Éd. du Cerf, "SC 387, 474 , 498," 993–2005. Ed. and trans. John Wortley, *The Anonymous Saying of the Desert Fathers: A Select Edition and Complete English Translation.* Cambridge: Cambridge University Press, 2013.

Select Narratives of Holy Women from the Syro-Antiochene or Sinai Palimpsest: As Written above the Old Syriac Gospels by John the Stylite, of Beth-Mari-Qanūn in A.D. *778.* Ed. and trans. Agnes Smith Lewis, 2 vols. London: C. J. Clay and Sons, 1900.

Sifra Levitucs. Ed. Jacob Weiss, *Sifra debi Rav: Sefer Torat Cohanim*. Jerusalem: Sifra, 1959 (Vienna, 1862).

Sifrei Deuteronomy. Ed. Louis Finkelstein, *Sifrei ʿal Sefer Devarim*. New York: Jewish Theological Seminary of America, 1969.

Sozomen. *Ecclesiastical History.* Ed. J. Bidez and G. C. Hansen, trans. André-Jean Festugière, *Histoire Ecclésiastique*. 4 vols., Paris: Éd. du Cerf, "SC 306, 418, 495, 516," 1983–1996.

Sylloge inscriptionum graecarum. Ed. Guilemo Dittenbergero, 4 vols. Hildesheim: G. Olms, 1960.

Synaxarium Ecclesiae Constantinopolitanae. Propylaeum ad Acta Sanctorum Novembris. Ed. Hippolyte Delehaye. Brussels: Société des Bollandistes, 1902.

The Syriac Life of Symeon the Stylite. In *Acta Sanctorum Martyrum Orientalium et Occidentalium, Acta S. Simeonis Stylitae*, vol. 2, pp. 268–412. Trans. Robert Doran, *The Lives of Simeon Stylites*, pp. 101–229. Spencer, MA: Cistercian Publications, 1992.

Tacitus. *Annales.* Ed. and trans. Henri Goelzer. 3 vols. Paris: Les Belles Lettres, 1923–1925.

Tertullian. *Apology.* Ed. and trans. Jean-Pierre Waltzing, *Apologétique*. Paris: Les Belles Lettres, 1961. Trans. Gerald H. Rendall. The Loeb Classical Library. Cambridge, MA: Harvard University Press, 1966.

———. *De anima.* Ed. J. H. Waszink. In Tertullian, *Opera*, vol. 1, vol. 2, pp. 779–869. Trans. Edwin A. Quain in *Tertullian Apologetical Works and Minucius Felix Octavius*, pp. 179–309. Washington DC: Catholic University of America Press, 1962 (1950).

———. *Opera.* Ed. Dom Eligius Dekkers, 2 vols. Turnhout: Brepols, "CCSL I–II," 1953–1954.

———. *To the Martyrs.* Ed. E. Dekkers. In Tertullian, *Opera*, vol. 1, pp. 1–8.

———. *To the Nations.* Ed. Jean-Pierre Waltzing. In Tertullian, *Opera*, vol. 1, pp. 11–75.

———. *To Scapula.* Ed. E. Dekkers. In Tertullian, *Opera*, vol. 2, pp. 1127–1132.

Theodore of Petra. *Life of Theodosius.* Ed. Hermann Usener, *Der heilige Theodosios: Schriften des Theodoros und Kyrillos.* Leipzig: Teubner, 1890.

Theodoret of Cyrrhus. *A History of the Monks in Syria.* Eds. and trans. Pierre Canivet and Alice Leroy-Molinghen, *Histoire des moines de Syrie.* 2 vols. Paris: Éd. du Cerf, "SC 234, 257," 1977, 1979.

———. *On divine love.* In *A History of the Monks in Syria*, vol. 2, pp. 253–315.

Tosefta. Ed. Saul Liberman. 5 vols. Newark: Jewish Theological Seminary of America, 1955–1973.

Treatise Semaḥot. Ed. Michael Higger. Jerusalem: Makor, 1970.

Secondary Sources

Ahonen, Mark. *Mental Disorders in Ancient Philosophy.* Cham: Springer, 2014.

Agazarian, Yvonne M. *System-Centered Therapy for Groups.* New York: Guilford Press, 1997.

Agazarian, Yvonne, and Richard Peter. *The Visible and Invisible Group: Two Perspectives on Group Psychotherapy and Group Process.* London: Routledge & Kegan Paul, 1981.

Amati Sas, Silvia. "L'interprétation dans le trans-subjectif. Réflexions sur l'ambiguité et les espaces psychiches." *Psychotérapies* 24/4 (2004): 207–213.

———. "Situations sociales traumatiques et processus de la cure." *Revue française de Psychanalyse* 66/3 (2002): 923–933.

Aron, Lewis. "The Patient's Experience of the Analyst's Subjectivity." *Psychoanalytic Dialogues* 1 (1992): 29–51.

Artaud, Antonin. *Le théâtre et son double.* Paris: Gallimard, 1964 (1938).

Ashbrook Harvey, Susan. *Asceticism and Society in Crisis: John of Ephesus and the Lives of the Eastern Saints.* Berkeley: University of California Press, 1990.

———. "The Sense of a Stylite: Perspectives on Simeon the Elder." *Vigiliae Christianae* 42 (1988): 376–394.

Artières, Philippe et al., eds. *Histoire de la folie à l'âge classique de Michel Foucault: Regards critiques 1961–2011.* Paris: Presses Universitaires de Caen, 2011.

Baars, Bernard J., "Why Volition Is a Foundation Problem for Psychology." *Consciousness and Cognition* 2 (1993): 281–309.

Bakhtin, Mikhail, M. "Author and Hero in Aesthetic Activity." In Mikhail, M. Bakhtin, *Art and Answerability: Early Philosophical Essays*, eds. Caryl Emerson and Michael Holquist, trans. Vadim Liapunov, pp. 4–256. Austin: University of Texas Press, 1990 (ca. 1920–1923).

———. "From Notes Made in 1970–71." In Mikhail, M. Bakhtin, *Speech Genres and Other Late Essays*, pp. 132–158 (1970–1971).

———. "The Problem of the Text in Linguistics, Philology, and the Human Sciences: An Experiment in Philosophical Analysis." In Mikhail, M. Bakhtin, *Speech Genres and Other Late Essays*, pp. 103–131 (1970).

———. *Rabelais and His World.* Trans. Hélène Iswolsky. Bloomington: Indiana University Press, 1984.

———. "Response to a Question from the *Novy Mir* Editorial Staff." In Mikhail, M. Bakhtin, *Speech Genres and Other Late Essays*, pp. 1–9 (1970).

———. *Speech Genres and Other Late Essays.* Eds. Caryl Emerson and Michael Holquist, trans. Vern W. McGee. Austin: University of Texas Press, 2006.

Bar-Asher Siegal, Michal. *Early Christian Monastic Literature and the Babylonian Talmud.* Cambridge: Cambridge University Press, 2013.

Barnes, Timothy David. *Early Christian Hagiography and Roman History.* Tübingen: Mohr Siebeck, 2010.

———. *Tertullian: A Historical and Literary Study.* Oxford: Clarendon Press, 1971.

Basaglia, Franco. *Psychiatry Inside Out: Selected Writings.* Eds. Nancy Scheper-Hughes and Anne M. Livell, trans. Anne M. Lovell and Teresa Shtob. New York: Columbia University Press, 1987.

Bateson, G., D. D. Jackson, J. Haley, and J. Weakland, "Toward a Theory of Schizophrenia." *Behavioral Science* 1 (1956): 251-264.

Beidelman, T. O. "The Moral Imagination of the Kaguru: Some Thoughts on Tricksters, Translation and Comparative Analysis." In *Mythical Trickster Figures: Contours, Contexts, and Criticism*, eds. William J. Hynes and William G. Doty, pp. 174–192. Tuscaloosa: University of Alabama Press, 1997.

Bell, Randolph M. *Holy Anorexia.* Chicago: University of Chicago Press, 1985.

Benjamin, Jessica, *The Bonds of Love: Psychoanalysis, Feminism, and the Problem of Domination.* New York: Pantheon, 1988.

———. "Recognition and Destruction: An Outline of Intersubjectivity." In *Relational Perspectives in Psychoanalysis*, eds. N. Skolnick and S. Warshaw, pp. 43–60. Hillsdale, NJ: Analytic Press, 1992.

Bennis, Warren G., and Herbert A. Shepard. "A Theory of Group Development." *Human Relations* 9 (1959): 415–437.

Berger, Peter L. *The Sacred Canopy: Elements of a Sociological Theory of Religion.* New York: Doubleday, 1990 (1967).

Berthelot, Katell. "L'idéologie maccabéenne: Entre idéologie de la résistance armée et idéologie du martyr." *Revue des Études Juives* 165/1–2 (2006): 99–122.

Bilu, Yoram. *The Saints' Impresarios: Dreamers, Healers, and Holy Men in Israel's Urban Periphery.* Trans. H. Watzman. Brighton, MA: Academic Studies Press, 2009 (2004).

Bion, Wilfred Ruprecht. *Experiences in Groups and other papers.* London: Tavistock, 1961.

Bisbee, Gary A. *Pre-Decian Acts of Martyrs and Commentarii.* Philadephia: Fortress Press, 1988.

Bleger, José. *Symbiosis and Ambiguity: A psychoanalytical study.* Eds. Leopoldo Bleger and John Churcher, trans. Leopoldo Bleger, John Churcher, and Susan Rogers. London: Routledge, 2013 (Buenos Aires: Paidós, 1967).

Bloch, Ernst. "Entfremdung, Verfremdung: Alienation, Estrangement." Trans. Anne Halley and Darko Suvin. *The Drama Review* 15 (1970): 120–125.

Bohak, Gideon. *Ancient Jewish Magic: A History.* Cambridge: Cambridge University Press, 2008.

Boustan, Ra'anan. "A Hebrew Hymn of Praise for a High-Priestly Rabbinic Martyr: A Note on the Relationship between the Synagogue Liturgy and Rabbinic Literary Culture." *Zutot* (2004): 27–34

Boustan, Ra'anan S. *From Martyr to Mystic.* Tübingen: Mohr Siebeck, 2005.

Bowersock, Glen Warren. *Martyrdom and Rome.* Cambridge: Cambridge University Press, 1995.

Boyarin, Daniel. *Dying for God: Martyrdom and the Creation of Christianity and Judaism.* Stanford, CA: Stanford University Press, 1999.

Brecht, Bertolt. "Alienation Effects in Chinese Acting." In *Brecht On Theatre: The Development of Aesthetic,* ed. and trans. John Willett, pp. 93–99. London: Methuen, 1974 (1935).

Brock, Sebastian. "Early Syrian Asceticism." In *Syriac perspectives on Late Antiquity,* pt. 1 (=*Numen* 20, 1973, pp. 1–19). London: Variorum Reprints, 1984.

Bromberg, Philip M. "Shadow and Substance: A Relational Perspective on Clinical Process." *Psychoanalytic Psychology* 10/1 (1993): 147–168.

———. *The Shadow of the Tsunami and the Growth of the Relational Mind.* New York: Routledge, 2011.

Brown, Peter. *The Body and Society: Men, Women, and Sexual Renunciation in Early Christianity.* New York: Columbia University Press, 1988.

———. *The Cult of the Saints: Its Rise and Function in Latin Christianity.* Chicago: University of Chicago Press, 1981.

———. "The Rise and Function of the Holy Man in Late Antiquity." *The Journal of Roman Studies* 61 (1971): 80–101. Repr. with addenda in *Society and the Holy in Late Antiquity,* pp. 103–152. London: Faber, 1982.

Brox, Norbert. *Zeuge und Märtyrer: Untersuchungen zur frühchristlichen Zeugnis-Terminologie.* Munich: Kosel Verlag, 1961.

Buc, Philippe. "Martyre et ritualité dans l'Antiquité tardive: Horizons de l'écriture médiévale des rituels." *Annales. Histoire, Sciences Sociales* 52/1 (1997): 63–92.

Buell, Denise Kimber. *Why This New Race: Ethnic Reasoning in Early Christianity.* New York: Columbia University Press, 2005.

Burston, Daniel. *The Wing of Madness: The Life and Work of R. D. Laing.* Cambridge, MA: Harvard University Press, 1996.

Bushell, William C. "Psychophysiological and Comparative Analysis of Ascetico-Meditational Discipline: Toward a New Theory of Asceticism." In *Asceticism,* eds. Vincent L. Wimbush and Richard Valantasis, pp. 553–575. Oxford: Oxford University Press, 1995.

Bynum, Caroline Walker. *Holy Feast and Holy Fast: The Religious Significance of Food to Medieval Women.* Berkeley: University of California Press, 1987.

———. "Women's Stories, Women's Symbols: A Critique of Victor Turner's Theory of Liminality." In *Anthropology and the Study of Religion*, eds. Frank Reynolds and Robert Moore, pp. 105–125. Chicago: Center for the Scientific Study of Religion, 1984.

Caner, Daniel. *Wandering, Begging Monks: Spiritual Authority and Promotion of Monasticism in Late Antiquity.* Berkeley: University of California Press, 2002.

Canivet, Pierre. "Erreurs de spiritualité et troubles psychiques: À propos d'un passage de la *Vie de S. Théodose par Théodore de Pétra* (530)." *Recherches de science religieuse* 50 (1962): 161–205.

Carney, Sean. *Brecht and Critical Theory: Dialectics and Contemporary Aesthetics.* London: Routledge, 2005.

Castelli, Elizabeth Anne. *Martyrdom and Memory: Early Chrisrtian Culture Making.* New York: Columbia Univesity Press, 2004.

Christo, Gus George. *Martyrdom According to John Chrysostom: "To live is Christ, to die is gain."* Lewiston, NY: Mellen University Press, 1997.

Clark, Elizabeth A. *Reading Renunciation: Asceticism and Scripture in Early Christianity.* Princeton, NJ: Princeton University Press, 1999.

Clément, Cathrine, and Sudhir Kakar. *La folle et le saint.* Trans. (of Sudhir Kakar's text) Marie-José Minassian. Paris: Éd. du Seuil, 1993.

Cohen, Jeremy. *Sanctifying the Name of God.* Philadelphia: University of Pennsylvania Press, 2004.

Cohen, Shaye J. D. "Masada: Literary Tradition, Archaeological Remains, and the Credibility of Josephus." *Journal of Jewish Studies* 33 (1982): 385–405.

Connors, Joanie V., and Richard B. Caple. "A Review of Group Systems Theory." *The Journal for Specialists in Group Work* 30/2 (2005): 93–110.

Cox, Martha J., and Blair Paley. "Families as Systems." *Annual Review of Psychology* 48 (1997): 243–267.

Crawford, Lawrence. "Viktor Shklovskij: Différenace in defamiliarization." *Comparative Literature* 36 (1984): 209–219.

Dagron, Gilbert. "L'homme sans honneur ou le saint scandaleux." *Annales. Histoire, Sciences Sociales* 45/4 (1990): 929–939.

Dalal, Farhad. *Taking the Group Seriously: Towards a Post-Foulkesian Group Analytic Theory.* London: Jessica Kingsley, 1998.

Damousi, Joy, and Robert Reynolds R., eds. *History on the Couch: Essays in History and Psychoanalysis.* Melbourne: Melbourne University Press, 2003.

Dan, Joseph. "*Aseret Harugei Malkhut*, Martyrology and Mysticism" [in Hebrew]. In *Mincha leMenachem: A Collection of Essays in Honor of Rabbi Menachem Hacohen*, eds. Hana Amit, Aviad Hacohen, and Haim Beer, pp. 367–390. Tel Aviv: haKibbutz haMeuhad, 2007.

Davis, Stephen J. "Crossed Texts, Crossed Sex: Intertextuality and Gender in Early Christian Legends of Holy Women Disguised as Men." *Journal of Early Christian Studies* 10/1 (2002): 1–36.

De Certeau, Michel. *La Possession de Loudun.* Paris: Julliard, 1970.

———. "Le 'roman' psychanalytique: histoire et littérature." In Michel De

Certeau, *Histoire et psychanalyse: entre science et fiction*, pp. 107–136. Paris: Gallimard, 1987.

———. "Le Silence de l'Absolu. Folles et Fous de Dieu." *Recherches de Science Religieuse* 67/4 (1979): 526–546.

———. *The Writing of History*. Trans. T. Conley. New York: Columbia University Press, 1988.

De Martino, Ernesto. *The Land of Remorse: A Study of Southern Italian Tarantism*. Trans. Dorothy Louise Zinn. London: Free Association Books, 2005 (Milan: Il Saggiatore, 1961).

Dehandschutter, Boudewijn. "Martyr—Martyrium: Quelques observations à propos d'un christianisme sémantique." *Instrumenta Patristica* 24 (1991): 33–39. Repr. in Boudewijn Dehandschutter, *Polycarpiana: Studies on Martyrdom and Persecution in Early Christianity: Collected Essays*, pp. 105–111.

———. *Polycarpiana: Studies On Martyrdom and Persecution in Early Christianity: Collected Essays*. Ed. Johan Leemans. Leuven: Leuven University Press, 2007.

Déroche, Vincent. *Études sur Léontios de Néapolis*. Uppsala: Almqvist & Wiksell International, Stockholm, 1995.

———. "Les variantes italiques de la folie en Christ." *Nea Rhōmē: Rivista di ricerche bizantinistiche* 2 (2005): 193–203.

Descola, Philippe. *Beyond Nature and Culture*. Trans. Janet Lloyd. Chicago: Chicago University Press, 2013 (Paris: Gallimard, 2005).

———. "Human Nature." *Social Anthropology/Anthropologie Sociale* 17/2 (2009): 145–157.

———. *In the Society of Nature: A Native Ecology in Amazonia*. Trans. Nora Scott. Cambridge: Cambridge University Press, 1994 (Paris: Éd. de la Maison des sciences de l'homme, 1986).

———. "Societies of Nature and the Nature of Society." In *Conceptualizing Society*, ed. Adam Kuper, pp. 107–126. London: Routledge, 1992.

De Ste. Croix, G. E. M. *Christian Persecution, Martyrdom, and Orthodoxy*. Eds. Michael Whitby and Joseph Streeter. Oxford: Oxford University Press, 2006.

———. "Why Were the Early Christians Persecuted?" *Past & Present* 20 (1963): 6–38.

Diamond, Eliezer, "Lions, Snakes, and Asses: Palestinian Jewish Holy Men as Masters of the Animal Kingdom." In *Jewish Culture and Society under the Christian Roman Empire*, eds. Eliezer Diamond and Seth Schwartz, pp. 253–283. Leuven: Peeters, 2003.

Dodds, Eric Robertson. *Pagan and Christian in an Age of Anxiety: Some Aspects of Religious Experience from Marcus Aurelius to Constantine*. Cambridge: Cambridge University Press, 1965.

Dols Michael, "Insanity in Byzantine and Islamic Medicine." *Dumbarton Oaks Papers* 38 (1984): 135–148.

———. *Majnūn: The Madman in Medieval Islamic Society*. Ed. Diana E. Immisch. Oxford: Clarendon Press, 1992.

Doran, Robert. *The Lives of Simeon Stylites.* Spencer, MA: Cistercian Publications, 1992.

Draguns, Juris G., and Junko Tanaka-Matsumi. "Assessment of Psychopathology across and within Cultures: Issues and Findings." *Behaviour Research and Therapy* 41 (2003): 755–776.

Dunn, Marilyn. *The Emergence of Monasticism: From the Desert Fathers to the Early Middle Ages.* Oxford: Blackwell, 2007 (2000).

Durkheim, Émile. *Les formes élémentaires de la vie religieuse: Le système totémique en Australie.* Paris: Presses Universitaires de France, 1912.

Durkheim, Émile, and Marcel Mauss. "De quelques formes de classification—Contribution à l'étude des représentations collectives." *Année sociologique* 6 (1901–1902): 1–72. Trans. Rodney Needham, *Primitive Classification.* Chicago: Chicago University Press, 1963.

Du Toit, David S. *Theios Anthropos: Zur Verwendung von θεῖος ἄνθρωπος und sinnverwandten Ausdrücken in der Literatur der Kaiserzeit.* Tübingen: Mohr Siebeck, 1997.

Elman, Yaakov. "The Suffering of the Righteous in Palestinian and Babylonian Sources." *The Jewish Quarterly Review* 80/3–4 (1990): 315–339.

Ende, Michael. *The Neverending Story.* Trans. Ralph Manheim. London: Penguin, 1983 (Stuttgart: K. Thienemann, 1979).

Erikson, Erik H. *Young Man Luther: A Study in Psychoanalysis and History.* New York: Norton, 1958.

Ettin, Mark, F. "From Identified Patient to Identifiable Group: The Alchemy of the Group as a Whole." *International Journal of Group Psychotherapy* 50/2 (2000): 137–162.

Ettin, Mark F., Bertram D. Cohen, and Jay W. Fidler. "Group-as-a-Whole Theory Viewed in Its 20th-Century Context." *Group Dynamics: Theory, Research, and Practice* 1/4 (1997): 329–340.

Feldman, Louis H. "Diaspora Synagogues: New Light from Inscriptions and Papyri." In *Sacred Realm: The Emergence of the Synagogue in the Ancient World,* ed. Steven Fine, pp. 48–66. New York: Oxford University Press, 1996.

Felman, Shoshana. *Writing and Madness (Literature/Philosophy/Psychoanalysis).* Trans. Martha Noel and Shoshana Felman, with Brian Massumi. Palo Alto, CA: Stanford University Press, 2003 (Paris: Éd. du Seuil, 1993).

Finn, Richard Damien. *Asceticism in the Graeco-Roman World.* Cambridge: Cambridge University Press, 2009.

Flood, Gavin. *The Ascetic Self: Subjectivity, Memory and Tradition.* Cambridge: Cambridge University Press, 2004.

Foucault, Michel. *Les anormaux: Cours au Collège de France. 1974–1975.* Paris: Gallimard-Seuil, 1999.

———. *Histoire de la folie à l'âge classique.* Paris: Gallimard, 1972.

Foulkes, Siegfried Heinrich. *Therapeutic Group Analysis.* London: George Allen & Unwin, 1964.

Foulkes, Siegfried Heinrich, and Elwyn James Anthony. *Group Psychotherapy: The Psychoanalytical Approach.* London: Pelican, 1965 (1957).

Fowden, Garth. "The Pagan Holy Man in Late Antique Society." *The Journal of Hellenic Studies* 102 (1982): 33–59.

Frankfurter, David T. M. "Stylites and Phallobates: Pillar Religions in Late Antique Syria." *Vigiliae Christianae* 44/2 (1990): 168–198.

Freud, Sigmund, "A Disturbance of Memory on the Acropolis: An Open Letter to Romain Rolland on the Occasion of His Seventieth Birthday." In *The Standard Edition of the Complete Psychological Works of Sigmund Freud,* vol. 22, pp. 239–250.

———. "A Seventeenth-Century Demonological Neurosis." In *The Standard Edition of the Complete Psychological Works,* vol. 19, pp. 96–105.

———. *The Standard Edition of the Complete Psychological Works.* Ed. and trans. James Strachey. 24 vols. London: Hogarth Press, 1956–1974.

———. "The 'Uncanny.' " In *The Standard Edition of the Complete Psychological Works of Sigmund Freud,* vol. 17, pp. 217–256.

Freud, Sigmund, and Romain Rolland, *Correspondence 1923–1936.* Eds. Henri Vermorel and Madeleine Vermorel, trans. Pierre Cotet and René Lainé. Paris: Presses Universitaires de France, 1993.

Fromm-Reichmann, Frieda, ed. *The Philosophy of Insanity by a Late Inmate of the Glasgow Royal Asylum for Lunatics at Gartnavel.* New York: Greenberg, 1947.

Gauchet, Marcel, and Gladys Swain. *La pratique de l'esprit humain: L'institution asilaire et la révolution démocratique.* Paris: Gallimard, 2007 (1980).

Gay, Peter. "Psychoanalysis in History." *Poetic Today* 9/1 (1988): 239–247.

Gerson, Mary-Joan. *The Embedded Self: A Psychoanalytic Guide to Family Therapy.* New York: Routledge, 2009 (Hillsdale, NJ: Analytic Press, 1996).

Gianfrancesco, Angelo. "Monachisme ancien et psychopathologie." *L'évolution psychiatrique* 73 (2008): 105–126.

Gibney, Paul. "The Double Bind Theory: Still Crazy-Making After All These Years." *Psychotherapy in Australia* 12/3 (2006): 48–55.

Girard, René. *La violence et le sacré.* Paris: Bernard Grasset, 1972.

Glucklich, Ariel. *Sacred Pain: Hurting the Body for the Sake of the Soul.* Oxford: Oxford University Press, 2001.

Gorelick, Nathan. "Life in Excess: Insurrection and Expenditure in Antonin Artaud's Theater of Cruelty." *Discourse* 33/2 (2011): 263–279.

Grosdidier de Matons, José. "Les Thèmes d'édification dans la Vie d'André Salos." *Travaux et Mémoires* 4 (1970): 277–329.

Guillaumont, Antoine. "Le dépaysement comme forme d'ascèse, dans le monachisme ancien." *École pratique des hautes études, Section des sciences religieuses. Annuaire 1968–1969* 76 (1967): 31–58.

Hadot, Pierre. *Philosophy as a Way of Life: Spiritual Exercises from Socrates to Foucault.* Ed. Arnold I. Davidson, trans. Michael Chase. Oxford: Blackwell, 1995 (1981).

Harker, Andrew. *Loyalty and Dissidence in Roman Egypt: The Case of the Acta Alexandrinorum.* Cambridge: Cambridge University Press, 2008.

Hill, Darryl. B., and Michael J. Kral, eds. *About Psychology: Essays at the Crossroads of History, Theory, and Philosophy.* Albany: State University of New York Press, 2003.

Hoffman, Irwin Z. "Discussion: Toward a Social-Constructivist View of the Psychoanalytic Situation." *Psychoanalytic Dialogues* 1 (1991): 74–105.

Honigman, Sylvie. *Tales of High Priests and Taxes: The Books of the Maccabees and the Judean Rebellion against Antiochos IV.* Berkeley: University of California Press, 2014.

Hoppenbrouwers, Henricus. *Recherches sur la terminologie du martyre de Tertullien à Lactance.* Nijmegen: Dekker & Van de Vegt, 1961.

Horden, Peregrine. "Responses to Possession and Insanity in the Earlier Byzantine World." *The Society for the Social History of Medicine* 6/2 (1993): 177–194.

Hynes, William J. "Mapping the Characteristics of Mythic Tricksters: A Heuristic Guide." In *Mythical Trickster Figures,* eds. Hynes and Doty, pp. 33–45.

Hynes, William J., and William G. Doty, eds. *Mythical Trickster Figures: Contours, Contexts, and Criticism.* Tuscaloosa: University of Alabama Press, 1997.

Ivanov, Sergey A. *Holy Fools in Byzantium and Beyond.* Trans. Simon Franklin. Oxford: Oxford Univeristy Press, 2006 (Moscow, 1994).

Jacobson, Lawrence. "The Group as an Object in the Cultural Field." *International Journal of Group Psychotherapy* 39/4 (1989): 475–497.

James, William. *The Varieties of Religious Experience: A Study in Human Nature. Being the Gifford Lectures on Natural Religion Delivered at Edinburgh in 1901–1902.* New York: New American Library, 1958 (London: Longmans Green, 1902).

Judge, E. A. "Fourth-Century Monasticism in the Papyri." In *Proceedings of the Sixteenth International Congress of Papyrology,* eds. Roger S. Bagnall et al., pp. 613–615. Chicago: Scholars Press, 1981.

Jung, Carl Gustav. *The Collected Works.* Eds. Herbert Read, Michael Fordham, Gerhard Adler, and William McGuire, trans. R. F. C. Hull and H. G. Baynes. Bollingen Series, 20 vols. in 21 pts. Princeton, NJ: Princeton University Press, 1945–1979.

———. "On the Psychology of the Trickster-Figure." *The Collected Works,* vol. 9i, § 456–488.

———. "Psychology of the Transference." In *The Collected Works,* vol. 16, pp. 163–325.

Kahana, Menahem I. "The Halakhic Midrashim." In *The Literature of the Sages,* eds. Shumel Safrai, Joshua Schwarts, Peter Tomson. Vol. 2: *Midrash and Targum: Liturgy, Poetry, Mysticism, Contracts, Inscriptions, Ancient Science, and the Languages of Rabbinic Literature,* pp. 3–105. Assen: Royal Van Gorcum, 2006.

Kalmin, Richard, "Holy Men, Rabbis, and Demonic Sages in Late Antiquity." In *Jewish Culture and Society under the Christian Roman Empire,* eds. Richard Kalmin and Seth Schwartz, pp. 213–249. Leuven: Peeters, 2003.

Kleinberg, Aviad. *Brother Ginepro's Pork Leg* [in Hebrew]. Tel Aviv: Zemora Bitan, 2000.

Kohut, Heinz. *The Analysis of the Self: A Systematic Approach to the Psychoanalytic Treatment of Narcissistic Personality Disorders.* New York: International Universities Press, 1971.

Kraemer, David. *Responses to Suffering in Classical Rabbinic Literature.* Oxford: Oxford University Press, 1995.

Kroll, Jerome, and Bernard Backrach. *The Mystic Mind: The Psychology of Medieval Mystics and Ascetics.* New York: Routledge, 2005.

Krueger, Derek. *Symeon the Holy Fool: Leontius's Life and the Late Antique City.* Berkeley: University of California Press, 1996.

———. *Writing and Holiness: The Practice of Authorship in the Early Christian East.* Philadelphia: University of Pennsylvania Press, 2004.

Laing, Ronald D. *The Divided Self: An Existential Study in Sanity and Madness.* London: Penguin, 1965 (1960).

Laing, Ronald D., and A. Esterson. *Sanity, Madness, and the Family: Families of Schizophrenics.* New York: Basic Books, 1971 (London: Tavistock, 1964).

Le Guin, Ursula K. "The Child and the Shadow." *Quarterly Journal of the Library of Congress* 32 (1975): 139–148. Repr. in *The Language of the Night: Essays on Fantasy and Science Fiction,* ed. Susan Wood, pp. 59–72. New York: Berkley Books, 1982.

Lévi-Strauss, Claude. "Le Sourcier et sa Magie." In *Anthropologie structurale,* ch. 9 (=*les Temps modernes,* 4e année, 41, 1949, pp. 3–24). Paris: Plon, 1996.

———. *Le Totémisme aujourd'hui.* Paris: Presses Universitaires de France, 1965 (1962).

Levine, Donald N. *The Flight from Ambiguity: Essays in Social and Cultural Theory.* Chicago: University of Chicago Press, 1985.

Levine, Lee I. *The Ancient Synagogue: The First Thousand Years.* New Haven, CT: Yale University Press, 2005.

Lewin, Kurt. *Resolving Social Conflicts: Selected Papers on Group Dynamics.* Ed. Gertrud Weiss. New York: Harper & Brothers, 1948.

Lewis, Ioan M. *Ecstatic Religion: An Anthropological Study of Spirit Possession and Shamanism.* Harmondsworth, UK: Penguin Books, 1971.

Lifshitz, Felice. "Beyond Positivism and Genre: 'Hagiographical' Text as Historical Narrative." *Viator* 25 (1994): 95–113.

———. "The Martyr, the Tomb, and the Matron: Constructing the (Masculine) 'Past' as a Female Power Base." In *Medieval Concepts of the Past: Ritual, Memory, Historiography,* eds. Gerd Althoff, Johannes Fried, and Patrick J. Geary, pp. 311–341. Cambridge: Cambridge University Press, 2002.

Lilienfeld, Scott O., and Lori Marino. "Mental Disorder as a Roschian Concept: A Critique of Wakefield's 'Harmful Dysfunction' Analysis." *Journal of Abnormal Psychology* 104/3 (1995): 411–420.

Logan, Donald, F. *The Medieval Historian and the Quest for Certitude.* Toronto: Pontifical Institute of Mediaeval Studies, 2005.

Luijendijk, AnneMarie. *Greetings in the Lord: Early Christians and the Oxyrhynchus Papyri.* Cambridge, MA: Harvard University Press, 2008.

MacDonald, Michael. "Insanity and the Realities of History in Early Modern England." *Psychological Medicine* 11 (1981): 11–25.

Mango, Cyril. "A Byzantine Hagiographer at Work: Leontios of Neapolis." In *Byzanz und der Westen: Studien zur Kunst des europäischen Mittelalters,* ed. Irmgard Hutter, pp. 25–41. Vienna: Österreichischen Akademie des Wissenschaften, 1984.

———. "The Life of Saint Andrew the Fool Reconsidered." *Rivista di studi bizantini e slavi* 2 (1982): 297–313.

Markus, Robert. *The End of Ancient Christianity.* Cambridge: Cambridge University Press, 1990.

Masschelein, Anneleen. *The Unconcept: The Freudian Uncanny in Late-Twentieth-Century Theory.* Albany: State University of New York Press, 2012.

McHugh, Paul R. "Striving for Coherence: Psychiatry's Efforts over Classification," *Journal of the American Medical Association* 293 (2005): 2526–2528.

McKinley Runyan, William, ed. "Reconceptualizing the Relationships between History and Psychology." In *Psychology and Historical Interpretation,* pp. 247–295. Oxford: Oxford University Press, 1988.

McNally, Richard J. *What Is Mental Illness?* Cambridge, MA: Belknap Press of Harvard University Press, 2011.

Miller, Patricia Cox. "Is There a Harlot in This Text? Hagiography and the Grotesque." *Journal of Medieval and Early Modern Studies* 33/3 (2003): 418–435.

———. "Shifting Selves in Late Antiquity." In *Religion and the Self in Antiquity,* eds. David Brakke, Michael L. Satlow, and Steven Weitzman, pp. 15–39. Bloomington: Indiana University Press, 2005.

Mitchell, Stephen A., *Relational Concepts in Psychoanalysis: An Integration.* Cambridge, MA: Harvard University Press, 1988.

Morson, Gary Saul, and Caryl Emerson. *Mikhail Bakhtin: Creation of a Prosaics.* Stanford, CA: Stanford University Press, 1990.

Moss, Candida, R. *Ancient Christian Martyrdom: Diverse Practices, Theologies, and Traditions.* New Haven, CT: Yale University Press, 2012.

———. *The Myth of Persecution: How Early Christian Invented a Story of Martyrdom.* New York: HarperCollins, 2013.

Napier, Augustus Y., and Carl A. Whitaker. *The Family Crucible.* New York: Harper & Row, 1978.

Nasrallah, Laura. *An Ecstasy of Folly: Prophecy and Authority in Early Christianity.* Cambridge, MA: Harvard University Press, 2003.

Noam, Vered. "A Tale of a Captured Story: Metamorphoses of a Tale between Eretz Israel and Babylon" [in Hebrew]. *Mekhkarei Yerushalaim beSafrut Ivrit* 19 (2003): 9–21.

Ogden, Thomas, H. *The Matrix of the Mind: Object Relations and the Psychoanalytical Dialogue.* Northvale, NJ: Jaon Aronson, 1990.

Oppenheimer, Aharon. "Heiligkeit und Hingabe des Lebens in der Folge des

Bar-Kochba Aufstands." In Aharon Oppenheimer, *Between Rome and Babylon*, pp. 320–333. Tübingen: Mohr Siebeck, 2005.

Papaconstantinou, Arietta, Muriel Debié, and Hugh Kennedy, eds. *Writing "True Stories": Historians and Hagiographers in the Late Antique and Medieval Near East.* Turnhout: Brepols, 2010.

Patlagean, Évelyne. "*Ancienne hagiographie* byzantine et histoire sociale." *Annales: Économies, Sociétés, Civilisations* 23/1 (1968):106–126. Repr. as "Ancient Byzantine Hagiography and Social History." In *Saints and Their Cults: Studies in Religious Sociology, Folklore and History*, ed. Stephen Wilson, trans. Jane Hodgkin, pp. 101–22. Cambridge: Cambridge University Press, 1983.

———. "L'histoire de la femme déguisée en moine et l'évolution de la sainteté féminine à Byzance." In *Structure sociale, famille, chrétienté à Byzance IVe–XIe siècle*, pt. XI (*Studi Medievali*, ser. 3, 17, 1976, pp. 597–623). London: Variorum, 1981.

Perkins, Judith. *The Suffering Self: Pain and Narrative Representation in the Early Christian Era.* London: Routledge, 2002.

Pichon-Rivière, Enrique. *El proceso grupal: Del psicoanalisis a la psicologia.* Buenos Aires: Nueva Vision, 1971.

Porter, Roy. "Foucault's Great Confinement." *History of the Human Sciences* 3/1 (1990): 47–54. Repr. in *Rewriting the History of Madness: Studies in Foucault's Histoire de la folie*, eds. Arthur Still and Irving Velody, pp. 119–25. London: Routledge, 1992.

———. *Mind-Forg'd Manacles: A History of Madness from the Restoration to the Regency.* London: Athlone, 1987.

———. *A Social History of Madness: The World through the Eyes of the Insane.* New York: Dutton, 1986.

Priel, Beatriz. "Bakhtin and Winnicott: On Dialogue, Self, and Cure." *Psychoanalytic Dialogues* 9 (1999): 487–503.

Radin, Paul. *The Trickster: A Study in American Indian Mythology.* New York: Schocken, 1955.

Rajak, Tessa. "Reflections on Jewish Resistance and the Discourse of Martyrdom in Josephus." In *Judaea-Palaestina, Babylon and Rome: Jews in Antiquity*, eds. Benjamin Isaac and Yuval Shahar, pp. 165–180. Tübingen: Mohr Siebeck, 2012.

Rapp, Claudia. "'For next to God, you are my salvation': Reflection on the Rise of the Holy Man in Late Antiquity." In *The Cult of Saints in Late Antiquity and the Early Middle Ages. Essays on the Contribution of Peter Brown*, eds. James Howard-Johnston and Paul Anthony Hayward, pp. 63–81. Oxford: Oxford University Press, 1999.

———. "The Origins of Hagiography and the Literature of Early Monasticism: Purpose and Genre between Tradition and Innovation." In *Unclassical Traditions: Alternatives to the Classical Past in Late Antiquity*, eds. Christopher Kelly, Richard Flower, and Michael Stuart Williams, pp. 119–130. Cambridge: Cambridge University Press 2010.

———. "Storytelling as Spiritual Communication in Early Greek Hagiography: The Use of *Diegesis*." *Journal of Early Christian Studies* 6/3 (1998): 431–448.

Reicher, Gideon. *Madness* [in Hebrew]. Tel Aviv: Zmora, Bitan, Modan, 1980.

Riley-Smith, Jonathan. "Crusading as an Act of Love." *History* 65 (1980): 177–192.

Rimmon, Shlomit. *The Concept of Ambiguity—the Example of James*. Chicago: University of Chicago Press, 1977.

Ruysschaert, José. "Les 'martyrs' et les 'confesseurs' de la lettre des églises de Lyon et de Vienne." In *Les Martyrs de Lyon (177): Actes du colloque International du CNRS, Lyon, 20–23 septembre 1977*, eds. Jean Rouge and Robert Turcan, pp. 155–166. Paris: Éd. du CNRS, 1978.

Rydén, Lennart. "The Date of the Life of Andreas Salos." *Dumbarton Oaks Papers* 32 (1978): 127–155.

Sacks, Oliver Wolf. *Migraine*. New York: Vintage Books, 1999.

Safrai, Shmuel. "Kiddush haShem in the Teaching of the Tannaim" [in Hebrew]. *Zion* 44 (1979) 28–42. Repr. in English in *Sjaloom*, eds. T. C. de Kruijf and H. van der Sandt, pp. 145–164. Hilversum: B. Folkertsma Stichting voor Talmudica, 1983.

Saward, John. *Perfect Fools*. Oxford: Oxford University Press, 1980.

Schachner, Lukas Amadeus. "The Archaeology of the Stylite." In *Religious Diversity in Late Antiquity*, eds. David Gwynn and Susanne Bangert, pp. 329–398. Leiden: Brill, 2010.

Schama, Simon. *Landscape and Memory*. New York: Vintage Books, 1996.

Scheff, Thomas J. *Being Mentally Ill: A Sociological Theory*. Hawthorne, NY: Aldine, 1999.

Scholem, Gershom. *Sabbatai Ṣevi: The Mystical Messiah*. Trans. R. J. Zwi Werblowsky. Princeton, NJ: Princeton University Press, 1973.

Schwartz, J. "Quelques réflexions à propos des Acta Alexandrinorum." *Zeitschrift für Papyrologie und Epigraphik* 54 (1984): 130–132.

Scott, W. Joan. "The Incommensurability of Psychoanalysis and History." *History and Theory* 51 (2012): 63–83.

Searles, Harold F. "Concerning Therapeutic Symbiosis: The Patient as Symbiotic Therapist, the Phase of Ambivalent Symbiosis, and the Role of Jealousy in the Fragmented Ego." In *Countertransference and Related Subject: Selected Papers*, pt. 10. New York: International Universities Press, 1979 (1973).

———. "Countertransference and Theoretical Model." In *Countertransference and Related Subject: Selected Papers*, pt. 18. New York: International Universities Press, 1979 (1975).

———. "The Patient as Therapist to His Analyst." In *Countertransference and Related Subject: Selected Papers*, pt. 19. New York: International Universities Press, 1979 (1975).

Sedikides, Constantine, and Marilynn B. Brewer, eds. *Individual Self, Relational Self, Collective Self*. Ann Arbor, MI: Sheridan Books, 2001.

Ševčenko, Nancy. "The Hermit as Stanger in the Desert." In *Strangers to Themselves:*

The Byzantine Outsider: Papers from the Thirty-second Spring Symposium of Byzantine Studies, University of Sussex, Brighton, March 1998, ed. Dion C. Smythe, pp. 75–86. Aldershot, UK: Ashgate Variorum, 2000.

Shannon, Claude E., and Warren Weaver. *The Mathematical Theory of Communication.* Urbana: University of Illinois Press, 1964.

Shepkaru, Shmuel. "From After Death to Afterlife: Martyrdom and Its Recompense." *Association for Jewish Studies Review* 24 (1999): 1–44.

Shklovsky, Viktor. "Art as Device." In *Theory of Prose*, trans. and intro. Benjamin Sher, pp. 1–14. Elmwood Park, IL: Dalkey Archive Press, 1991.

Shoham-Steiner, Ephraim, "The Humble Sage and the Wandering Madman: Madness and Madmen in an Exemplum from *Sefer Ḥasidim." The Jewish Quarterly Review* 96/1 (2006): 38-49.

Shorter, Edward. "Still Tilting at Windmills: Commentary on . . . The Myth of Mental Illness." *The Psychiatrist* 35/5 (2011): 183–184

Shweder, Richard A. *Thinking through Cultures: Expeditions in Cultural Psychology.* Cambridge, MA: Harvard University Press, 1991.

Sinyavsky, Andrei. *Ivan the Fool: Russian Folk Belief: A Cultural History.* Trans. Joanne Turnbull and Nikolai Formozov. Moscow: Glas, 2007.

Sokoloff, Michael. *A Syriac Lexicon: A Translation from the Latin, Correction, Expansion, and Update of C. Brockelmann's Lexicon Syriacum.* Winona Lake, IN: Eisenbrauns, 2009.

Stein, Ruth. "Evil as Love and as Liberation: The Mind of a Suicidal Religious Terrorist." *Psychoanalytic Dialogues* 12/3 (2002): 393–420. Repub. in *PSYART: A Hyperlink Journal for the Psychological Study of the Arts* (2004). Accessed December 15, 2009. http://www.psyartjournal.com/article/show/stein-evil_as_love_and_as_liberation_the_mind_.

Still, Arthur, and Irving Velody, eds. *Rewriting the History of Madness: Studies in Foucault's Histoire de la folie.* London: Routledge, 1992.

Straw, Carol. "Martyrdom and Christian Identity: Gregory the Great, Augustine, and Tradition." In *The Limits of Ancient Christianity: Essays on Late Antique Thought and Culture in Honor of R. A. Markus*, eds. William E. Klingshorn and Mark Vessey, pp. 250–266. Ann Arbor: University of Michigan Press, 1999.

Stroumsa, Guy. *La fin du sacrifice: Les mutations religieuses de l'antiquité tardive.* Paris: Odile Jacob, 2005.

———. "Madness and Divinization in Early Christian Monasticism." In *Self and Self-Transformations in the History of Religions*, eds. David Shulman and Guy Stroumsa, pp. 73–88. New York: Oxford University Press, 2002.

Swain, Gladys. *Le sujet de la folie: Naissance de la psychiatrie.* Toulouse: Privat, 1977.

Syrkin, Alexander. "On the Behavior of the 'Fool for Christ's Sake.' " *History of Religions* 22/2 (1982): 150–171.

Szakolczai, Arpad. "Liminality and Experience: Structuring Transitory Situations and Transformative Events." *International Political Anthropology* 2/1 (2009): 141–172.

Szasz, Thomas Stephen, ed. *The Age of Madness: The History of Involuntary Mental Hospitalization Presented in Selected Texts.* Garden City, NY: Anchor Press/ Doubleday, 1974.

———. *The Myth of Mental Illness: Foundations of a Theory of Personal Conduct.* New York: Harper & Row, 1961.

Thomas, Andrew. *The Holy Fools: A Theological Enquiry: Thesis submitted to the University of Nottingham for the degree of PhD* (2009). Accessed November 20, 2013. http://etheses.nottingham.ac.uk/797/1/The_Holy_Fools_A_Theological_Enquiry.pdf.

Thomassen, Bjørn. "The Uses and Meanings of Liminality." *International Political Anthropology* 2/1 (2009): 5–27.

Tian, Min. *The Poetics of Difference and Displace: Twentieth-Century Chinese-Western Intercultural Theatre.* Hong Kong: Hong Kong University Press, 2008.

Todorov, Tzvetan. *The Fantastic: A Structural Approach to a Literary Genre.* Trans. Richard Howard. Ithaca, NY: Cornell University Press, 1975 (1971).

———. *Mikhaïl Bakhtine: Le principe dialogique.* Paris: Éd. du Seuil, 1989.

Turner, Victor Witter. "Liminality and Communitas." In *The Ritual Process: Structure and anti-structure (The Lewis Henry Morgan Lectures, 1966)*, pp. 94–130. London: Routledge & Kegan Paul, 1969.

Vaage, Leif E., and Vincent L. Wimbush, eds. *Asceticism and the New Testament.* London: Routledge, 1999.

Valantasis, Richard. "A Theory of the Social Function of Asceticism." In *Asceticism*, eds. Vincent L. Wimbush and Richard Valantasis, pp. 544–552. Oxford: Oxford University Press, 1995.

Van Esbroeck, Michel, "The Saint as a Symbol." In *The Byzantine Saint / University of Birmingham Fourteenth Spring Symposium of Byzantine Studies*, ed. Sergei Hackel, trans. Michael Breck, pp. 128–140. Crestwood, NY: St. Vladimir's Seminary Press, 2001.

Van Gennep, Arnold. *Les rites de passage.* Paris: E. Nourry, 1909.

Van Hanten, Jan Willem, *The Maccabean Martyrs as Saviours of the Jewish People: A Study of 2 and 4 Maccabees.* Supplement to the *Journal for the Study of Judaism* 57. Leiden: Brill, 1997.

———. "The Martyrs as Heroes of the Christian People: Some Remarks on the Continuity between Jewish and Christian Martyrology, with Pagan Analogies." In *Martyrium in Multidisciplinary Perspective: Memorial Louis Reekmans*, eds. M. Lamberigts and P. van Deun, pp. 303–322. Leuven: Leuven University Press, 1995.

Van Hanten, Jan Willem, and Friedrich Avemarie. *Martyrdom and Noble Death: Selected texts from Graeco-Roman, Jewish and Christian Antiquity.* London: Routledge, 2002.

Virmaux, Odette. *Le théatre et son double: Antonin Artaud.* Paris: Hatier, 1975.

Vööbus, Arthur. *History of Asceticism in the Syrian Orient: A Contribution to the History of Culture in the Near East*, 3 vols. Louvain: Secrétariat du CSCO, "CSCO 184, 197, 500, Subsidia, 14, 17, 81," 1958–1988.

Wachtel Paul L. *Relational Theory and the Practice of Psychotherapy.* New York: Guilford Press, 2008.

Wakefield, Jerome C. "The Concept of Mental Disorder: On the Boundary between Biological Facts and Social Values." *American Psychologist* 47/3 (1992): 373–388.

———. "Evolutionary versus Prototype Analyses of the Concept of Disorder." *Journal of Abnormal Psychology* 108 (1999): 374–399.

Weber, Max. *The Sociology of Religion.* Trans. Ephraim Fischoff. London: Methuen, 1965 (*Wirtschaft und Gesellscahft.* Tübingen: J. C. B. Mohr, 1922, vol. 2, pp. 227–363).

Weiner, Eugene and Anita Weiner. *The Martyr's Conviction: A Sociological Analysis.* Atlanta: Scholar Press, 1990.

Weingarten, Susan. *The Saint's Saints: Hagiography and Geography in Jerome.* Leiden: Brill, 2005.

Welner, Althar. *The Ten Slain by the Kingdom in the Midrash and Piyyut* [in Hebrew]. Jerusalem: Mosad haRav Kook, 2005.

Whitby, Michael. "Maro the Dendrite: An Anti-Social Holy Man?" In *Homo Viator: Classical Essays for John Bramble,* eds. Michael Whitby, Philip Hardie, and Mary Whitby, pp. 310–318. Bristol: Bristol Classical Press, 1987.

Wilson, Edmund. "The Ambiguity of Henry James." *Hound and Horn* 7 (1933–34): 385–406. Repr. in *The Triple Thinkers: Twelve Essays on Literary Subjects.* London: J. Lehmann, 1952.

Wimbush, Vincent L., and Richard Valantasis, eds. *Asceticism.* New York: Oxford University Press, 1995.

Winnicott, Donald M. "Ego Distortion in Terms of True and False Self." In *The Maturational Processes and the Facilitating Environment: Studies in the Theory of Emotional Development,* pt. 12. London: Karnac, 1990 (1960).

———. "Hate in the Countertransference." *The International Journal of Psycho-Analysis* 30 (1949): 69–74.

———. *The Maturational Processes and the Facilitating Environment: Studies in the Theory of Emotional Development.* London: Karnac, 1990.

———. "Mirror-Role of Mother and Family in Child Development." In *Playing and Reality,* pt. 9. London: Tavistock, 1971 (1967).

———. *Playing and Reality.* London: Tavistock, 1971.

———. "Primitive Emotional Development." *The International Journal of Psycho-Analysis* 26/3–4 (1945): 137–43.

———. "The Theory of the Parent-Infant Relationship." *The International Journal of Psycho-Analysis* 41 (1960): 585–595.

Woolfenden, Gregory W. *Daily Liturgical Prayer: Origins and Theology.* Aldershot, UK: Ashgate, 2004.

Yarom, Nitza. *Body, Blood, and Sexuality: A Psychoanalytic Study of St. Francis' Stigmata and Their Historical Context.* New York: P. Lang, 1992.

Young-Eisendrath, Polly. "The Self in Analysis." *Journal of Analytical Psychology* 42 (1997): 157–166.

Zalkhah, Yafa. "The Prayer, the Miracle and the Miracle-Worker: On the Border between an Aggadah in the Yerushalmi and an Aggadah in the Bavli" [in Hebrew]. *Masekhet* 8 (2008): 159–185.

Ziadé Raphaëlle, *Les martyrs Maccabées: De l'histoire juive au culte chrétien: Les homélies de Grégoire de Nazianze et de Jean Chrysostome.* Leiden: Brill, 2007.

Acknowledgments

This book came to being in a graduate seminar I taught at Yale on the question of insanity and sanctity in medieval societies, which examined how religious language appropriated the borderline between sanity and insanity and used it as an undefined space of ambiguity by sanctifying forms of abnormal behavior. My research on this topic started with Byzantine Christianity but did not remain there. It became engaged with psychology, literary criticism, anthropology, and sociology of religion, and soon comprised different religious communities in the Romano-Byzantine world in the time of its transformation into a monotheistic world. My work greatly benefited from conversions I had with friends and colleagues from different fields who contributed much to its writing. I am grateful to them all.

I am deeply thankful to Henry Abramovitch, Daniel Boyarin, Marcel Gauchet, Misgav Har-Peled, and Guy Stroumsa for the great interest they took in this book and their encouragement, especially at times when I needed it the most. I am grateful to Benjamin Isaac and Aharon Oppenheimer for their constant support, and to Benjamin Beit-Hallahmi, Yoram Bilu, Gideon Bohak, and Joan Scott for reading, commenting on, and enriching the discussion. I thank Orit Bashkin, Orna Harari, Irène Leontakianakou, Anna Mirabella, Ioanna Rapti, Susan Reynolds, Ruth Sarig, Alexander Segal, Gideon Segal, Kostis Smyrlis, Francesca Trivellato, and Marina Ville for their support, feedback, and contributions to the book.

I thank Yad Hanadiv and Asher Ragen for the grant I was awarded for the research of this project, Sharmila Sen for her initiative and the care she has taken with the book, Susan Weingarten for her great help in accompanying the writing of the book and for her wise suggestions, Bar Belinitzky and Inbar Graiver, who contributed much to both the research and the discussion, as well as Leslie Connor and John Shannon. And I also thank my ten brave students who followed me in the seminar on the same topic at Yale, and with whom I had a unique and stimulating experience.

This work could not have been started, realized, and accomplished without the continuous support of Kobi Auslander, whose human perspective and psychoanalytical eye were essential for the intellectual process and individual involvement needed for such a project, and to whom I am ever indebted.

Index

www.ingramcontent.com/pod-product-compliance
Ingram Content Group UK Ltd.
Pitfield, Milton Keynes, MK11 3LW, UK
UKHW041421290926
475585UK00013B/31/J

9 780674 057616